D1713579

Breaking the Gender Code

Breaking the Gender Code

WOMEN AND URBAN PUBLIC SPACE
IN THE TWENTIETH-CENTURY UNITED STATES

Georgina Hickey

University of Texas Press, Austin

The Louann Atkins Temple Women & Culture Endowment is supported by Allison, Doug, Taylor, and Andy Bacon; Margaret, Lawrence, Will, John, and Annie Temple; Larry Temple; the Temple-Inland Foundation; and the National Endowment for the Humanities.

Short sections of the book have been developed from Georgina Hickey, "Barred from the Barroom: Second Wave Feminists and Public Accommodations in US Cities," originally published in *Feminist Studies* 34 (Fall 2008): 382–408, by permission of the publisher, Feminist Studies Inc.; Georgina Hickey, "The Geography of Pornography: Neighborhoods, Feminism, and Battles against 'Dirty Bookstores' in Minneapolis," *Frontiers: A Journal of Women's Studies* 32 (Spring 2011): 125–151, by permission of the publisher, University of Nebraska Press; and Georgina Hickey, "From Civility to Self-Defense: Modern Advice to Women on the Privileges and Dangers of Public Space," *Women's Studies Quarterly* 39 (Spring/Summer 2011): 77–94, copyright © 2011 by the Feminist Press at the City University of New York, used by permission of The Permissions Company, LLC on behalf of the publishers, feministpress.org (all rights reserved).

Requests for permission to reproduce material from this work should be sent to:
Permissions
University of Texas Press
P.O. Box 7819
Austin, TX 78713-7819
utpress.utexas.edu

♾ The paper used in this book meets the minimum requirements of ANSI/NISO Z39.48-1992 (R1997) (Permanence of Paper).

Library of Congress Cataloging-in-Publication Data

Names: Hickey, Georgina, 1968– author.
Title: Breaking the gender code : women and urban public space in the twentieth century United States / Georgina Hickey.
Description: First edition. | Austin : University of Texas Press, 2023. | Includes bibliographical references and index.
Identifiers: LCCN 2023002712 (print) | LCCN 2023002713 (ebook)
    ISBN 978-1-4773-2822-4 (hardcover)
    ISBN 978-1-4773-2823-1 (pdf)
    ISBN 978-1-4773-2824-8 (epub)
Subjects: LCSH: Urban women —Political activity —United States —History—20th century. | Urban women —United States —Social conditions —History —20th century. | Women political activists —United States —History —20th century. | Public spaces —Social aspects —United States —History —20th century. | Urban women —Services for —United States —History —20th century. | Urban women —Protection —United States —History —20th century. | Cities and towns —Social aspects —United States —History —20th century. | Feminist geography —United States —History —20th century.
Classification: LCC HQ1420 (ebook) | LCC HQ1420 .H54 2023 (print) | DDC 305.420973 23/ eng/20230 —dc17

doi:10.7560/328224

The publication of this book was made possible by the generous support of the Louann Atkins Temple Women & Culture Endowment.

Contents

Preface

My first book considered the social and cultural history of women in early twentieth-century Atlanta. It explored how images of white and African American working class women served larger debates about the direction of the city's growth. Narratives about cleaning up the city and restoring order relied heavily on curtailing and surveilling women's presence in public. Women, however, often ignored or challenged efforts to control them—calling for police to protect them from harassment, taking to the streets to demand suffrage or better working conditions, and filling the city's dance halls and other sites of leisure despite dire warnings of the danger these spaces held.

I was impressed by the confidence these early twentieth-century women demonstrated when it came to accessing public space. When I later came across news footage of a group of women protesting street harassment on the crowded sidewalks of Wall Street in the early 1970s, catcalling at the men they passed and telling reporters they did not want to be treated like "sexual objects," the broad shape of this book started to come together. I saw women on both ends of the twentieth century rejecting messages that told them the streets were not for them and challenging old ideas that a woman who was in public could not be good or moral. This is how I began to see a thread connecting activists, reformers, and different groups of women across the century.

Beyond this new understanding of women's activism, I was also drawn to the topic because it spoke to my own experience, particularly the experience of being a feminist scholar who was supposedly savvy about power relationships yet still often felt out of place when walking alone. Being approached on the street—"Smile!" "You out here all alone?"—left me unnerved. Although my scholarly credentials haven't helped me much when I'm out in public, they have equipped me with the skills to head into the archives and discover both history and context for what many individuals experience daily. The goal of this book, then, is to explain the history that created patterns of harassment, narratives of danger, and the deep sense of unease many women experience in public. More than just answering the question of why women seem so vulnerable to fear and harassment when out in the world, I really wanted to know what has been done to confront and interrupt these patterns. As it turns out, a lot has been done. By understanding where society has been on these issues, I mean to arm the readers of this book with a keener understanding of what is at stake when people encounter an urban landscape in which their presence is questioned or restricted because of their gender presentation, however normative or transgressive that presentation is.

I want anyone who has ever felt out of place in public—be they someone who identifies as a woman or someone from another disadvantaged group—to feel validated in their discomfort, frustration, or even fear instead of diminished or dismissed. I want them to see that these experiences are not trivial or anomalous, but part of a larger system, an institutionalized hierarchy that generally privileges men, especially straight white men. It does so through a pattern of gender segregation that extends from the workplace to domestic roles, to how, why, and when people move through public space. Gender segregation is intertwined with other systems of social control and rooted in institutions and practices that were built over time—which means that, if understood, they could be rebuilt differently.

If you have lived as a girl or woman in American society, you are likely to read something in this book that will revive old memories and provoke feelings of frustration, fear, or anger. I wrote this book for you. Your reactions are valid and have meaning.

Introduction

In 1876, author Robert Macoy offered New York tourists guidance on visiting "the Great Metropolis," promising his book would "assist those who wish to know what to see, and how to see it with the greatest degree of comfort and convenience." He offered advice to "strangers"—first-time visitors to the city—telling them to arrive in daylight, be cautious in interactions with strangers, negotiate with drivers before engaging a carriage, ask police for directions, and "avoid all crowds, particularly at night." He assured readers that following these instructions would "insure freedom from annoyance or interruption."[1] Substitute "taxis" for "carriages" and this advice will surely sound familiar. But when I assign an excerpt from Macoy's book to undergraduates in an urban history class, they invariably read it through a gendered lens. My students ascribe to women the vulnerability that Macoy attributed to newcomers who would not know big-city ways. "Go back," I say. "Show me where you see him addressing women." Eventually, they concede that they cannot find the words that lead them to this conclusion. These twenty-first-century students are a fair representation of how more than a century of history has taught us good and well that cities are dangerous for women.

The connection of women and danger in urban public space takes many forms and fulfills many functions. It is not necessarily true, however, and neither is it static. There is a history to how the association became so deeply entrenched in American society, a story that is intertwined with ideas not only about gender, but also about race, class, and sexuality. There is also an even more unrecognized history of individuals and organizations challenging the variety of assumptions, institutions, policies, structures, and practices that restricted women's access to public space.

Breaking the Gender Code tells the story of both the danger narrative and the resistance to it across the long arc of the twentieth century, from their roots in the closing years of the nineteenth century to their reverberations early in the twenty-first century. Throughout women received subtle—and not so subtle—messages that they shouldn't be in public. Or that, if they were, they were not safe, needed special accommodations, or were not entitled to civil treatment because they had chosen to expose themselves to abuse by being out in the world in the first place. Individual women and a variety of organizations, however, confronted the danger, hostility, racism, homophobia, and violence attached to women's presence in public spaces. They especially challenged "commonsense" advice that told women to "just" avoid dangerous situations and inhospitable spaces—advice essentially telling them to stay home. They demanded that American cities and society better accommodate, serve, and respect women's rights and autonomy. Many also laid bare the connections between gendered urban practices and other power hierarchies, particularly those attached to class, sexuality, and race. These fights continue today in the efforts of a new generation of activists seeking to redefine the parameters of civil and human rights. They have raised awareness of the violence faced by trans individuals, called for full access to public bathrooms, brought visibility to police violence against women of color and missing indigenous women, and, in the #MeToo era, expanded public discussions of "rape culture."

Beginning in the nineteenth century, gender was used as an important tool for organizing and controlling urban space, and women who wanted to avoid being labeled immoral, accused of prostitution, or seen as predators had to limit where they went and with whom. I refer to this system as "urban gender segregation." Nineteenth-century women venturing out into American cities faced numerous challenges, not the least of which was that their very presence in public spaces belied the association of women with the private sphere. Rapid urban growth in the nineteenth century had encouraged various forms of division and segmentation that provided a sense of order amid swift changes by assigning specific uses and meanings to different urban spaces. Among the many forms taken by this segmentation was a deeply gendered distinction between public and private, which historian Glenna Matthews labeled the "social geography of gender."[2] These new and gendered understandings of urban space marked women's presence in public as out of place and problematic and thus a threat to the moral and social order.

Gender did not exist, however, as a monolithic or independent variable. It often stood in for and intertwined with race, class, sexuality, and ethnicity. As historian Mary Ryan notes of the nineteenth century, "Female behavior, so obsessively charted on the streets, might stand in for other social differences

In the second half of the nineteenth century, some public services offered separate windows, count-ers, and entrances for women. Arthur Lumley, American Sketches: The Ladies' Window at the New York Post-Office, *1875, wood engraving on paper. (Clark Art Institute, 1955.4578, www.clarkart.edu)*

that were imperfectly ranked and ordered in everyday life and poorly sorted in urban space."[3] Reserving spaces for "ladies," yet recognizing only white women of economic means as members of that category, functioned to exclude people of color, the working classes, and ethnic minorities. One jus-tification given for dismissing the dire circumstances of the immigrant urban poor who languished in tenements and worked long hours in sweatshops was that they lacked the gender distinctions of more comfortably classed white urbanites and the respectability implied by those distinctions. Excluding people of color from first-class railcars reserved for "ladies" shored up white supremacy in the South in the decades following the end of slavery by imbu-ing ladies' accommodations with racial exclusion and denying gender and class privilege to women of color.[4]

The patterns and practices of nineteenth-century gender segregation shel-tered women from the morally harmful elements of the public realm, linking the prize of respectability to only the most guarded forays out of domestic space. Etiquette told women to shield their reputations through reserved presentation and behavior in public and instructed men to offer themselves up to aid the women in their lives in achieving this standard. The gender-specific accommodations—ladies' entrances, rooms, and service counters—dotting the urban landscape by the second half of the nineteenth century promised to further shield women from the vagaries of public spaces and crowds and to protect their reputations in situations that might otherwise obscure social differences and create chaos. The trend toward gender-specific accommodations for women represented a kind of inclusion. It was a significant, if incomplete, shift away from the exclusion that had been such a strong cultural force earlier in the century, when a woman's presence in public raised moral alarms. Built heavily around privileges of class and race, however, the protection this version of gender segregation offered women extended only to more privileged women, leaving others exposed to harassment, violence, and allegations of immorality for not staying within these restrictive structures.

Separation may have limited women's access to public space by reserving specific places for them, but it also made them a visible part of the public landscape. Ladies' accommodations garnered plenty of criticisms—for removing women from the protective eyes of their families, encouraging them to develop secret relationships, and leaving them vulnerable to social and financial exploitation. These concerns inadvertently revealed the freedoms and options such accommodations afforded women. As critics clearly understood, the provision of women-specific public spaces and services was the entering wedge to an expanded and autonomous public presence for women.

In the twentieth century, gender segregation underwent a significant, though not wholesale, transformation. Moralistic assessments of women's public presence, gender-specific accommodations, and an etiquette of respectable deference and reserve dissolved with the rapid expansion of cities, and what was purportedly a more democratic gender code emerged. Gender-specific public toilets are one of the few legacies of the earlier system to persist past the nineteenth century. Twentieth-century gender segregation generally recognized women in public as a hallmark of the modern era, but still restricted women's presence. Those restrictions were enforced through limited accommodations, racialized and classed expectations for behavior, and clear messages that women brought danger on themselves. Periodic moral panics over epidemics of sexual violence reinforced notions of women's vulnerability. A new system of etiquette privileging self-sufficiency over gendered courtesies essentially told women they could rely only on themselves when out and about. The implication was that if a woman found herself in need of assistance, threatened, or underserved, it was her fault for having ventured out in the first place. Whatever negative experiences women had, the twentieth-century code suggested they could have anticipated and avoided them. Much of the work of women and activists addressing gender segregation across the twentieth century attempted to counter this individualized and dismissive understanding of women's limited access to public space. If nineteenth-century gender segregation aimed to lock women away, the twentieth-century version tried to scare them away.

Fundamental to understanding gender segregation is understanding that women have never experienced the public spaces of American cities in the same way men do because of factors such as race, age, ethnicity, ability, sexual orientation, and class. Gender segregation rarely had absolute boundaries, especially in the twentieth century, and was enforced through both formal (*de jure*) and informal (*de facto*) practices. It manifested in a variety of ways, including everything from the exclusion of women to the use of gender privileges to enforce racial discrimination, access restrictions based on place or time of day, and what we know of today as street harassment and other types of gender-based violence targeting women who broke the code. The system governed behavior in public spaces, interactions with others, and the services one could expect based on a host of perceived social identities and never just on gender alone.[5] That gender segregation was also naturalized and obscured by assumptions about the inherent characteristics associated with women and other categories of identity both increased the complexity of the system and hid it from view. "Until you bumped into it, you didn't know it was there," recalled one white urban dweller of the mid–twentieth century.[6] The frequent framing of the most visible aspects of gender segregation as privileges extended to protect women in their moral and physical vulnerability made the system particularly hard to question—at least for the women who could access these privileges—as a source of discrimination or limitation.

As much as gender segregation promised to protect some women, it also justified harassment and violence against other women. Using a different set of gendered assumptions about some women's inherent depravity, these justifications invoked negative ideas that often targeted women of color and immigrant, queer, and working-class women for interference, torment, and exclusion. Like any social system, urban gender segregation contained nuances, inconsistencies, and contradictions that complicated the experience of living under it. Individual women developed techniques to maneuver through urban spaces, in spite of gender segregation, by creating personal maps of cities. Mentally coding how safe, dangerous, welcoming, or inaccessible particular neighborhoods and urban areas would be for them based on their gender and other identities, they organized their daily lives accordingly.[7]

Breaking the Gender Code focuses more on organized challenges to urban gender segregation, which tended to produce explicit critiques of the system and often offered a better way to understand the meaning women ascribed to the gendered landscape. These efforts reflected the larger social stratification of the twentieth century. Heterosexual white women often privileged gender over other identities that shaped the experience of public space, particularly when it came to race and sexual orientation. Not surprisingly, their stories are often the easiest to find and the most explicitly tied to gender segregation. Their experiences point to how the notions of "protection" and "danger" functioned to both control and divide women. White women were excluded, segregated, and controlled under the guise of being protected, while the exclusion, harassment, and targeting of women of color, queer women, and working-class women communicated again and again that much of society believed them to be unworthy of protection. Twentieth-century efforts to challenge entrenched social practices and laws reflect this complexity. Sometimes women confronted aspects of the code through movements for gender reform or equity; at other times challenging the gender code was part of movements for racial justice, workers' rights, gay rights, or other identities or causes. By focusing on the key ways in which women of different social backgrounds interacted with urban public space, as well the ideas, traditions, and structures that shaped that interaction, this book captures some of this variety.

In exploring the history of organized challenges to urban gender segregation, this book tells a wide range of stories, covers more than a century of history, and includes material from many cities. Those who wish to follow a discrete series of events, a particular organization, or the history of just one city may find this approach frustrating, but the larger shape of urban gender segregation and the history of breaking gender codes are best revealed in this breadth. From this perspective, three broad patterns emerge. First, in moments of great social change, women have often found unexpected reasons and opportunities to articulate a vision of the public sphere in which they might more fully participate. Second, in these moments of great opportunity, conservative cultural narratives have arisen in response, often limiting women's ability to take advantage of these new options by at least partly invoking or expanding urban gender segregation. Consequently, gains have often proved uneven and transitions incomplete. Finally, the desire to secure autonomy for women and full standing in the public sphere has most often translated into concrete demands and reforms seeking to secure access for women. Such demands have included not just a tolerance of women's presence but also an insistence on their right to be free from interference, suspicion, harassment, or fear.

At times, these efforts revealed fissures and ignorances as some groups of women pressed their own agenda at the expense of others, especially when white women's demands made public space harder to access or more dangerous for people of color. But the range of organizations and individuals who have returned to the idea of women's right to access to public space have presented a surprisingly coherent set of demands for economic options, political inclusion, bodily autonomy, and a sense of independence. Women have long wanted to determine for themselves how and when they use the spaces around them and they want to do so without restrictions, fear of judgment, or violence.

As much as gender segregation reflects a variety of political and economic trends, efforts to challenge it also reveal core tensions in American society. The gendered codes of public space have often served as tools for other agendas. Privileged accommodations for women, for example, and concern over women being harassed on the street have enforced a racialized public space in which white women need protecting, most often from men of color or lower-class status. These arguments both control white women—by reinforcing the idea that being in public is dangerous to them—and make these public spaces more dangerous to certain groups of men by casting them all as potential predators. That women from some backgrounds are left out entirely suggests they are due no consideration and dismisses the dangers and discomfort they face. When women have behaved in ways that challenged certain power structures, such as picketing during labor strikes, the press and police often responded by accusing them of being immoral for not following gendered behavioral codes and not confining themselves to demure and necessary public appearances.[8] Questioning their respectability as women allowed critics to skirt recognition of them as workers with potentially valid complaints about working conditions. These issues point to the tensions between privileges and rights, between protection and control, and between the private and public realms found at the core of gender segregation and sometimes also within the efforts to challenge the system.

Those who challenged gender segregation never formed a national organization, nor did they come from a single demographic. Efforts to dismantle gender segregation were never movements in their own right; instead, they emerged from and within other movements for social change that ran the gamut from liberal to radical. Focusing on public space, then, offers a fresh way to view the interplay of various twentieth-century social movements, capturing moments of awareness, cooperation, and tension.

As for those who drove collective efforts to challenge gender segregation, I generally use one of three terms: reformer, activist, or feminist. These admittedly imperfect labels can help place them in the movements from which their work sprang. "Reformers" came out of liberal efforts to better use the state to smooth the sharpest edges of capitalism; in the early twentieth century, such reformers included those we generally associate with the Progressive movement. They created settlement houses to serve immigrant neighborhoods, fought for better conditions for women in the labor force, pioneered the fields of public health and social work, and endorsed women's voting rights as a tool for cleaning up politics and creating a social safety net, particularly for women and children. Reformers dominated in a second historic moment in the late twentieth century, when the Democratic Party initiated another wave of policy reform.

Demanding more transformative change to political and economic structures, "activists" tied their efforts to theory building in order to question traditional power relationships. Although activists operated across the twentieth century, they were particularly likely to be found in circles challenging institutionalized racism. The broadest spectrum of activists emerged in the 1960s and 1970s, embedded in the civil and human rights movements of the period. "Feminist" is a term in use over the entire twentieth century, though it was and remains a controversial label. I use it to refer to those who explicitly define gender as central to their activism and who seek transformational social and cultural change along with political and economic goals. Whenever possible, I use terminology that reflects how individuals and groups defined themselves.

This book rests, in part, on the excellent work of other scholars who became interested in the intertwined history of women and cities in the closing decades of the twentieth century. Dominant themes in this literature emphasize the ways in which space influences experience and identity, shapes ideas about authority, and structures power relationships. For example, studies by Kathy Peiss, Christine Stansell, and Joanne Meyerowitz of working-class women in New York and Chicago in the nineteenth and early twentieth centuries counter decades of urban history that ignored neighborhoods in favor of city halls and business districts.[9] These and other historians sought to understand the city through the eyes of the women who worked, played, and raised children there. They discovered rich networks of women who sought to make their own way in the world, often providing crucial economic support to working-class households and communities. Succeeding generations of historical scholarship expanded the cities and groups of women under consideration. More importantly, these scholars examined how women created new types of spaces through their actions and activism that ultimately led to their own "political empowerment," in the words of historian Sarah Deutsch.[10] Taken together, the work of Nan Enstad, A. Finn Enke, Maureen Flanagan, Jessica Sewell, LaKisha Simmons, Daphne Spain, Victoria Wolcott, Sharon Wood, and many others cited throughout this book reveals that women have been active city builders in their own right, shaping the political, cultural, social, and economic terrain of the urban worlds they inhabited.[11]

Building on this work, *Breaking the Gender Code* takes up a particular theme—public space—to broadly examine women's interventions in the ongoing process of urban development in the United States across the twentieth century. Race, class, and ethnicity, perhaps largely because of their deep connection to urban housing and economic patterns, have long been studied by urban historians. By comparison, the role of gender in organizing cities and shaping the experience of urban living has largely been overlooked; most of the studies noted earlier have rarely found an audience outside women's history circles. Perceptions of women, however, often track with Americans' perception of cities as places of opportunity, exclusion, excitement, decline, or danger. Approaching the urban experience through a focus on gender, then, reveals new ways to understand the interplay of multiple social identities and to assess the impact of broad cultural and economic changes on the experience of living in a city.

As these patterns suggest, gender segregation refracted the contours of twentieth-century history. Challenges to the system are easiest to find in moments when great change was accompanied by extensive social movements. It was also most pronounced when Americans understood their cities to be in crisis and saw them as places where divisions, competition, neglect, and discrimination often manifested in violence. These moments reflected fears that old mechanisms of social order had begun to break down, creating opportunity but also anxiety over what would come next. The first of these periods, marked by massive urban growth and the rise of Progressive reform, came in the early twentieth century and is explored in the early chapters of the book. Chapter 1 examines the gender codes applied to women migrating to American cities in the early decades of the twentieth century. While sexual panics over the kidnapping and exploitation of "girls" infused urban culture with tales of the dangers that women faced, women themselves and social reformers defended and justified women's increased public presence. Chapter 2 considers institution building, demands for urban services, and advocacy for infrastructure reform that accompanied arguments for women's need and right to access public space early in the century.

Organized challenges to gender segregation are harder to find in the decades when the nation appeared to be less interested in its cities and more focused on the economy or world politics than on social safety nets or human rights. During the economic depression of the 1930s, World War II, and the early Cold War, a masculinist language of self-determination dominated in movements around racial justice and labor rights, and protest shifted to shop floors and courtrooms. Chapter 3 looks at these middle decades of the century, when women's presence in public space raised markedly less concern, but the expectations for women's appearance and behavior while there remained constrained and even narrowed. Nevertheless, women from marginalized social groups found opportunities in America's prosperous postwar cities to push against these boundaries, and their actions sparked the civil rights movement of the 1950s and 1960s.

Another broad moment of opportunity came with the "rights revolutions" of the 1960s and 1970s. Chapters 4 and 5 explore the efforts of self-identified feminists of these decades to recognize ways in which the urban environment restrained, excluded, segregated, and troubled women. These activists targeted gender-based exclusions from public accommodations, named street harassment, and launched broad-based antiviolence campaigns that problematized the "commonsense" advice that women needed to stay away from public places. Chapter 6 looks at multigenerational and multiracial efforts to establish spaces that explicitly catered to women, offering a wide range of services not provided by family, the private marketplace, or government.

The rise of right-wing conservatism in the closing decades of the twentieth century provides perhaps the clearest evidence of the relationship between gender segregation and a broad array of civil and human rights. When Phyllis Schlafly and other conservatives sought to undermine ratification of the Equal Rights Amendment (ERA) in the 1970s and 1980s, they often invoked the end of gender-specific public toilets as a symbol of the social chaos the ERA would bring. Despite this backlash, by the closing decade of the century the work of previous generations had translated into aspects of gender segregation receiving sustained popular and policy attention, which created a third moment of attention to the gendering of public space. Chapter 7 examines the resulting policy work done in the 1990s to address a century of modern gender segregation. Reflecting women's unprecedented access to legislative, administrative, and economic power, cities, states, and the nation embraced new policies to improve public restroom access for women, address stalking and other forms of gender-based violence, and protect women breastfeeding in public. The epilogue reflects on the implications of this long history of organizing around access to public space for understanding contemporary debates within feminism, the progress of the women's movement, and current political arguments surrounding rights and access.

Although the specific narratives of danger, women's vulnerability, and their need or desire for protection in public spaces changed shape over the course of the twentieth century, they never disappeared; instead, these narratives remained relatively constant, as did their functions. Women's mobility was limited by depictions of women being accosted on the streets, lured into prostitution, or raped by strangers, as well as by the harassment and violence that women, particularly women of color, experienced. These narratives told women that the public spaces of cities would not be safe for them. Even when sympathetic voices called attention to women's plight, they often conveyed a message that women did not need to be in public, where they put themselves at risk of being preyed upon by the city's darker forces. Whether they featured the "white slaver" of the 1910s (what we might now label a "human trafficker") or the mugger of the 1970s, American society's narratives proclaimed public spaces for leisure, mass transit, and city sidewalks to be where women were most vulnerable. These narratives propagated a culture of fear that not only erased the harassment of individuals who were not white, straight, or cisgendered, but also deflected attention away from private spaces, where women have always been statistically far more likely to experience harm.

One of the key lessons offered by the stories in this book is that when women act as independent and autonomous individuals, they are often perceived as a threat to moral and social order. Women who challenge the norms of their day—whether motivated by necessity, determination, or even whimsy—are courageous in their self-reliance. Their actions are harder to see than those of participants in organized mass public protests whose motivations are overtly political. Whether it was the African American woman riding a streetcar at the turn of the twentieth century, the immigrant woman seeking to support herself in the 1910s, the lesbian searching out social connections in a bar in the 1950s, a lone white woman entering a bar in the 1970s, or a woman breastfeeding in a restaurant in the 1990s, their actions functioned as a form of what historian Leila Rupp has dubbed "everyday resistance."[12]

At particular moments, however, these instances of everyday resistance were joined by organized political attempts to change American society by challenging urban gender segregation. These were not the great battles for reform or social change in which women fought during the twentieth century—ending child labor, reforming prisons and the judicial system, confronting racial segregation, fighting tuberculosis, securing voting rights, ending workplace discrimination and sexual harassment, securing reproductive justice, creating gender equity in education, challenging rape culture, or critiquing a popular culture that demeaned and undermined women and minorities. Rather, challenges to urban gender segregation addressed a wide range of secondary issues that activists—mostly women but not exclusively so—encountered in their daily lives along the way to those major crusades. These issues, by themselves, might seem superfluous, minor, or even just silly. Taken together, however, they reveal the role of gender in organizing and stratifying American society. In the context of fighting for meaningful reforms or creating deep social change, such "little" issues add up.

Harassment on the street, exclusion from public accommodations, and a lack of public facilities represent the myriad ways in which women's access to public space—and by extension the larger public sphere—has been restricted by American laws, institutionalized racism, social customs, and even the built environment. If women cannot even prove their standing as members of the public enough to freely access "public" space, then how can they hope to establish their standing to advocate for deep social change, or to act as autonomous social and political beings? Seen in this light, customs, laws, public accommodations, and public services take on a deeply symbolic meaning, and activists across the twentieth century came to embrace them as worthy of action.

---- 1 ----

Right and Reason

Understandings of Women's Presence in the Modern City

"No, I'm not surprised," began a 1911 letter from a native-born white woman to her younger sister, but "it is going to give me a great deal of anxiety to think of your battling to make your own way in the city."[1] The elder sibling spoke from experience, having migrated ten years earlier when she joined a rising tide of immigrant, rural white, and Southern African American women arriving in cities in the early twentieth century. Another elder sister, an African American transplant to Chicago, wrote to her sibling advising her to come north, but warning, "We don't have much time to play but it is a matter of a dollar with me."[2] Whatever their ethnic or racial background, most of these newcomers were young, single, and working-class. Many fled racial or ethnic persecution, and virtually all sought economic opportunities that would allow them to support themselves. These elder sisters drew on their experience of urban living to offer practical suggestions on how to find work and housing. Nowhere in their advice did they suggest that the younger sisters needed to worry over moral dangers in the city. Rather, the elders warned of potential loneliness and financially lean years while they got themselves established. The tone and content of these letters indicate an important thread in the discussion of urban women taking place in the early decades of the twentieth century, namely women's emphasis on practicality and autonomy over sentimental morality.

Stories about self-supporting women like these sisters held an important place in the gendered cultural landscape of urban America at the turn of the twentieth century and provided the lens through which many urban women's experiences would be viewed. Women could draw on their language and interpretations to articulate their own experiences. These stories also represented both what women could expect from the city and the mixed response that society at large had to them, even those who were not newcomers. The new arrival—so often cast as young and single, with some variations according to race, ethnicity, or class—was often "everywoman." Talking about her real or imagined experiences was a commonplace mechanism for introducing and discussing women's needs in public space. And talk about her people did.

Early twentieth-century disruptions to the old order of urban life, fueled by urban growth, a maturing industrial economy, and the increased visibility of women's independent lives, gave rise to a new system of gender segregation built more on de facto, informal practices and tied to codifying notions of propriety surrounding women's behavior. Periodic moral panics over the abduction of women and their sexual vulnerability broadcast the alleged dangers women would face in cities. The messages of warning largely absolved society from ensuring women's safety, effectively telling women they needed to go out and about with caution. Racialized and classed expectations for behavior further communicated to women that their presence and actions in public were under scrutiny by community leaders and law enforcement. For some women, surveillance took the form of protections that restricted their presence; for others it was the threat of questioning, harassment, or removal at any time.

The concerns over moral danger and social order, however, existed alongside newer social, cultural, and commercial trends that welcomed and defended women's presence in cities. This distinctly modern perspective presented newly arrived women and those who lived and worked outside the confines of family as self-reliant and responsible agents, capable of sidestepping moral traps far more easily than they could sidestep poverty, ill health, harassment, loneliness, or poor working conditions. Many of these women and their defenders rejected men's protection and proclaimed women's ability to take care of themselves, while asserting their right to autonomy, independence, and even pleasure. Despite the dangers that, as American society promised, awaited lone women in the turn-of-the-century city, women continued to migrate to cities, where they took on paid employment, lived apart from family, and enjoyed at least some of the pleasures the city had to offer. They found allies in a commercializing leisure economy, shifting standards of etiquette, and at least some reformers and civil rights activists who rejected nineteenth-century sentimentality to focus instead on the material conditions of urban women's lives.

"The Girl Beginner in City Life": New Arrivals in Early Twentieth-Century Cities

When women arrived in American cities in record numbers in the decades surrounding the turn of the twentieth century, they greatly expanded their presence in the workforce and their visibility in urban public spaces. The number of women in the paid labor force rose from 18 percent of all women in 1890 to almost 24 percent in 1920. Demand for female workers in the industrial and service sectors of America's cities soared, pushing urban employment rates up far higher than in the nation generally. By 1920, over 40 percent of adult women in Boston and Atlanta worked for wages.[3] By 1930, 67 percent of women in Chicago held paying jobs.[4] As the proportion of women working for wages grew, so did the number of women living independent of family. A survey of twenty-eight American cities conducted in 1900 revealed that 19 percent of all employed women lodged away from relatives, and this number would increase tenfold over the next decade alone.[5] The newly arrived "girl beginner" seeking her fortune in the city became a familiar figure in newspapers, women's magazines, popular novels, and films of the early twentieth century. The titular character in Theodore Dreiser's 1900 novel *Sister Carrie* embodied the white, native-born version: Carrie came to Chicago from rural Wisconsin "full of the illusions of ignorance and youth."[6] Other versions of her could be glimpsed in tales of the immigrant girl landing in America and the "Negro girl" coming to the urban North. "Girls" of all types suddenly seemed to be everywhere.

Economic opportunity drove most of these "girls" to the city and often shaped their experiences with public space. Some, particularly immigrant women, arrived with or soon joined a family unit. Their contribution often came in the form of care work they provided for relations, which kept them close to home. Those who joined the ranks of waged labor—especially those who came alone or in advance of other family members—had much to master in order to successfully negotiate the urban environment. Reflecting on that learning curve, one migrant concluded, "It takes brave hearts and strong constitutions to battle with the hard, cruel ways of the city."[7]

Many of the "cruel ways" encountered by women migrants came down to economics. As young women seeking employment quickly learned, employers preferred women who lived at home with their family so that they might be paid less. Those who made their home in a boardinghouse or shared flat or even a tiny bedroom partitioned off from a hallway struggled—and often failed—to make ends meet in a wage structure based on the assumption that all women were dependents.[8] Women often chose living quarters based on cost but also took proximity to work into account. If an unskilled woman earning only a few dollars a week lived close enough to take her lunch at home, she could avoid paying streetcar fare and save precious nickels.[9] Renting a bedroom with housekeeping privileges or a studio fixed up with a rudimentary kitchen allowed women to do laundry and prepare some of their meals, so that they might need to rely on the budget restaurants common in furnished-room districts for only one meal a day. A not-insignificant amount of migrants' energy went into strategizing about where to find better-paying jobs and how to economize on living expenses.

A strong theme of self-reliance runs through the accounts that self-supporting women gave of their experiences in the city. "I always had confidence in myself," explained a resident of Spokane, Washington, reflecting on the source of her success.[10] Only later realizing the enormity of what she had taken on, an African American woman who arrived in Philadelphia in 1923 with only a suitcase and $100 quipped years later, "That's nerve, isn't it?"[11] They proclaimed their accomplishments and successes, in part, by pointing to their independent status: "Everything I've got . . . I've worked for it. I've worked hard for it." "I had really no help from any source—only my own determination." "I count my experience a success . . . [but] I never knew what responsibility was until I made my way in the world alone."[12] These new arrivals took pride in overcoming the challenges of adjusting to the new environment, earning their own way, and avoiding the pitfalls of urban living.

Women living in early twentieth-century cities understood that their physical appearance when in public shaped how they would be perceived and treated. Immigrant women arriving in America, if they had friends or family to help them, would be whisked off to buy new clothes immediately so that they would not look like "greenhorns."[13] Those seeking work learned "that to be well dressed was nearly half the battle in obtaining . . . a decent position."[14] Being recognized as new, uncertain, or needy could provide someone with an opening to intrude upon them under the guise of offering assistance or commentary. Women learned to hide any uncertainty or neediness they felt while they overcame their "greenness" and learned to navigate the city geographically as well as socially.[15]

Self-supporting women's approach to urban living—self-reliance and carefully crafted appearances—meshed well with shifting standards of etiquette. The codes of behavior embedded in the hundreds of advice manuals published in the late nineteenth and early twentieth centuries envisioned public space as truly shared, at least potentially civil, and very much open to women. At the turn of the twentieth century, etiquette manuals advised women not about when or why they might be out and about, but rather on how they might make their presence both pleasant and respectable. Self-possession and civility toward others served as the guiding principles behind the approach of twentieth-century advice manuals to public space, where everyone needed to show "true courtesy" to those around them.[16] Women should avoid spectacle, helplessness, and selfishness at all costs, lest they call attention to themselves or inconvenience others. Women were to show "quiet reserve," as was believed fitting for their sex, "but not haughty reserve" when in public.[17] Etiquette advisers instructed women to ask for and expect little assistance, recommending self-reliance when it came to paying a street-car fare, securing a seat, transporting packages, or managing an umbrella.[18] The most venerable voice in twentieth-century etiquette, Emily Post, was emphatic on the point that if a woman followed these rules, she could travel freely, "without the slightest risk of a disagreeable occurrence if she is herself dignified and reserved."[19]

This type of advice, which was typical in the early twentieth-century literature, tended to be phrased in positive terms of women exercising and expecting their freedoms. Lurking behind this language, however, were hints of what might await women who did not follow the rules and thereby opened themselves up to strangers on the street. Based in a relatively strict system of etiquette that urged women to ask for nothing from those around them, this advice was also a method of protection. If a woman took care of herself and otherwise limited her interactions—practicing what historian Sarah Deutsch has referred to as "personal restraint and bodily integrity"—then her intentions were less likely to be misinterpreted and her vulnerabilities were less susceptible to exploitation.[20] Although the etiquette manuals focused on women's rights, the subtext suggested women should guard their person and behavior closely in order to earn the privilege of safe access to public space. To encounter interference in public as imagined by this literature was not so much to face a physical attack as to have one's respectability questioned, or to face the intrusion of a stranger into one's private world. "The woman of to-day," explained a manual from the 1920s, "has much more freedom in pleasing herself regarding when and with whom she goes." That is, if she followed the rules.[21]

The connection between etiquette and respectability had special significance to African American women. Elite Black women challenged the arguments that African American depravity justified Jim Crow segregation by promoting an image of African Americans, especially women, as refined and cultured.[22] Deportment and appearance played a large role in these efforts, and advice manuals served as one means of promoting respectability and uplifting the race. In fostering an image of respectability, Charlotte Hawkins Brown, a prominent early twentieth-century African American reformer and educator from North Carolina, made no mention in her book *The Correct Thing to Do—to Say—to Wear* of her own race or how her advice might be tempered by the race of her readers. Her approach, and that of other advocates for African American rights in this era, was to insist, perhaps even to demand, that the "correct thing" was correct regardless of race.[23]

Immigrant and racial-minority women often faced similar expectations for their behavior and appearance in public. Unmarried Italian women living in urban America in the early twentieth century were under intense pressure from their families and communities to display public respectability. Since many of these women worked for wages and so had to leave their home neighborhood, men from the family usually escorted them to and from their workplace.[24] The nineteenth-century American association of Chinese women with immorality and prostitution cast a long shadow over women's presence in public until at least World War II. Chinese families monitored their daughters closely, often limiting their exposure to men and shielding them from white men in particular.[25] To avoid the intrusions and harassment white American society condoned for "loose" women, women of Chinese ancestry had to present themselves carefully in public, often relying on men to escort them around the city or staying within the boundaries of Chinese neighborhoods.[26] To distance their young women—and by extension their whole community—from the negative portrayals of African American and Chinese women, Japanese immigrant communities placed heavy expectations on them to present an image of cultured grace.[27] In this way, gender performance served as a race project.

In telling their own stories of living in early twentieth-century cities, self-supporting women often described their experiences in public space, revealing an awareness of the expectations for "correct" behavior. "It is very trying," explained an African American migrant, "for a good girl to be out in a large city by [her]self among strangers."[28] Whether learning to get around, traveling to find work and housing, commuting daily to work, or just enjoying the leisure-time offerings and the spectacle of the city, independent women invariably spent a great deal of time out and about. The close association of public space with moral vulnerability in the nineteenth century did not fade entirely in the early twentieth century, as women recognized. The frequency with which women commented on their experiences moving

through the city certainly suggests an awareness of the possibility of harassment and victimization on the street, but their stories put these dangers in
perspective and highlighted their own capabilities. "I don't think there was
one evening . . . that I went home unmolested," a white shop clerk reported
of her nightly walk home from work. This Bostonian felt unable to traverse
the business district without "a man at my side questioning me as to where
I lived, and if I would not like to go to dinner, how I was going to spend the
evening, etc." Revealing both the anxiety these encounters produced and her
clear feeling that her autonomy was being unjustly imposed upon, she "never
answered, except to threaten to speak to the police." Although she felt that
she could threaten to call the police to her defense, she also confessed that
she would have felt "ashamed to do it."[29] She ultimately seemed to think that
if she only presented herself with enough "dignity," she could ward off intrusions. Whether her protection was to come from her own comportment or
from police officers, she clearly felt entitled to her privacy as she traversed her
routes between home and work.

After the turn of the century, the willingness of women who encountered
gender-based harassment while in public to respond directly to harassers—in
surprisingly forthright ways—began attracting attention. Dorothy Richardson, an undercover reporter passing as an unskilled woman seeking to eke out
a living in New York City in the early 1900s, reported on one such encounter.
In Richardson's telling, a young woman waged a "heroic defense" of herself
by physically pushing away a man who offered her an "unwarranted" invitation to the theater and touched her arm.[30] Women's actions on sidewalks and
streetcars in defense of their personal space indicated that they felt entitled
to be in public and would rely on themselves to defend that right. As historian Estelle Freedman argues, this stance was driven by a feminist "political
critique of male sexual privilege" akin to campaigns to secure the vote for
women and protect girls from exploitation by raising the legal age for sexual
consent.[31] However, it also reflected a shifting understanding of women's unescorted presence in public: a woman alone in public was no longer regarded
as an unfortunate circumstance but as a sign of the modern era.

The "masher" began appearing in the press in the late nineteenth century,
but the height of attention to this stock urban character came in the 1900s
and 1910s, when attention—and praise—fell on women who rebuffed his
advances. The masher, unlike the *flâneur*, who merely observed the urban tab-
leau, took pleasure in approaching women on the street, on trains and streetcars, and in public accommodations, offering comments on their appearance,
inviting them to go out, and sometimes even taking their arm. When a man

jumped out of a dark alley to intercept two women on their way home from a Chicago theater in 1903, one of the women grabbed the man's umbrella and began beating him while the other alerted the police. The judge, who fined the man $50, praised the women's actions, saying, "If more girls had the spirit of these two, 'mashing' would be stopped in short order." The *Chicago Daily Tribune* also reported the women's defense of themselves, particularly the "full force" umbrella blow to the assailant's face, in congratulatory tones.[32] Backing up the "plucky" girls fending off mashers, some authors of etiquette manuals further encouraged women to defend their independence in public. "Be merry and pleasant and have a good time, but don't let any man feel that he can treat you with aught but respect," instructed a 1913 book. The author went on to explain that "a young girl who is a victim of persistent and unwanted attentions must be excused for defending herself even roughly."[33]

Women defending themselves were a new addition to the cultural narratives of the early decades of the century. In 1907, young white Chicago women from a Michigan Avenue factory laid plans to teach a lesson to the masher who frequented the sidewalk in front of their workplace, annoying them on their way to and from work. While her coworkers went across the street to watch, the appointed "teacher" artfully unfurled her umbrella at just the right moment to send the masher's fine silk hat into a muddy puddle.[34] An Atlanta woman on her way home from work answered the "insults" a man offered her on the streets with a series of blows that sent the masher sprawling on the sidewalk. The press, obviously delighted in stories of women beating up men who sought to prey upon their presence in public spaces, added these new "heroines" to the cultural story of this era. When a police officer asked the Atlanta woman if she wished to press charges, she responded, "I think he has been punished enough . . . but I would like to get him in some place where I could teach him a good lesson."[35] Perhaps more telling is that nowhere in these sometimes humorous—but always admiring—press accounts did the reporters, the police, or, apparently, the public at large question women's choice or right to answer unknown men's "smiles" with "punches."[36]

While tales of women's physical or humorous actions against harassment in public most often attracted the press, some women raised the issue of harassment only to question whether it existed. White women in particular, when recounting their experiences as self-supporting urban women, often noted they had not had negative encounters: "I never had any unpleasant experiences." "I have yet to be spoken to in a way that any girl would resent." "I have never met with any incivility either in the cars or on the street." "I have never had a stranger speak to me or any one make any advances."[37] That women frequently addressed the issue of harassment, even though they denied having encountered it, testifies to the power of the masher trope and the limits that concerns over harassment put on women's mobility. Women who spoke about the issue felt they had to explain themselves, justify their actions, and correct misperceptions. If the purported danger did not prove to be real, then what was to prevent them from going out as they chose? Both their proclamations of safety and comfort on city streets at night and their indignation at not being able to travel "unmolested" served as clear indicators that they claimed for themselves the right to be there.

The racialized public discourse of the early twentieth century left little room for the existence of nonwhite mashers. Where mashers were generally recognized as annoyances, most men of color, particularly African American men, who flirted with a woman on the street would have been read as a sexual predator. Reluctant to fuel the myth of the Black rapist used to justify lynching Black men and the political disenfranchisement of African Americans, the African American press, not surprisingly, shied away from reporting on Black men "mashing" on women. When the Black masher figure did appear in these accounts, he was depicted as a source of humor and his actions were not reported as actual news or a crime but as relatively innocent, with African American women being his unconcerned targets.[38] Under the shadow of Jim Crow and early twentieth-century racial politics, there was little room for Black women to raise alarm over being accosted by Black men without reinforcing the myth of the Black rapist, and both the Black press and most Black women were loath to do so. White men harassing Black women, however, triggered long-standing grievances, and the African American press championed Black women who defended themselves against such harassment. Accounts circulated of Black women successfully defending their sexual respectability against the white men who propositioned them. Sometimes these women physically fended off a man, but more often the stories ended with police intervention, jail time, and a fine for the masher.[39]

African American women's sexual vulnerability to white men was certainly not new, but the narratives surrounding it in the early twentieth century moved their vulnerability out of the white home—where a lone domestic worker might find herself cornered by any of the men in the family employing her—and into urban public space. Black leaders condemned "renegade men, who would not dare approach the women of their own race" but who harassed African American women on the street.[40] Black newspapers faithfully reported stories of the "woman of culture" and the "plucky" young woman resisting the advances of white mashers or harassment from white mobs.[41] These stories served as a political tool in a larger fight to undermine white supremacy. Their retelling asserted African American women's entitlement to safety from harassment when in public, based explicitly on their status as women. Not surprisingly, the white press failed to report on these stories. The Black woman did not fit in the white media's narrative of a respectable heroine righteously defending herself.

The racialized gender harassment of Black women from multiple sources expanded the layers of danger they needed to negotiate when in public. Willie Mae Cartwright, an Atlanta domestic worker with a sense of style, proudly recalled "wanting to put on the dog" (dress stylishly) when she went out at night after work. Her style, however, attracted the attention of a white police officer. Assuming she was dressed too nicely to have come by her ensemble honestly, he felt perfectly entitled to bring her into the station and telephone her employer. "I was," she remembered, "so scared I was weak" after his intrusive questioning.[42] Even though the police officer let her go, the racialized gender code that determined how a woman of color should appear when in the public spaces of this early twentieth-century city had clearly been enforced.

African American women also faced particularly frequent harassment from white transit workers and white passengers on public transportation. For African American women, streetcars and buses proved a crucial tool for transitioning away from live-in domestic work, common in the nineteenth century, to the increasingly common domestic day-work positions of the twentieth century. Owing to the racial residential segregation common in American cities, African American women, 90 percent of whom worked as domestics, needed a reliable means of transportation if they were to get from their own homes to those of the white families that employed them. As one DC domestic worker reported, "The streetcar took up most of the time I got."[43] This almost daily reliance on public transportation exposed African American women to harassment driven by the racialized and gendered practices of the city during the Jim Crow era. African American women, however, responded in surprisingly confrontational ways to harassment on public conveyances. During the 1906 Atlanta race riot, when white mobs rampaged through the city's public spaces, Black women traveling through the city's downtown became targets of white male violence. One woman was pulled from a car and stripped, while those who attempted to assist her were beaten away with barrel staves. Other women more successfully fought back. A Black woman riding a streetcar defended herself like "a savage wildcat" with her umbrella; another wielded her hatpin as a weapon.[44] Although African

American women often avoided conflict in other public spaces, they proved remarkably unwilling to cede quietly their rights on public transportation.

Whether their motivation sprang from economic need or a desire to enjoy the spectacle of the modern city, early twentieth-century women took to the city streets with some amount of both confidence and caution. As the African American women riding public transportation demonstrated, urban women had a keen willingness to act on their perceived right to be in public, even when challenged by mashers, police, or popular tales of moral danger. The "girl beginner" might have arrived in the city with little knowledge of how to negotiate it, but popular and firsthand accounts from the early twentieth century indicate that she was a fast learner. Accounts of her experiences, particularly those appearing in magazines, newspapers, and novels, also reveal that the cultural narrative had shifted to accommodate women's increasing visibility in urban public space and to popularize images of them as plucky, determined, and independent.

Commercial developments reinforced the expectation of women in public, and even its desirability. Department store owners relied on women to make up much of their clientele, and they designed their establishments specifically to attract women and serve their needs with everything from lunchrooms to lounges and childcare facilities.[45] Theater owners looking to profit from the growing popularity of vaudeville sought female audience members in order to counter the rough reputation of male-dominated burlesque.[46] New Orleans, a city struggling to alter its reputation for "male-centered attractions," encouraged entertainment and businesses that would attract both men and women. A sociology professor studying this transformation in 1919 credited women with rescuing "civic virtue by seeking a less offensive urban society devoid of rowdy behavior."[47] Women apparently accomplished this feat through their very presence and the good behavior that their presence was expected to encourage in both genders. And for their part, many women eagerly accepted the opportunities that desire for their patronage created.

"Unseen Danger Is Lurking": Twentieth-Century Moral Panics

In what would become a familiar pattern throughout the twentieth century, the changes and opportunities that seemed to appear almost suddenly for women provoked a wave of moral panics. The lurid tales of exploitation and abduction of lone women in the nation's cities that circulated in the 1900s and 1910s signaled women's sexual vulnerability. Under the guise of protection, city officials and newly created anti-vice commissions enacted policies to detain lone women arriving in cities and even to send some back home. Urged on by social purity reformers, they also turned women away from commercial amusements and restricted their presence in other public spaces. As women's own accounts of city living reveal, the messages embedded in these moral panics hit home; though many claimed not to have encountered issues, they had absorbed the message that they should be expecting interference as an inherent part of urban living. It would be easy to read these cultural messages of danger as a throwback to an earlier time, but they played an integral role in creating and maintaining twentieth-century gender segregation by broadcasting the alleged dangers women faced in public.

Perhaps the most pronounced of these early twentieth-century moral panics were embodied in the shocking and nearly obsessive stories of "white slavery"—young women being lured to the city and trapped into lives of prostitution. The Women's Christian Temperance Union (WCTU), which had been the largest women's organization in the nineteenth century, joined forces with other social purity reformers and newly created anti-vice commissions to raise the alarm over violent abduction, drugging, and coercion of women into sexual slavery that some likened to African American slavery before the Civil War (an analogy that did not sit well with many Black people).[48] Concern over sex trafficking through cities almost always centered white women, focusing heavily on the procurement of native-born women from the countryside and small towns and generally excluding women of color from the calls for protection. In this way, the white slavery scare was particularly revealing of nativist and racist responses to early twentieth-century immigration and African American migration. White Americans often refused to see women of color involved in sex work as potential victims, be they Chinese immigrants or African Americans. And the traffickers in white slavery tales were almost invariably cast as men of color or foreign birth.[49] The policies and laws that followed from the white slavery scare point to the complicated ways in which gender segregation threaded through other systems of control. When police surveilled white women in public places, particularly at commercial amusements, they promised protection, but this protection came with a price. It reinforced assumptions of women's naivete and privileged restrictions on their behaviors over their autonomy. For most immigrant women and women of color, such protection generally excluded them from gender privileges altogether, further aligning the category of "women" with American-ness and whiteness. This pattern of restricting white women's behavior in the name of protection

Moral panics of the early twentieth century cast cities as dangerous places for young women. "The Traffic in Girls: White Slavery as Now Practiced in America," c. 1900. (University of Wisconsin Digital Collections)

while relegating other women to categories deemed unworthy of protection became common across the twentieth century.

These moral panics also subtly suggested that women were ultimately responsible for any ill treatment they received by having entered public space in the first place.[50] If they had stayed home or under the watchful eye of their family, they would not have been available targets for exploitation. Typical of this view, one reformer wrote in 1910, "Perhaps more girls, craving amusement and fun, have travelled to their ruin over the smooth, glistening floors of innocent looking public dance halls, than in any other way."[51] Suggesting it was women who made themselves available to be lured into prostitution, another white anti-vice crusader declared, "Those who know the danger will not put themselves into a position of risk."[52] Clifford Roe, an Illinois state prosecutor who followed numerous cases related to white slavery, shared the story of "Agnes" as an example of a young woman who thought herself clever enough to attend a dance alone. There a young man "'jollied' her and told her how pretty she was . . . she went with him willingly, simply because he had pleased her by his artful gratifying of her vanity."[53] These accounts removed women's agency, painting them as vain and naive creatures too "mystified by the glare and light of the large cities after night" to resist the wiles of white slavers. Roe's accounts of white slavery identified public spaces as dangerous for women and offered only one solution: women were to avoid entering these spaces.

Other moral and sexual panics created similar narratives of danger for women of color and immigrant women. Neglect, censure, and harassment fell particularly hard on women who exhibited racial, ethnic, or class characteristics that associated them with populations that whites believed to be hypersexual or prone to sexual impropriety. In the cities of the American West, white women reformers raised alarm over Chinese immigrant women being lured or forced into prostitution, and they created institutions to reform Chinese women by settling them into marriage, often away from the city.[54] Public health officials also targeted Chinese women as agents of contagion who spread venereal diseases to white men, who then brought them into white homes.[55]

Leaders in African American urban communities, particularly those in the urban North and Midwest, raised concerns over what W.E.B. Du Bois called the "excess" of single Black women migrating to cities.[56] Many long-standing members of African American communities in the North feared these women would be exploited by unscrupulous labor agents or employment bureaus and forced into prostitution or work as domestics in brothels. As the number of migrants rose, so too did the cries of alarm that the "lure of pretty clothes and stories of gay life" would draw Black women to cities where they would be abandoned or exploited by whites.[57] Concern over the sexual vulnerability of single women intertwined, however, with suspicion of the moral corruption these migrants brought with them and the harm that corruption might inflict on the larger population. In this way, lone women migrants often carried the weight of racial advancement on their backs. Race leaders endorsed an agenda of racial uplift in which African American demands for civil rights rested heavily upon the restrained, industrious, and respectable behavior of women.[58] Such inherently political behavior was meant to counter racist stereotypes of laziness and licentiousness that supported segregation and discrimination. This confrontational aspect of respectability focused the attention of some race leaders on the behaviors and bodies of young and single Black women migrants, particularly in public space.

In the resulting moral panics surrounding African American women migrants, concern over women's safety often found expression through condemnation of the latest arrivals and their presence and presentation in public.[59] Commentators seemed to accept the existence of corrupting forces in the urban environment, and their response reinforced an image of women's sexual vulnerability. "Unseen danger is lurking around them upon every side," one African American minister explained. As he continued, however, it became clear that his solution did not confront those dangers and instead focused on the women, who, he declared, would need to stop "walk[ing] unattended the streets of our cities." They needed to guard against "overtures" from white men. If a woman did not present herself with "modesty" and the "greatest reserve," she would be taking the "first step to infamy and ruin," by which "she unfits herself for the loving office of either mother or wife" and "both defiles her body and destroys her soul." "Unchaste" women, he argued, must be thoroughly shunned for the good of the race. "The leniency with which sexual offenses are treated by colored society is largely responsible for the universal and slanderous charges which thoughtless white men indiscriminately make against our women as a whole." While admitting that men had a part to play in the image and treatment of the race, he chose not to address them, instead saying to young women, "You have it almost entirely in your power to make the social standard what you please."[60] These narratives of moral danger created a less than welcoming message for new arrivals. Stressing both the danger they faced and their own responsibility to avoid it, this message warned these women that they would be monitored by the larger community for any indication that they were further dragging down the already abused race.

The efforts to preserve and present African American respectability permeated Black newspapers and other media, middle-class women's organizational work, and many other efforts to assist newly arrived migrants, creating a culture of surveillance around African American women. Women who did not behave in ways deemed appropriate were labeled loose, disorderly, or immoral. Advice columns in the Black press, manuals on manners and health, advice books, and the organizational efforts of Black and white reformers instructed women of color to manage their bodies, behaviors, and thoughts so as not to further feed negative stereotypes of African Americans as sexually licentious. As literary scholar Nazera Sadiq Wright's analysis of this advice reveals, young Black women were told that "ignoring social rules was a tacit message that they would be willing participants in any violence inflicted on their bodies."[61] To be a "Loud Girl" or "Don't-Care Girl"—to be too rowdy, take up too much space, or be too bold—was to risk having one's character questioned and consequently hindering the progress of the race. When reformers, particularly middle-class African Americans, challenged the racial politics of the early twentieth century, they also perpetuated tropes of cities as dangerous for women and held women responsible for not just the negative experiences they might have but also the poor treatment of the race. The respectability envisioned by racial uplift ideology often centered heavily on a proper home lovingly and thriftily cared for by a demure and capable African American woman. This grounding in a private, domestic space cast Black women in public as socially and sexually suspect and brought censure to women whose attire, behavior, or presence in crowded commercial amusements suggested anything other than sexual restraint, thrift, and hard work. While often purporting to support women, proponents of racial uplift ideology laid claim to a narrowly defined respectability, and their rhetoric about the need to "uplift the standards of true womanhood" often cast women's public presence as disgraceful or improper.[62] The assimilationist and uplift strategies pursued by elite members of immigrant and nonwhite communities exacerbated the obstacles some women faced when accessing public space.

As a result of the various early twentieth-century moral panics, many middle-class Americans supported legal, institutional, and social measures designed to keep unescorted women away from public accommodations and commercial amusements.[63] Some reformers, writers, and politicians, for example, proclaimed that "women must keep off the streets," and they endorsed policies that restricted women's presence in dance halls and saloons.[64] Sensationalized tales of abduction and exploitation also translated into greater concerns over women traveling alone at precisely the same time as opportunities for travel on railroads and streetcars expanded. Although the specific dangers women faced would change, the dual trope of vulnerability and just desserts proved to have remarkable staying power, forming a core element of twentieth-century gender segregation.

"To Take Her Place in the World": Defending Women in Public Space

Tales of danger and the judgments embedded in the moral panics empha-sized women's vulnerability and justified heavy scrutiny of their behaviors. Even when police and reformers purportedly addressed these threats, their rhetoric and solutions focused heavily on restricting women's mobility, ques-tioning their presence in public, and instructing them that staying away was the only safe path. However, these narratives, the cornerstone of de facto twentieth-century urban gender segregation, did not go unchallenged. The actions of women themselves and their allies combined with emerging cul-tural and commercial trends that defended and even celebrated women's pub-lic presence.

The actions of urban women reveal that many not only used public space, but also reveled in it. Women who chose new forms of mobility and pub-lic leisure, such as driving their own carriage (for those rich enough to have such resources) or riding a bicycle (a more accessible trend at the turn of the century), accepted and sometimes encouraged the attention their presence drew.[65] Despite the association of visibility with danger embedded in moral panics, some women enjoyed the attention of strangers and even sought it out. Thomas Edison's short 1901 film *What Happened on Twenty-Third Street, New York City* captures a small slice of the transitions afoot in women's use of public space.[66] As a young white woman passes over a grate in the sidewalk, a rush of air blows up her skirt to reveal stocking-clad lower legs. She rushes to hold her skirt from rising any further while her befuddled male companion struggles to pull her along. But then she throws her head back with a roar of laughter, acknowledging with good humor the responses of those around her who have observed the episode. As the film ends a second later, her face holds a wide smile as she walks on. This woman clearly embraced the urban adventure. And she was not alone. The intersection of Twenty-Third Street and Sixth Avenue in New York at the foot of the new Flatiron Building, near the setting of Edison's film, developed a reputation for frequent wind gusts that played with women's clothing. Both men and women gathered at the intersection to watch and display. While police officers told the men who lin-gered to "skidoo" (origins of the phrase "23 skidoo"), women apparently did

I am seeing great things.

New York's Flatiron Building developed a reputation as a tourist attraction for men. Wind gusting through the intersection of Twenty-Third Street and Sixth Avenue played with women's clothing, offering tantalizing glimpses of legs. "I am seeing great things," postcard, c. 1910. (Museum of the City of New York, X2011.34.106) not avoid the area. Clearly, for some women, flirting and being watched had become more exciting than threatening.

By embracing the spectacle and even comfort of a bustling city street, women claimed their right to derive pleasure from the public realms of the city. The beautiful sister in *Bread Givers*, Anzia Yezierska's 1925 novel about young Jewish immigrant women, pretends to complain about the "freshness" of men she encounters while looking for work, but she obviously enjoys the "million eyes" that follow her as she walks the street.[67] As a real-life stenographer reflected, "There is something about the noises, the teeming life, of New York which always puts new life into me."[68] Poor living conditions and oppressive work spaces often made streets, parks, and whatever commercial amusements women could access welcome refuges from the "ugly" and "loveless" spaces in which they slept and worked.[69] Whatever their struggles to find work and adequate housing, the excitement and diversions of the early twentieth-century city captivated independent women, and they eagerly joined the "hurrying crowds."[70]

Women in cities found allies in an emerging and often more pluralistically minded collection of social reformers eager to defend women's desire for respectable self-reliance. Drawn primarily from the ranks of educated, urban, comfortably classed women, these reformers eschewed overly moralistic approaches in favor of practical solutions to material problems. They challenged religious and law-and-order reformers who obsessed over women's sexual vulnerability and the inherent danger cities posed to women by arguing for women's dignity and right to bodily autonomy. Jane Addams, the white founder of the best-known settlement house in the United States and a champion of Progressive reform, took up an earnest defense of America's youth, and particularly young women, in her 1909 book *The Spirit of Youth and the City Streets.* "The mass of [these] young people are possessed of good intentions," she argued, "and they are equipped with a certain understanding of city life."[71] She chided American society for taking advantage of the labor of young people, offering meager earnings while overworking them during the day, and exploiting their "love of pleasure" at night for profit. She expected that modern cities of the early twentieth century could and should do better by making opportunities available to those in their midst who were willing to live industriously. This kind of thinking represented a notable shift in the cultural landscape from the nineteenth-century safeguarding of morality to an argument for safeguarding women instead.

Although Addams's position as an educated, genteel, middle-aged white woman often led her to call for an oversimplified and race-blind civic good, her sympathies clearly lay with the youth, especially young working-class women.[72] "As these overworked girls stream along the streets," she wrote, "the rest of us see only the self-conscious walk, the giggling speech, the preposterous clothing. And yet through the huge hat, with its wilderness of bedraggled feathers, the girl announces to the world that she is here."[73] Histories of cross-class relationships during this period certainly provide ample evidence that middle-class women often objected to the flamboyant clothing of young working-class women.[74] Addams, however, asked her readers to look past the style and accept young women's desire for autonomy. "She demands attention to the fact of her existence, she states that she is ready to live, to take her place in the world . . . and has an individual contribution to make."[75] To aid young women in taking up their rightful place in the city and making their mark on the world, Addams and her cohort of clubwomen and social reformers argued that cities could not leave recreation to unscrupulous entrepreneurs. Instead, they insisted, cities needed to better "organize" play, as they were beginning to do for labor with the regulation of workplaces. City officials should recognize youth's need for recreation and "make safe the street in which the majority of our young people find their recreation and form their permanent relationships."[76] Reformers also argued for better pay and safer streets to aid single and working women in their quest to take up "their rightful place in the world." This was a new vision for the new century, one that demanded that cities be remade to accommodate and accept women's presence. "Whose duty is it, good people, to help her find herself and get the most out of city life?" queried one proponent of more supports for young women.[77] Progressive Era reformers' efforts on behalf of independent urban women did much to draw the nation's attention to the plight of the "girl beginner."

Although the moralizing tone of some of the reformers' language would be easy to read as judgmental and often revealed a deep elitism, their efforts to improve the lives of working women indicate an unwavering sympathy for the challenges they faced. This tension is particularly clear in the work of African American clubwomen in cities such as New York, Chicago, Boston, Atlanta, Washington, DC, and Philadelphia. Fannie Barrier Williams, an African American educator and activist, took up the defense of Black women early in the first Great Migration, declaring that, though they might arrive unaware of the "snares and pitfalls" of a city, they would come to thrive and be "confident in their own worth" with only a bit of assistance.[78] Jane Edna Hunter, who took up the cause of migrant women in Cleveland, used similar language: "A girl alone in a large city must needs know the angers and pitfalls awaiting her."[79] Both reformers noted the particular problems faced by African

American women. As Williams sympathetically explained, "There has been no fixed public opinion to which they could appeal; no protection against the libelous attacks upon their characters, and no chivalry generous enough to guarantee their safety against man's inhumanity to woman."[80] Activist and educator Mary Church Terrell stated the problem even more boldly: "Colored women have been regarded as the rightful prey of every white man."[81] Reformers sought to be working women's allies and defenders in the face of laws and "public sentiment" that allowed these conditions to flourish. They believed women had a right to work and play in the city without endangering their health or reputation. Reformers' visions of the city certainly encouraged women to curtail some of their activities, but their efforts to reform institutions, rules, infrastructure, and customs to support women's independent existence reveal at least some motivation to better equip women to act upon their rights.

The defense of self-supporting women offered by Addams, Williams, Hunter, and others reveals that many reformers themselves believed that cities posed a threat to young and single women, but their response differed markedly from that of moralizing anti-vice crusaders. Rather than seeking to send women away or reinstall them in their families of origin, this new breed of reformer hoped to arm women with the tools they needed for an independent life. They advocated for a form of etiquette and respectability that women could use as a shield against harassment, hassling, judging, and intrusions. To be sure, there were limits to the rights reformers sought to protect for women. They generally did not support women's right to go anywhere they pleased, whenever they wanted, and with whomever, but they did endorse women's right to earn their living and have access to enough money, a decent living space, and some recreation in order to enjoy life without being questioned, blamed, harassed, or stigmatized. These reformers believed self-supporting women had the right to live a decent life (though their own class biases were revealed in what they considered decent) without being victimized by employers, landlords, strange men, and entrepreneurs of the leisure trades. However tinged with middle-class morality and virtue their approach might have been, the women who promoted this response saw it as a pragmatic way to negotiate the many obstacles women encountered in the city.

Pronouncements that both subtly and obviously defended women's presence in the public realm stood alongside sentimental tales of young girls being "rescued" from dangerous dance halls and boardinghouses. Some women's organizations advocated for (and even paid for) women matrons and police to patrol streets and commercial leisure venues—not to remove women but rather to arrest the men who preyed upon young women who were seeking amusement.[82] The white Atlanta Woman's Club approached the "so-called 'fall' of these young women" not by calling up images of moral ruin but by explaining that "young girls are generally attracted to the motion picture shows and cheap vaudeville by a lack of proper amusement and recreation in their homes."[83] The solution that they and their counterparts in cities across the country suggested was not to ban women from public space, but rather to accept "nature's demand for the free, joyous social life" and provide women with better recreation venues.[84] To lump these efforts in with the work of anti-vice crusaders is to ignore the practical advice and supportive efforts of the organizations that created or lobbied for such services.

In their attempts to support women and build their self-reliance, reformers sometimes targeted women themselves as the objects of reform. Middle-class women's clubs launched efforts to convince working-class women to present themselves more carefully in public. These women were encouraged to practice self-reliance and restraint to limit interference or unwanted attention. Women were told to avoid pausing in public, lest they attract attention from "corner loafers."[85] They were told to adorn themselves with care when out in public. As pamphlets for Detroit's African American "Dress Well Club" explained, "Carelessness in regards to dress will lead to discrimination and segregation."[86] Reformers assumed that women of any race would experience fewer impediments in their public lives if they appeared demure, urban, and respectable in their dress and deportment. Although it is easy to dismiss these efforts as the judgmental actions of wealthier women toward their poorer counterparts, better dress advocates explained their efforts as a practical means by which women could negotiate the landscape of public urban space with the least amount of friction.

In further defense of independent women, many reformers of the Progressive Era argued for two interrelated points when it came to what women needed. First, they called for more protection for women in the form of better policing, employment laws, and regulation of commercial amusements. For African American reformers, such calls very much included challenging Jim Crow racial segregation as well. Second, they supported changes that could help eliminate the need for protection by improving women's economic and social position. Policies ensuring better pay, for example, would allow women to become economically self-sufficient and could protect them from predatory employers and landlords. But reformers also had a message for women on how to be their own best allies. Activist and artist Mabel Dodge offered this to young women: "Don't allow your men to be too familiar in words or action. Don't visit a young man at his place of business. . . . Don't accept a present from a young man if you are not engaged to him."[87] And while all those "don'ts" surely encouraged restrained behavior, they can also be read as advice meant to support women: free from entanglements with men and unwanted attention, women could maintain their independence.

Although the dealings of some social reformers, community leaders, and "race women" with the women migrating to American cities in the early twentieth century sometimes smacked of elitism, they generally sought to foster the independence of those they saw as their less-privileged sisters. Similarly, the magazines and newspapers that printed migrants' letters and stories about the "girl beginner" often chose material that offered insights on practical matters such as adjusting to city life, getting work, finding housing, and budgeting for city living. Certainly, the behaviors being encouraged in women through etiquette and reform activities disciplined their conduct in ways that resonated with middle-class mores, but such encouragement did not preclude the cultivation of empowerment, self-reliance, and a sense of autonomy in women of other classes. Reformers respected working-class women and advocated that society only "give her a fair chance."[88] This early twentieth-century transition in how women's presence in public space was understood, while incomplete, was still profound.

Conclusion

Clear evidence that women had achieved a new status in public space came with a short-lived attempt to return to gender-specific accommodations. "Ladies'" entrances, counters, waiting rooms, and hours had been the hallmark of nineteenth-century gender segregation, reinforcing gender distinctions and preserving male spaces in hotels, banks, theaters, post offices, train stations, railcars, and pharmacies. These accommodations created supposedly "safe" spaces and practices for respectable women who were drawn into public so that they might retain the virtue usually associated with the private sphere. These spaces never offered enough access or services, not even to white, middle- and upper-class women, and they had largely fallen out of favor by the twentieth century. When a rapid transit line on the East Coast revived the practice in 1909 by reserving the last car on rush-hour trains for women only, controversy erupted. Proponents argued that a "ladies' car" would appeal to "those who are physically unable to cope with the fearful crushes, those who travel with children, and those who have suffered from insults and indignities which they have been powerless to avoid."[89] The experiment on the rail line in question, which ran from New Jersey to Manhattan, sparked interest across the country.

The image of women as powerless did not sit well with many women's rights advocates. Some responded that "men would consider that all the rest of the train belonged to them." Florence Kelley, a prominent white reformer in Chicago, declared the idea "perfect nonsense," explaining, "The last thing in the world women want is to be segregated."[90] Harriot Stanton Blatch, president of the Equality League of Self-Supporting Women, was quick to point out that "the women crowd as much as the men."[91] She recognized women's claim to public space, even when that claim took physical form in the battle for seats and standing space on crowded trains, and she made no apology for it. To her mind, women held their own and needed no special accommodations. Echoing Blatch's sentiment, one woman rider dodged a porter trying to direct her to the ladies' car, explaining simply, "I am no better than the men."[92]

While these comments reveal an acceptance of women's presence in public, they also hint at the frank and gendered discussion of public behavior this experiment provoked. One woman complained that women did not use transportation correctly; she had been forced to "take protection behind the backs of men when a scrambling, jamming crowd of women was trying to get on the cars."[93] A man moaned over women's pushing, "sour faces," and "bad tempers."[94] Women complained of men who stood holding newspapers in both hands, expecting those around them to hold them up on swaying cars; men who acted like the "star hog" by crossing their legs and letting one "hoof project . . . into the centre of the car"; and men who "push and jam" to get to seats first.[95] When proponents referenced the need for a ladies' car because men no longer offered their seats to women, men vented their frustrations. "The kindliness of our nature," one man's letter to the editor of the *New York Times* began, "has been unequal to the pressure of the rush hour." Men reported feeling there were no good options left to "conserve some . . . self-respect and also avoid scenes."[96]

In light of the controversial response, the cost of employing porters to serve women specifically and keep men off the designated cars, and the number of women who jumped on the first open car rather than traipse along to the ladies' car at the back, the company abandoned its experiment after only four months.[97] While appropriate etiquette for public conveyances continued to be questioned through the middle of the century, popular wisdom finally settled on the custom of giving up one's seat, if one were able, only to someone in obvious need or to someone who appeared more worthy than oneself—a concept that often invoked racial and class distinctions. Merely being a particular gender would no longer be sufficient cause in and of itself for anyone to relinquish the prize of a perch in a crowded car. The battle over personal space in public places continues to this day. Anyone who has ridden public transportation in the twenty-first century or followed discussions of it on social media might realize that the "star hog" has now been replaced by the "man spreading" rider.

Gender segregation came to look different in the twentieth century than it had in the nineteenth. The contours of the system surfaced in the discussions about new arrivals in the early decades of the century. Women found tacit—and sometimes even enthusiastic—acceptance of their presence in public, but moral panics also strengthened the message that women faced danger there. Such danger was often accepted as inevitable, and as something that women themselves would need to manage. The tensions of this era laid out a pattern that persisted across the century. Narratives of danger; messages that women could, and must, behave their way out of or around danger; censure and hostility toward women who were judged to act too casually or freely; and pressure on racially and ethnically marginalized women to represent their communities—all ultimately constrained women's access to public space and formed the core elements of twentieth-century gender segregation. Women's own actions, however, along with organized efforts to amplify women's rights, presented a different vision of women's options. No longer seen as just the result of unfortunate circumstances, women's public presence became a hallmark of the modern era.

Building Women into the City

Infrastructure and Services in the Early Twentieth Century

In 1909, in the midst of the argument over "ladies' cars" on trains, one group of white Chicago women took advantage of the public eye being on women's mass transit experiences to lobby for adjusting the handrail height on subways to better accommodate women.[1] They also called for streetcar steps to be lowered so that women, in their skirts, would be able to climb them more comfortably. San Francisco women called for similar changes on the city's famed cable cars.[2] Demanding access to public transportation and fair treatment, African American women launched protests against the spread of Jim Crow racial segregation in Washington, DC, and elsewhere. Cities at the height of the industrial age needed new infrastructure to move, house, and otherwise accommodate their growing populations and size. Women took advantage of this moment of rapid expansion to mount what historian Maureen Flanagan calls an "intrusion" into political and economic realms.[3] They campaigned for altering the built environment to better suit women, for better services, for access, and for new institutions geared toward the needs of the women who had begun to occupy in ever greater numbers and more visible ways the public spaces of early twentieth-century cities.

These initiatives, and the arguments behind them, spoke to the options women found in early twentieth-century cities. They also suggest the way some urbanites of this period imagined cities might develop if they were truly to recognize women's presence and contributions. Going beyond women's right to be in public, discussions of what could make cities good for women often merged with other discourse. White reformers tended to tie

Women often found that urban infrastructure, including the height of streetcar steps, was not designed to accommodate women's fashions or stature. Woman boarding New York City streetcar by jumping onto a running board, 1913. (Library of Congress Prints and Photographs Division, Washington, DC)

their efforts to the language of urban boosterism as they strove to promote growth and civic order. African American leaders sometimes used a similar language of progress. Even when aimed at the obstacles women faced, however, their approach to infrastructure and institutions framed the work as part of a broader race rights agenda. Championing the cause of working women also served as a means for some women from the more elite classes to enter the public realm of urban politics. Filtered through the language of civic good and progress, the relatively privileged women advocating reform spoke most often of the needs of others—new arrivals, travelers, young women, working women, African American women, immigrant women. But by arguing for new and altered infrastructure, demanding policy and legal changes, challenging racial segregation, and establishing services and institutions, women reformers gained authority in the public sphere, as well as a place to have lunch when they were downtown.

Even as a new acceptance of women's right to occupy public space emerged in the decades around the turn of the twentieth century, sympathetic observers recognized that women faced many obstacles in acting upon that right. Some of these obstacles sprang from gender specifically, but most arose from the intertwining of gender with race and class and the links of gender segregation to white supremacy. A range of reformers, civil rights activists, and policymakers—all of whom believed that urban women were at a disadvantage when it came to making a life in the city—launched an unprecedented series of initiatives designed to make the public spaces and services of cities more accessible, safe, and hospitable. In the nineteenth century, reformers and the state built homes, schools, and similar institutions to remove problematic women from society. In the early twentieth century, however, a new generation of reformers supported institutions, laws, public accommodations, and infrastructure that bolstered women's ability to participate more fully in urban life.

"Anyone Who Needs a Friend": Institutions to Serve Women

Efforts to provide better urban services for women often began in local women's organizations. Key to these efforts was understanding and delineating women's needs and the resources available for meeting those needs. Researchers working under the guise of reform and social service agencies conducted extensive studies of women's lives and experiences. They surveyed eating establishments, boarding and rooming houses, major employers of women, and recreation centers. Through this research, reformers found that few public resources existed and that private ones either turned women away or exploited their needs for profit. This finding led a host of reform and service organizations to step in. They established large and permanent institutions—such as settlement houses (turn-of-the-century community centers in working-class neighborhoods) and local branches of the Young Women's Christian Association (YWCA)—in many cities during the early twentieth century. They also lobbied for local governments to institutionalize and codify many of these services in the 1910s and 1920s.

Reformers concerned with the fate of the "girl beginner" logically focused on providing assistance at sites of women's arrival in cities. Local volunteers positioned themselves at railroad stations and docks, spaces they perceived as "dangerous places" for women.[4] Although tales of young women lured from the train to the brothel abounded in the popular press through the 1910s, the records of organizations that took up this work reveal far more mundane problems to be solved: travelers who arrived unannounced or without a relative's address, ran short of funds, ended up on a late train, or missed their connection. What started as "sympathy" offered to "anyone who needs a friend" became organized efforts in many cities "to guard and guide young women, traveling alone."[5] The YWCA initially aided Christian white women, but other organizations, such as the Young Hebrew Women's Association, local Urban League branches, and many church- and synagogue-based groups, assisted new arrivals from other religions and races. By 1917, the scattered efforts of local organizations merged into a new national organization, the Traveler's Aid Society, with a more inclusive mission to assist new arrivals regardless of race, religion, or ethnicity.

Traveler's Aid workers referred women to vetted boardinghouses, helped locate friends and family, and gave directions to local hospitals, restaurants, and other resources. Reformers wanted to ensure that "unprincipled men and women" would not prey upon the young women who arrived with little knowledge of the "ways of a large, bustling city."[6] They tackled the unregulated service economy as a part of this work and used "their influence with the voters in the city" to back better licensing of hack drivers and porters.[7] In some cities, Traveler's Aid even maintained small houses to provide emergency shelter and meals to new arrivals. The mostly volunteer staff quickly became a ubiquitous sight in the nation's train stations and later in its bus stations and airports. Traveler's Aid desks remain in many of these urban spaces even today, a lingering symbol of efforts to provide newcomers with a positive introduction to urban life.[8]

New arrivals, once temporarily settled, needed to quickly find a job and longer-term housing, and so they joined the throngs searching for better employment and accommodations. Few resources existed to assist women in their search. They wasted time and energy wandering through unfamiliar areas, only to come across unscrupulous employers or recruiters who undervalued their work and landlords who would either turn them away or rent them drafty and crowded spaces. Reformers again decided the only way to challenge these conditions was to create appropriate services themselves. Consequently, a variety of local organizations, including YWCAs, benevolent associations, and women's clubs, launched their own employment bureaus, housing referral services, recreation programs, and cafeterias, either to fill in gaps in existing public services or to counter the predatory services offered in the private marketplace.

Referral services offered women guidance and information on negotiating a highly sex-segmented urban environment. Employment bureaus and vocational training aimed to keep women out of brothels and sweatshops by guiding them to legitimate and well-paying jobs. As part of its effort to make Seattle a "safer, healthier, and more desirable place to live," the YWCA committed itself to "the training and fitting of girls to enable them to earn at least minimum wage."[9] Minneapolis's YWCA evaluated boarding and rooming house opportunities for women and kept a registry of "satisfactory" places to which it would refer them. In Cleveland, the YWCA kept a "white list" of boardinghouses and brought the keepers of those houses together in a club. This local association committed to sending business to these houses if the owners would maintain the YWCA's standards: only women boarders, heated bedrooms, separate beds, a bath with hot and cold water in the house, and a parlor room to entertain male guests.[10] Through referral programs such as these, allies cultivated a market niche to meet the social and economic needs of women living apart from their families.

Beyond investigations and referrals, many of these organizations created their own institutions through which to provide direct services. These institutions offered facilities and programs that supported women's new social and economic roles and reinforced the message that women belonged in urban places. Boardinghouses, lunchrooms, and gymnasiums run by women's organizations provided urban women with safe, economical, and respectable accommodations. The "brave and venturesome women" of the Women's Building and Rest Room Association of Sandusky, Ohio, for example, sought to meet the "need for a place . . . where women who were spending a few hours in the city could find wholesome food, and a place to rest."[11] Beginning in 1908, the organization published a newspaper to fund its work and secured rooms in which to offer the first "self-serve lunch room" in the city as well as meeting space for girls' clubs and classes. In 1926, the association donated assets so that the local women's club could purchase a "club home for the women and girls of the city."[12] A few nineteenth-century institutions, such as the YWCA, proved resilient enough to continue providing services into the new century, adapting as necessary. More common, however, were new endeavors that emerged in the transition zones surrounding downtowns and in working-class, immigrant, and African American neighborhoods. Needing to claim their own space to do this work, many of the women's organizations created outposts in central business districts or retrofitted more modest structures in surrounding neighborhoods.

The rise in service work for women through the 1920s, particularly in department stores and offices, brought more and more working-class women downtown, where their concentration increased the visibility of women in the urban landscape.[13] Middle-class reformers responded to these trends with something of a building frenzy in the early 1900s. The purpose-built women's spaces that resulted, many of them designed by women architects such as Julia Morgan, appeared in American downtowns from Brooklyn to Cleveland to San Francisco, literally making a place for women in the middle of the most "public" areas of cities.[14] These buildings functioned as sites of crucial services that alleviated some of the pressures independent women faced; while supporting their public presence at times, they also gave women respite from the publicness of the workplace and city street. The staff and boards who ran these institutions hoped to provide alternatives to free market and underground businesses that took advantage of women's need for housing, employment, and entertainment or ignored women altogether.

Perhaps the most recognizable of these buildings were the YWCAs built by local chapters, owing to their common name and notable numbers. Two hundred YWCA buildings appeared in cities across the country by 1922.[15] Formally chartered in 1908, for example, the San Diego Young Women's Christian Association experienced explosive growth during its first two decades, reaching out to the women and girls of San Diego who "found cities unfriendly places."[16] Very much a part of the "voluntary vernacular" described by Daphne Spain, San Diego's YWCA rented offices, meeting space, and a basement cafeteria in three different buildings.[17] The organization also purchased a lot for future expansion. The Panama-California Exposition of 1915–1916 and mobilization for World War I drew thousands to San Diego. The YWCA responded with cafeterias and "rest-lounges" for exposition visitors, war workers, and military personnel, generating enough income and donations for the Y to buy the rest of the block on which it already owned property. The Y erected recreation facilities there in 1917 and launched an aggressive citywide campaign for residents to "give back" to the city. Its slogan centered the needs of women: "San Diego needs it—our girls and women deserve it—let's build it."[18] The successful campaign allowed the Y to construct a five-floor building containing 137 beds, restrooms, clubrooms, and

Women's organizations built substantial institutions to serve the needs of urban women in the early twentieth century. YWCA, San Jose, CA. Original building designed by the renowned architect Julia Morgan. (Photo by John C. Gordon, courtesy of San Jose State University, Special Collections and Archives)

offices; and a library, kitchen, lobby, sewing room, committee room, and auditorium. By the end of the 1920s, the building housed three thousand transient women and over one hundred long-term female residents a year, and the cafeteria served women twelve thousand meals a month.

In some significant ways, the erection of this building in the 1920s represented the transition of the San Diego YWCA from a voluntary organization into something much more settled, known, and, essentially, institutionalized. Rather than operating on the margins of the public and private worlds of San Diego, the YWCA physically anchored itself—and the urban women it served—in the city's downtown. The building gave women a permanent physical and programmatic place in the twentieth-century city. Conscious of this status, the YWCA took pride in the building itself, its "beautiful detailing" and stylish "Spanish Renaissance themed architecture," both of which lent weight to the organization's presence in the city's downtown and signaled its legitimate claim to occupy such a space.[19] That visibility and institutionalization further stabilized the organization by drawing a steady stream of financial support from public and private elements. As the organization would soon learn, however, permanency could not lapse into stagnancy. The building housed new programming and services over the decades to come, revising programs and renovating the building to meet the shifting needs of urban woman.

The San Diego story was not unique. The Cleveland YWCA operated residences for women almost from its inception in 1869, but the location and nature of these institutions changed over time. Originally run out of existing housing stock on the west side of the city and serving white women, the organization opened a purpose-built structure with fifty-four rooms and fifty-one suites in the late 1920s. Cleveland's Phillis Wheatley Association served African American women, primarily newly arrived migrants from the South, by offering space for recreation, an employment office, and residences beginning in 1916. Two moves and a little over a decade later, the association built a nine-story community center with space for one hundred residents and a host of activities designed to "balance the scales of justice for Negro women" by offering "safe shelter" and "special opportunities."[20] In Seattle, responding to a call from working women for a place to spend their lunch hours, the local YWCA opened a lunchroom and restroom on the second floor of a downtown building. The organization moved and expanded services several times over its first few years before acquiring its own building. There it served women twenty-four hours a day with a pool, cafeteria, and room registry for local, private boardinghouses. In 1929, the organization opened another building downtown to provide recreation and temporary rooms for women in need of housing.[21]

Even as they provided what they believed to be practical responses to local conditions, most of these organizations had lofty goals for their residences. Perhaps the most common example was the lunchroom. Most local YWCAs established lunchrooms in the 1900s and 1910s for the "ever-growing army of young women workers," and the national association issued a formal cafeteria handbook in 1917.[22] Organizers touted the restorative effects of "a bright, sunny place of rest and refreshment for body and spirit."[23] These spaces would offer "untold relief and comfort" by allowing women a place to rest as well as facilities for her to "arrange" herself before going back into public. An important aspect of fulfilling these goals was keeping these spaces for women only, since men "take up space" and "create a different atmosphere."[24] Apart from the service mission cafeterias fulfilled, they proved to be important revenue sources for organizations, funding many programs and underwriting the costs of renting or owning properties.[25]

While maintaining their work on behalf of women in the urban core, many YWCAs across the country came to realize that they needed to expand their efforts in industrial, working-class, and immigrant neighborhoods. The Minneapolis association, for example, conducted an extensive survey of the city in 1919 and concluded that women needed more options for housing, eating, and recreation in all but the wealthiest neighborhoods. Inventories of boardinghouses revealed that even where an ample supply could be found, they were "undesirable" in that they had too many "men in the houses" and no space for entertaining guests.[26] By highlighting these two factors, reformers revealed their belief that women needed living spaces apart from men, lest they find themselves in vulnerable situations on stairways and in their rooms. Similarly, investigators became concerned about the welfare of women who worked split-shift jobs that gave them only a few hours off between shifts, such as telephone operators and restaurant workers. Without enough time to go home, women might find themselves with no place to be except on the streets, where the "familiarity of men was unchecked."[27] After gathering extensive data on all districts in the city, the Minneapolis YWCA drew up plans to expand new programs, build new branches, and establish new boardinghouses in neighborhoods and factory districts across the city. The organization prioritized working-class districts with significant numbers of working women as well as African American neighborhoods, where few other social service agencies were already active.[28] Other cities saw similar patterns of proliferation. By the 1920s, YWCAs and other women-focused organizations had become important outposts and alternatives to a public space that was, in many ways, hostile toward women.

Although residences convenient to downtown and serving primarily native-born white women led the way, their success encouraged local YWCAs to build institutions that offered a whole range of services in ethnic and racial-minority neighborhoods. The San Francisco Neighborhood House for Unprotected Jewish Girls opened in 1915, and the Emanu-El Sisterhood, which operated a boardinghouse for Jewish women, moved into a building designed by Julia Morgan in 1923. The Sisterhood sought to "assist . . . girls in adjusting themselves to this community" and "encourage independence" in young women just starting out in the city and life.[29] African American branches (often called Phillis or Phyllis Wheatley Clubs) operated in cities across the country by the 1910s and for much of the twentieth century.[30]

After the first of these opened in Nashville in 1895, Phillis Wheatley Clubs spread quickly to Northern cities and then to the West and South to support young Black women arriving in cities there during migration booms before and after both world wars. Many of these institutions operating in neighborhoods outside downtowns blended multiple functions in one physical space, including referral offices, recreation, and housing.

The YWCA in particular expected the cafeterias and boardinghouses it maintained to be not just a "real service to girls and women" but also a "large money-making proposition" for local organizations, since the private marketplace underserved working women. These institutions supported women's efforts to live independently, underscoring reformers'—and women's—demands that women be treated as respectable and worthy members of society. They also showed that profit could be made through fair dealings with women. Local YWCA organizations saw themselves as competitors with the for-profit market when it came to running residences, and they hoped to prove their worth through both a positive "economic result" and a positive "social result."[31] The YWCA wanted to demonstrate that a "high class hotel" for women could be profitable, hoping to encourage the private market to take on similar projects.[32] Pioneering historian Mary Beard found a similar sentiment among other reformers in the early twentieth century; in her book *Woman's Work in Municipalities*, she quotes one reformer: "And if we cannot get the housing of girls taken up as a community duty, then all the more must we struggle by private enterprise to find out the way."[33]

The "autonomy," or "self-reliance," theme of YWCAs and similar organizations proved fundamental to the residences and cafeterias. These institutions operated "on a self-supporting basis." The YWCA in particular refused to treat these endeavors—or those who patronized them—as a charity. All women, it argued, needed to be paid a "living wage" so that they could afford "the dignity and delight of a private room" and decent food and the sense of independence that came with such amenities.[34] This argument maintained, in effect, that subsidized housing supported a fundamentally unfair system that underpaid women.

While the YWCA did much to defend women's right to earn their living and make their way in the city, the organization also realized that women often remained exposed to hostility and exploitation as they moved through their days. YWCA residences, with their myriad services, allowed women the option to circumvent many public spaces by providing alternatives in the less public—though not entirely private—spaces. By the 1920s, the YWCA and similar organizations had made a "chain of safe places across the country" for women who worked for wages and did not live with family.[35] These efforts, particularly in successfully demonstrating that serving women's needs could be profitable, underscored a message that women could and should be approached as a normal, even desirable, part of the urban landscape in the twentieth-century city.

"The Need Is a Public One": Urban Infrastructure

Alongside this impressive institution building came a related wave of demands for urban infrastructure to better serve women's needs. Androcentric urban design revealed itself in the height of handrails, seats, and steps. These "unremarked" elements—spatial arrangements that few notice or question—reveal the "truth" of how fundamental a gender divide is to the organization of urban spaces, according to scholar Elizabeth Wilson.[36] Clubwomen, volunteers, visiting nurses, and civil rights advocates, however, began to bring attention to these elements of the built environment in the early twentieth century. Reformers from different cities, organizations, and causes raised numerous issues with municipal government and public service providers, demanding that infrastructure better serve urban residents, particularly women. These demands complemented reformers' institution building and further supported women's access to public space. While these efforts were happening in cities across the country, they were notably muted in the South; driven at least in part by institutionalized racism, Southern cities offered far fewer amenities overall.

Where reformers did take up these issues, they advocated for everything from curb markets and places to rest to covered transit stops and better lighting. Of all the demands, however, public toilets topped the list. With varying amounts of success, an array of "physicians, health officers, and public-spirited men and women" demanded that toilets "be regarded as a public function" that should be publicly funded and administered. The rationale provided by these mostly white women reveals a conception of the public emerging around the turn of the twentieth century that clearly included women as constituents and entitled, as such, to make demands and expect services from municipal governments.

Toilet facilities—often called "comfort stations" or "public conveniences" in this period—became a necessary element of the modern city. The mobility at the heart of modernization led both men and women to travel farther and more frequently. Increased transportation options made mobility more possible, but secondary services were needed if people were to take regular advantage of their greater mobility. When away from home, nineteenth-century Americans could usually find a toilet in a train station—at least if they were white or outside the South. Often located on the edges of business districts, train station toilets did not meet daily needs. Men could turn to saloons, offices, and private clubs. For women, department stores sometimes filled this need. Some theaters, hotels, tearooms, lunchrooms, and a few women's clubs might also have facilities, but all placed class, ethnic, or racial restrictions (formal or informal) on who might access them and when they were open.

By the twentieth century, however, advocates for building truly public facilities declared the reliance on private businesses and associations an "unfair and unprofitable" imposition. Some noted that noncustomers were, at best, "unwelcomely tolerated," and many establishments were not open sufficient hours.[37] "It is clearly the duty of the municipality," explained one Florida official, "to care for the public in this matter."[38] Civic leaders, business owners, urban boosters, public health reformers, and women's clubs increasingly endorsed the idea of public facilities, lobbied for their funding, designed the actual stations, and monitored their upkeep in the decades following the turn of the twentieth century. For these civic-minded proponents—who were already steeped in the ideology of other Progressive reforms—public toilets were a "public necessity" akin to street lighting and trash removal.[39] As an official of the American Civic Association declared in 1908, public comfort stations were of "too great importance and too closely related to 'the health of the people' to be further neglected" by American municipalities.[40] For women, these facilities carried a further significance: they marked their entrée into the public sphere. Special accommodations for women in the nineteenth-century city—waiting rooms and separate entrances—treated women as patrons. By contrast, publicly funded comfort stations recognized women as part of the "public."

Early twentieth-century women's civic organizations played a vital role in the movement for public comfort stations, especially, though not exclusively, in creating facilities for women. Public toilets appeared regularly on the agendas of women's clubs alongside calls for improved city services, streetscapes, and transportation. To secure public funding, these clubs allied themselves with men's civic organizations. Together they drew on the rhetoric of urban boosterism and made the case that facilities could aid in the competition for new businesses and economic growth.[41] "Already a number of our larger eastern cities," noted a 1908 Chicago editorial, "have realized the public need in this direction and have constructed comfort stations in the hearts of their business districts, where they are much used and greatly appreciated by the general public."[42] Time and again proponents cited an extensive system of public facilities in much-idealized European cities and bemoaned the failure of their own city to keep up with its American counterparts, especially New York, Brooklyn, Cleveland, Boston, and Seattle.[43]

Women's clubs surveyed existing facilities, consulted on design and location, and campaigned hard for bond issues to fund the projects. They often used the boosterish, pro-business language of growth and progress. The work of the Woman's City Club of Chicago in particular reveals the political maneuverings employed by advocates for public toilets and women's inclusion. Not waiting for the city to act, a club committee undertook the task of mapping out locations for comfort stations. The organization supported the city's 1916 survey of facilities and regularly sent its officers to lobby city officials to address stalled projects.[44] A standing committee of the Woman's City Club kept up pressure on the city over the next three years to fund new facilities and then, finally, to break ground on the facilities at Madison and Market Streets. The committee's chair approached the building of comfort stations as a foregone conclusion and cast her remarks in the language of "intelligent economy," which promised both "financial restraint" and "reasonable growth" if the facilities were folded into funded street-widening projects.[45] Like many of the Progressive reformers of her day, she was well schooled in the ways of municipal politics and understood the effectiveness of the promise to "help us to prevent . . . a waste of city money."[46]

Keeping up the pressure, women's clubs continued to present bold visions for public conveniences, including comfort stations. In Chicago, women's clubs called on the city to plan for all future public buildings to have public toilets "accessible from the street" and a "definite plan for an adequate system of comfort station facilities" in the city's master plan.[47] Although women's organizations played a key role in the campaigns for public toilets, advocates envisioned an infrastructure that would provide comfort and safety to many others besides women. Women, however, stood to gain tremendously from this movement, which reworked urban infrastructure to include them. "Public comfort stations," proponents argued, "are just as valuable municipal assets as playgrounds which contribute so directly and so largely to public health and happiness."[48]

In Chicago and other US cities, those working to build public comfort stations assumed that men and women needed separate facilities. Public comfort stations would serve the public, but men and women represented wholly distinct groups within the public. The public toilets movement began at a

time when the landscape of urban public space remained firmly gendered—
some nineteenth-century ladies' entrances and service counters still lingered
on—and in places where clear gender distinctions indicated orderliness. Men
needed public comfort stations because so many, from construction workers
to letter carriers, worked outdoors. Away from an office or factory that might
make facilities available, men turned to the saloon. As one Chicago bar owner
admitted, the toilet often brought in more business than the free lunch.[49]
Women could not avail themselves of the masculine space of the saloon (at
least not if they were to keep their reputation and safety intact). Few American cities had any public facilities at all for women before 1900, though some
urinals and comfort stations for men did exist. Department stores closed
early enough to leave women without even that option in off-hours, and in
any event, these establishments, such as theaters and hotels, expected to serve
customers. "You may be able to find some place," one Pittsburgh editorial
reminded "Mr. Voter," "but how about your wife or daughter?"[50] Advocates
for public toilets fit their arguments to these contours of gender segregation:
they recommended separate facilities for women that would be geographically distinct and in many cases would have somewhat different provisions
than those planned for men.

Considering the tendency of municipal officials to overlook women
entirely, getting any facilities at all for women signaled a substantial victory.
Opponents invoked nineteenth-century judgments of women's public presence, arguing that respectable women would not want to see a public toilets
facility, or be seen entering one. The implication, of course, was that only
"unworthy" women—prostitutes and street peddlers—would use public toilets.[51] In response, advocates cast women as worthy, if vulnerable, figures by
making reference to the woman who, "through a sense of delicacy, suffers in
silence."[52] "A Taxpayer" expressed his "indignation" at finding a downtown
women's comfort station closed on a Sunday evening, "for no doubt there are
many women who would express their opinion on this same matter except
that modesty forbids."[53] Nevertheless, when plans for public facilities faltered,
money and not morality was always the cause.[54]

Design trends for public toilets reveal the fundamental assumptions about
gender at work in early twentieth-century America.[55] A national movement—
built through the work of state and local boards of health and departments of
public welfare, the American Civic Association, urban planning journals, and
transportation-oriented organizations such as the National Highways Association—codified gendered design practices.[56] Women's facilities tended to be
open for significantly shorter hours and generally contained fewer free toilet

options than men's facilities, factoring urinals into the count. Women's facilities often had more sinks as well as more pay compartments, some of which had lounge facilities that included a table, mirror, and couch.[57] Women's stations also offered rooms for rest, "sick compartments," or at least "a couch on which to rest from the strenuous ordeal of city shopping"; these amenities were not included in men's facilities.[58] Driving these design standards were assumptions that fewer women than men ventured into the public spaces of American cities. Those who did go out had a greater need for cleanliness, required a place to retreat from the public, were not out past evening, and often had a great enough desire for more privacy that they were willing to pay for it.[59] Pay toilets failed to attract enough use to justify the space they took up in both women's and men's facilities, and they quickly fell out of favor. The other conventions, however, especially providing fewer fixtures for women than for men, remained in place for decades. These assumptions were built into the landscape of cities and shaped behaviors accordingly. Americans came to expect (and many continue to do so) that public toilets must be restricted by gender, yet women often could not count on finding adequate or open facilities.

While hours, locations, and numbers of stations for men and women differed across cities, standard practice by the 1910s was to provide facilities for both genders.[60] A Wisconsin statute required cities to "provide and maintain a sufficient number of suitable and adequate public comfort stations for both sexes," which the state's board of health defined as a "convenient, safe and properly regulated place open at all reasonable hours to the general public—men, women and children." Women had clearly become a part of the "public" to be served by these "public conveniences."[61] As early as 1908, the American Civic Association reported on public comfort stations, including facilities for women, in New York City, Boston, Worcester (Massachusetts), Brooklyn, Cleveland, Washington, DC, Baltimore, Columbus (Ohio), Denver, St. Louis, Seattle, and Hartford, with plans for stations brewing in Indianapolis, Louisville, Milwaukee, Brookline, Providence, and Bridgeport.[62] A 1916 study listed seventy-four cities with public facilities, from Hoboken, New Jersey, to Kansas City, Missouri, to Salt Lake City, Utah.[63] By 1938, *The American City* estimated, there were "about 1,000 municipally owned comfort stations in the United States."[64]

Once built, proponents set about ensuring that these facilities served their intended audience. Beginning during World War I, public comfort station advocates lobbied to have many standardized signs prominently placed in the most public sections of cities to make these facilities more accessible and

Restrooms reveal the ways in which gender and racial segregation often intertwined in public space. Bus station restroom for white women in Durham, North Carolina, 1940. (Library of Congress Prints and Photographs Division, Washington, DC)

literally more readable to the greatest number of people.[65] Ultimately, these signs became ubiquitous in the twentieth-century city, pointing the direction to facilities for "MEN" and "WOMEN." To this day bathrooms are segregated by gender and the built environment is marked with signs indicating the population to be served, not the function of the space. Gender-segregated bathrooms have ensured that these categories remain salient markers of the gendered geography of public space. By labeling at least some facilities for "WOMEN," public toilet advocates succeeded in marking the masculinized spaces of urban downtowns as places where women did belong, albeit in ways that reinforced gender distinctions.

In some cities, particularly those in the South, signs for "MEN" and "WOMEN" shared the landscape with other signs of segregation: those for race. Like most public facilities in the early twentieth century, public toilets fell prey to Jim Crow, revealing the complicated relationship between gender and racial segregation.[66] Emerging in the decades after the Civil War, the formal and informal practices that made up the system of Jim Crow reinscribed the racialized power relationships built under slavery and confined African Americans to subordinate social positions. Jim Crow is commonly thought of as a set of social rules (such as an African American being expected to step off a sidewalk so that a white person could pass) and institutions designed to keep the races separate (such as schools), but in fact it imposed demands much more actively and pervasively with expectation that both whites and Blacks would "perform" their racial positioning repeatedly in the context of daily life. White supremacy embedded gender in that performance. An African American woman faced signs reading "FOR LADIES" and "FOR COLORED PEOPLE" would be left "wondering under which head I come."[67] In noting the "thousand times . . . without a single word being said," that African Americans were reminded of their inferior position every day, educator Mary McLeod Bethune pointed to the common Southern practice of providing "only one set of toilet accommodations for men and for women which means white men and women," thus erasing African Americans from public space altogether.[68] Mary Burks, an African American teacher who grew up in Montgomery, Alabama, in the early twentieth century, proudly recalled using public bathrooms as a site of resistance: "I went into rest rooms with signs FOR WHITE LADIES ONLY." Confronted with this hostile environment, some women waged their own "private guerrilla warfare" against the humiliation of Jim Crow.[69]

Train stations might have more facilities, but with signs that read "WHITE MEN," "WHITE WOMEN," and "COLORED," gender-specific accommodations even more clearly enforced white privilege. Race leaders who were women understood the significance of this and clearly demanded the privileges of gender segregation in an effort to challenge racial segregation. Nannie Helen Burroughs called on fellow Baptist activists to demand "a separate toilet for colored women, just as they have a separate toilet for white women." "We pay the same fare," she noted, "and are entitled to the same treatment."[70] In a few Southern cities, including Atlanta and Nashville, boosters embraced a modern image and provided separate facilities for each race and gender in rail stations.[71] Most Southern cities, however, avoided this expensive model for providing services by having no public toilets at all. While African Americans read the signs of Jim Crow on the urban landscape as constant reminders of the limited place they had in the public sphere, signs indicating gender separation generally raised no such negative associations.[72] Labeling toilet facilities by gender normalized gender distinctions, often entwining a gender binary with racial privilege, while allowing American cities that had invested in them to claim success at meeting their obligation to promote the civic good.

As the 1920s progressed, the location for urban comfort stations shifted from streetscapes and public buildings of downtowns to the more open spaces of parks, beaches, and similar sites of recreation.[73] New Deal funding in the 1930s furthered this transition, although the design standards established in the earliest decades of the twentieth century continued to prevail, particularly the tradition of building multi-user, gender-specific facilities. World War II brought construction to a halt, and the postwar highway obsession shifted public money toward building rest stops for long-distance motorists. Despite having dotted the city landscape with public facilities for the better part of three decades, municipalities struggled to maintain the structures they had, curtailing hours and eliminating attendant service in the face of budget cuts. Increasingly, American cities opted either to forgo all but the most minimal maintenance or to shutter the facilities entirely. However troubled these facilities would become later in the century, at least in the first three decades of the twentieth century improvements in infrastructure, including public toilets and wayfinding signs, marked a sea change in the gendered—and sometimes racialized—geography of the city by explicitly including some women in the public spaces of modern downtowns.

"Our Self-Respect Demands That We Walk": Public Conveyances and the Issue of Access

For African American women activists, access often mattered more than design. The arrangements of railcars in particular starkly revealed the workings of gender segregation as a tool of white supremacy, a connection that African American women highlighted through both words and actions. They challenged racial segregation by demanding access to public spaces and gender privileges. In spaces reserved specifically for women, such as first-class train cars, the resistance that African American women met revealed just how much gender-separated services and spaces had been racialized as white—and how long a history there was of Black women challenging this pattern.

In 1883, a schoolteacher bought a first-class ticket for her trip to Memphis. When she boarded the train, she settled herself in the "ladies' car," but her presence soon drew the attention of the conductor, who demanded that she move to the second-class "Negro car."[74] She reasoned that since she had paid for a first-class ticket, she was entitled to a seat in the first-class coach. The white male conductor disagreed and placed a hand on her shoulder in an attempt to remove her. The teacher, Ida B. Wells, who would go on to become a leading voice in the early civil rights movement, responded to this physical incursion into her personal space by sinking her teeth into his hand. It ultimately took the conductor and two other men to remove her from her seat.

Many of the complicated threads of gender segregation in the late nineteenth and early twentieth centuries run through Wells's experiences—as was the case for many other African American women. Etiquette dictated that men did not touch a "respectable" woman in public, yet none of the white women in the coach moved to defend Wells from the ejection or the rough handling. The conductor's breach of gender norms and the acquiescence of bystanders clearly indicated an unwillingness to recognize Wells's gender or class presentation in the face of her race. In this way, a gender-specific accommodation meant to "protect" women from the vagaries of public space functioned to reinforce other forms of discrimination. Those who could access the privileged spaces reserved for women rarely acknowledged the class- and race-based exclusions they perpetuated. African American women, however, developed a keen understanding of the connections. Protesting their exclusion from the privileges of gender became a foundational form of protest deep into the twentieth century.

Wells challenged what was, in the 1880s, the nascent system of segregation that would come to be known as Jim Crow by claiming entitlement to better treatment as a respectable woman. She was not alone. Historian Barbara Welke cataloged forty-seven cases of women seeking legal redress for treatment on public conveyances between 1855 and 1914.[75] Wells filed a lawsuit against the rail company for the 1883 incident and another in 1884.[76] The court rejected her attempts to access gender privileges, declaring her "purpose" was to "harass" rather than to "obtain a comfortable seat for the short ride."[77] In the context of the late nineteenth century, with the landmark *Plessy v. Ferguson* Supreme Court case endorsing racial segregation on the horizon, the court's reaction is perhaps not surprising. For Wells, these experiences solidified her growing understanding of the magnitude of the fight for legal protection that Black women would face and served as a "catalyst" for her later activism against lynching and for women's voting rights.[78] She also realized that the rulings denying her the status and gender protection of the ladies' car as a loss for the race generally, but her efforts received little recognition among African Americans at the time. "None of my people ever seemed to feel it was a race matter," she explained, "so I trod the winepress alone."[79]

Within a decade, Wells was very much no longer alone. Beginning in the 1890s, elite African American women articulated a new vision for race progress that centered their own lived experiences and highlighted the intertwining of race and gender. Achieving the "undisputed dignity of my womanhood," promised Dr. Anna Julia Cooper, would ensure "the whole Negro race enters with me" into a new era.[80] Cooper repeated this theme throughout her 1892 essay collection, *A Voice from the South*: considering African American women's unique perspective and position in American society, "the race cannot be effectually lifted up till its women are truly elevated."[81] At the heart of the Black women's club movement, begun in earnest in the closing years of the nineteenth century and carried forward deep into the twentieth, lay African American women's efforts to defend Black womanhood. When the white press called Wells a "black harlot" for exposing the economic and political motivations behind lynching in her work as a journalist, elite Black Boston women came together to form the Woman's Era Club. They took on the mantle of anti-lynching work and, using gendered language, defended Wells's "purity of purpose and character."[82] Other organizations soon appeared and took on a similar slate of activities that challenged discrimination and confronted the indignities that Black women faced in Jim Crow America.[83] They established broader networks and came together as the National Association of Colored Women's Clubs in 1914.

The work of the Black women's club movement of the early twentieth century encompassed a range of issues pertaining to civil rights and social welfare, including votes for women, anti-lynching work, and opposition to Jim Crow segregation. These predominantly middle-class women of color challenged the "masculinist cast" that had dominated race politics in the previous century by often seeking out gender-specific accommodations precisely because these spaces represented and reinforced racial segregation.[84] African American women made claims to the privileges associated with "womanhood" when they purchased the first-class tickets required to ride in the ladies' cars of trains. Rather than directly discuss rape and other forms of sexual and gender-based violence rooted in US racial discrimination, they embedded challenges to racial segregation in positive images of respectable Black womanhood.[85] Wells, in her direct style, argued that the privileges of gender could not be confined only to "women who happen to be white."[86] Believing that recognition of their "respectable womanhood" lay at the heart of racial progress, they adorned themselves carefully before heading into public.[87] They fashioned themselves, often literally, into the modern, autonomous, and respectable individuals they wanted to be as part of a larger project of self-determination.

By showing up as stylish and feminine protesters, Black women claimed space in debates over racial segregation and voting and demanded respect as modern political actors. "Black women could not escape myths about their hypersexuality, depravity, uncontrollable anger, and impropriety," writes historian Treva Lindsay, "they therefore fashioned and performed a distinct form of feminine propriety while engaging in political activism."[88] But they did so in the face of Jim Crow laws and customs that, as Wells experienced, often made a "mockery of claims by African American females to womanhood" by explicitly denying Black women access to ladies' accommodations and the gender-based courtesies embedded in popular etiquette.[89] Cooper understood African American women "to be leaders of thought and guardians of society" and charged them with taking up the work of "tutoring" the country in "manners and morals."[90] Far more than mere etiquette or propriety, Cooper and her peers sought to undermine the institutions and practices that enforced the subordination of African Americans, especially those that did so under the guise of protecting womanhood inherently defined by whiteness.

While their ambitious agendas included work on many political, economic, and social fronts, women's daily experiences in public space, particularly their ill treatment on public transportation, repeatedly appeared on their agendas for social change. When African American women took up issues of public space, they did so both as a form of self-defense and a challenge to racial segregation and violence. Their work took on particular urgency around the turn of the twentieth century as racial violence and Jim Crow peaked and followed the Great Migration of African Americans leaving the rural South to settle in the urban North. Called "race women" in their day, these activists refused to acquiesce to expanding racial segregation laws and practices. The treatment of Black women in public laid bare the humiliation and brutality at the foundation of Jim Crow. "No pen can describe and no tongue portray," argued Mary Church Terrell in her autobiography, "the indignities, insults and assaults to which colored women and girls have been subjected in Jim Crow cars."[91] Cooper described the "unnamable burden" of Black women in public who might, at any time, be "forcibly ejected from cars, thrown out of seats, their garments rudely torn, their person wantonly and cruelly injured," with no expectation that anyone would come to their aid.[92] Chicago reformer Fannie Barrier Williams echoed a similar sentiment: "Certain it is that colored women have been the least known, and the most ill-favored class of women in this country."[93] African American women used their bodies to demonstrate the hypocrisy of a system that largely justified segregation with the presumption that white women required protection from Black men. Black women did not represent a threat to the purity of white womanhood—indeed, they often occupied the most intimate areas of white home life as cooks and maids—yet they could not use the same public toilet facilities or sit next to whites.

Public conveyances brought the racialized nature of gender segregation into stark relief, as Ida B. Wells had learned in 1883. White women and women of color encountered a different urban environment, depending on their perceived racial identity. By the turn of the century, with a rise in women's organized reform efforts, especially the renewed effort to achieve voting rights for women, some Black activists believed the moment to challenge gender segregation's role in upholding racial discrimination had arrived. Lottie Wilson Jackson, an African American clubwoman from Bay City, Michigan, laid the issue in front of her white suffrage allies in 1899. Jackson's proposed resolution asked the National Woman Suffrage Association to declare that "the colored women ought not to be compelled to ride in smoking cars, and that suitable accommodations should be provided for them."[94] Her call for this organization to endorse the right of all women (who could afford the fare) to access the ladies' car failed, being deemed "outside the province of the convention."[95] Rarely did affluent white women eschew the privileges of gender segregation and even when allies such as Jackson pointed out the connection, they sometimes denied it. In 1899, and again when women of other races pointed to the privileges of gender denied to women of color by segregation, white suffrage activists chose to make their movement white by dismissing the experiences of women of color. They accepted individual Black women as allies, but they rejected the larger agenda of the African American women's movement.

Challenging segregation on trains could be written off as a project of middle-class and elite African Americans largely because few working-class and poor African Americans had reason or resources to ride the train or pay for a first-class ticket. However, a wave of protests against racial segregation on streetcars that emerged in the late nineteenth century and then spread in the early twentieth century suggests that challenging segregation on public conveyances was far more than just a class-based project.[96] The organized action behind the streetcar boycotts represented a collective effort to challenge the dehumanizing aspects of segregation. A confluence of trends in the early twentieth century explains the particular focus on Jim Crow streetcars. The electrification of streetcars substantially expanded their service in cities across the country. Americans of all races and classes in the country's rapidly expanding cities relied on them daily for both work and leisure. In the urban

South, however, white urban boosters touted racial segregation as a sign of modern, progressive growth, and Jim Crow proliferated as quickly as the transit systems.

African Americans launched more than two dozen boycotts against segregation policies on streetcars in cities across the South, including Little Rock, Richmond, Nashville, Jacksonville, New Orleans, Houston, Memphis, and Chattanooga.[97] These protests represented an important effort to secure African American rights. As Maggie Lena Walker, a leading figure in the Richmond boycott, explained, "Our self-respect demands that we walk."[98] Her efforts and those of the other women who formed the backbone of the protests invoked their standing as both respectable women and citizens. As more and more Southern cities enacted segregation ordinances for public conveyances, the Black community responded and women proved central to the boycotts that ensued. Black clubwomen often first called for a boycott, as was the case in New Orleans in 1902, but once it started, men took over the leadership.[99] For these women, the call to act reflected their negative experiences on the cars as well as "the responsibility of mothers" to make a better world for their children. They sought dignity for both the community and themselves.[100] Once launched, the boycotts were primarily carried out by Black women—working-class women who needed to travel substantial distances to work as domestics in white homes and middle-class women toting groceries and packages for their households. It was women, in historian Blair Kelley's estimation, who paid the greatest price to demand "dignity, respect, and equity of first-class treatment."[101] And though the boycotts of the first decade of the twentieth century failed to overturn that era's segregation policies, they served as a symbolically important moment in a long movement to defend African American dignity and rights.

In challenging the gendered aspects of streetcar boycotts and carrying on the tradition of individual women demanding respect on the cars, African American clubwomen revealed the political nature of their work. They promoted a vision of racial uplift that had the potential to challenge justifications for segregation and discrimination that relied on a mythology of Black inferiority and backwardness. "Respectability was not just about manners and morals, although this was always present," explain historians Anne Valk and Leslie Brown. "Rather, respectability was a way for black women to claim themselves, for it required taking ownership and control of one's body and repelling unwanted advances."[102] Respectability could also serve as a form of protection. Parents and reformers hoped that Black children trained in respectability within the African American community would behave properly outside the Black community. As historian Jennifer Ritterhouse explains, "Knowing that they were behaving properly would, in turn, protect them—at least psychologically—from whites who treated them as if they and their behavior were improper and unworthy of respect."[103] Decades after the fact, Mary Church Terrell recalled her childhood bafflement at being removed from a first-class railcar despite "behaving like a little lady."[104] She understood the gendered expectations for her public behavior instilled so clearly by her mother, but had no context for the racial realities she encountered. Terrell's mother was not alone in instilling an "unshakeable understanding of what proper behavior was" in her daughter so that she could maintain a sense of self and self-worth when facing the demoralizing world of Jim Crow.[105] These lessons intimately linked race and gender.

By promoting racial uplift and respectability, African American women called attention to the frequent violations of their bodily integrity. In the words of DC educator Nannie Helen Burroughs, it was "the duty of Negro Women to rise in the pride of their womanhood and vindicate themselves . . . by teaching all men that black womanhood is as sacred as white womanhood."[106] Black women's organizations responded in a variety of ways, including with calls for more responsive policing. In Chicago, New York, and Washington, DC, for example, activists demanded African American women be employed as police officers to protect Black women in public spaces. According to historian Estelle Freedman, these efforts "signaled new expectations among African Americans that sexual protection could provide an entry point for expanding public authority."[107] Writing in 1925, Elsie Johnson McDougald explained, "We find the Negro woman, figuratively, struck in the face daily by contempt from the world about her."[108] For Black women, no firm line existed between gender-based harassment and the insults of Jim Crow. Reinforcing one another, they came together to create a particular kind of harassment in public space. But in the arena of public space women often fought back. In July 1908, Mary Church Terrell, now an adult and herself a mother of two daughters, had what she called "a disagreeable experience" on a DC streetcar. She was carrying many packages and asked a white man to give her a space to sit, but he refused. She sat anyway and confronted him for not moving for her: "When I tell you to move, you move." When he replied, "I won't be sassed by a nigger," she slapped him. He almost hit her back, while another white man threatened her with his umbrella. Even though she "didn't believe a hand would have been lifted in my defense if the man had struck me," she had both stood her ground and demanded the courtesy that etiquette reserved for women.[109]

Black women used any vestiges of gender segregation that offered respite to women as an opportunity to strike a blow (sometimes literally) at racial segregation. When they claimed streetcar segregation as a particular focus for their work, they did so in ways that demanded recognition of Black women's inherent worth and right to protection. Their efforts countered white society's sexualization and exploitation of Black women's bodies by demanding both respect and bodily autonomy. Their agenda centered the struggle against white culture's denial of African American womanhood. In this context, challenges to gender segregation and Black women's insistence that their intrinsic dignity be recognized were radical acts.

Conclusion

In many ways the institution building and calls for infrastructure and services were logical results of demographic, economic, and cultural shifts of the early twentieth century. As women took on new roles, they had new needs, and these efforts directly addressed some of the obstacles women faced, including a marketplace and municipal governments that did not question forms of twentieth-century gender segregation that overlooked women or failed to recognize them as potential patrons or important constituencies or, as was the case with African American women, erased them altogether.

Middle-class reformers and activists—those who led organized attempts to make cities more responsive and hospitable to women through institutions, infrastructure, and access—did not get everything they wanted, nor did they get everything right. Though many white reformers tried to assist working-class women, the gulf between socioeconomic classes, races, and ethnicities sometimes proved too large to bridge. White reformers generally failed to recognize how their efforts reinforced racial segregation in particular, even when women of color brought the issue to them directly. African American women approached gender segregation as racial activists and sometimes promoted gender-based restrictions on women in an effort to undermine arguments supporting institutionalized racism. In spite of such limitations, the foundational motivation and work of reformers still sometimes proved sound. Some, such as the YWCAs, created space in which working-class women could advocate for their own priorities. Other institutions and emerging urban infrastructure created during the Progressive Era of the 1900s and 1910s proved both adaptable and resilient in the decades that followed, supporting women's self-reliance long after these reform movements faded.

One paradox of the early decades of the twentieth century was that many institutional and infrastructural changes reinforced gender distinctions even as they offered a respite to women, who still moved through public space as something of a suspect class, and not on equal footing with men. Some legitimate purposes for women to be in public space had gained wide acceptance, such as shopping, while others, including work, travel, and leisure, remained suspect activities, or at least scrutinized. Gender-segregated respites such as cafeterias, comfort stations, and restrooms offered women a reprieve from the public gaze. The gender-specific accommodations of the early twentieth century repudiated the exclusions of the nineteenth century, but they also created a different kind of segregation through their emphasis on serving women as women. These institutions created homosocial outposts on the urban landscape of the patriarchal city, though they sometimes reinforced class, race, and ethnic distinctions and inequities in the process. These developments continued a familiar pattern of uneven gains, incomplete transitions, unexpected opportunities, and moments of backlash in the history of women's relationship to public space across the long twentieth century.

---3---

The City and the Girl

Midcentury Consumption, Civil Rights, and (In)Visibility

"How should a man assist a woman in ascending a streetcar or bus?" asked a reader. Etiquette columnist Roberta Lee responded, "By a light touch on her elbow."[1] This question and brief answer seem, upon first glance, rather unremarkable. In their time and place, however, they carry a deeper meaning. This exchange appeared in the Baltimore-based *Afro-American* newspaper in the spring of 1950, at the height of Jim Crow segregation. The action suggested—"a light touch"—would not physically "assist" someone in mounting the steps to board (though women had long complained about the steps on streetcars being too steep). Instead, the touch to the elbow was a gendered courtesy offered to a woman, presumably an African American woman, at a time when African American women generally received no deference in the scrum of public transportation. Recognition and performance of such a small gesture suggested a quiet insistence that African Americans were entitled to access public space. Performing this courtesy was a challenge to racial segregation tucked inside a ritual of gendered propriety. Considering the deep connections between white supremacy and gender segregation, it held the potential to destabilize both.

Although women seemed to have made a significant mark on the landscape of urban America through their institution-building efforts, the middle decades of the century reinforced and extended aspects of gender segregation. Midcentury urban American culture accepted women in public space, but did so in a way that placed the responsibility for their safety and civil treatment on each individual woman's ability and willingness to meet informal but rigid behavioral expectations. Particularly in the relatively prosperous period following World War II, normative gender roles contracted, strengthening the implicit messages of danger directed at women who did not follow the rules. Overt challenges to gender segregation rarely emerged in this atmosphere, leaving women to develop more subtle techniques to circumvent limitations on their access to public space. Celebrations of women in American culture presented them as domesticated creatures at the center of American family life. More sexual than her historical counterparts, the midcentury American woman was imagined with her sexuality safely ensconced within heterosexual marriage (or the promise of such).[2] Having met the challenges of depression and war, American prosperity promised women that family and material abundance would guarantee fulfillment in their lives. For women who could not (or would not) fit this mold, particularly women of color, single women, and lesbians, the normative and narrow message that all women's destiny lay in a "fulfilled womanhood" chafed against the lived realities of their lives.

Some historians labeled the middle decades of the twentieth century the "doldrums" when it came to activism tied explicitly to women's rights, but it might be more accurate to say that such activism entered a quiet phase.[3] Images of men queueing up for soup or jobs dominated the 1930s. When labor and capital clashed in those years, attention fell on the men on the picket line or the shop floor. Men in uniforms going to war symbolized the 1940s. Men in gray flannel suits headed to downtown offices held firm in the American imagination of the 1950s. Political, economic, and social changes during the decades of the Great Depression, World War II, and the early Cold War narrowed notions of women's proper role in society and cast a masculinist shadow over most overt American activism.[4] Historian Robyn Muncy refers to the "long" decade of the 1950s as a period of "reversal" in a longer tradition of progressive reform that had begun in the 1890s and stretched into the 1970s. This framing tracks well with the history of organized challenges to gender segregation.

Women did not abandon their activism or causes necessarily, but their agendas became harder to see as they moved further away from causes specifically associated with women, poured their efforts into government bureaucracies or service organizations, or brought their activism to the workplace.[5] Women activists often found that leaning into their identities as mothers could mute the confrontational aspects of their actions. Women involved in the 1937 sit-down strike against General Motors in Flint, Michigan, presented themselves as concerned wives, mothers, and girlfriends, and they distracted guards and police with chatter while strikers took over sections of the plant.[6] Women Strike for Peace, a loosely organized group of women opposed to nuclear weapons in the 1960s, built an image of the decorous middle-class woman into their activism. They counted on the power of a matronly figure in hat and gloves to deflect public criticism, delay police interference with their demonstrations on public sidewalks, and deter accusations of being communist sympathizers.[7] Even within the African American freedom movement, the midcentury focus on lynching, housing, school segregation, and political disfranchisement tended to erase African American women's unique contributions as women. Women had played a central role in challenging racial discrimination in earlier decades, and their tradition of protest continued into the 1960s with remarkable consistency; however, the gendered aspects shaping women's experience of racism rarely entered the public dialogue surrounding race and rights after the 1920s. The relative silence of this period would hold until the emergence of Black feminism in the 1970s.

A narrow rendering of women's public presence—including sexuality embedded in heterosexual marriage, strong gender differentiation, and promises of fulfillment to be found in consumption and the nuclear family—limited the emancipating potential of the early twentieth-century challenges to gender segregation. American culture cast women living visibly outside these prescribed roles as sexual deviants, delinquents, and "seducers." This kind of "sexualization," observes Estelle Freedman, "could entail a loss of protection," as African American women knew only too well from long experience.[8] Even white women who did not fit this era's narrow image of ideal womanhood found little room to maneuver in the public spaces of American cities. In the years after World War II, the American cultural imagination relegated married women to the rapidly growing suburbs, where children and strip malls would domesticate them. Lesbians established urban subcultures and alternative social spaces to counter a public culture that was remarkably—and even violently—hostile to their presence, but they also suffered mightily for their nonconformity when they became visible in public. For African American women, however, an opportunity to make their case for better access arose in these same years. Black women continued to be targeted when in public space, but they persisted in their efforts to fight back, providing a crucial spark that triggered the growth of a mass-based civil rights movement beginning in the 1950s.

"A Chance to Breathe for Once": Civil Rights and Public Space

It was African American women who perhaps found the most room to press their claims to public space at midcentury, since demanding privileges as respectable women had long been a mainstay of their activism and protests against Jim Crow segregation. They refused to give way to white men. Nor would they accommodate a white woman if a white man was available to do so, even if doing so led to their ejection or arrest. They also fought back, often choosing a legal route by filing formal charges rather than resorting to the hatpin or umbrella of an earlier era. These women sought to disrupt racial segregation, but they often chose to do so by interrupting the white supremacy embedded in gender segregation. In demanding access, accommodation, and protection as women, they continued to tie their activism to a conservative gender code of behavior. Even if they did not explicitly align their actions with those of others in earlier eras, their efforts carried political meaning. They reflected a tradition of troubling core elements of a gender code that reserved privileges for white women. Insisting on being granted respect as women became a strategy to mute the confrontational racial aspects of their behavior, but this strategy also hid in plain sight their challenges to urban gender segregation. The problems and promises of access to public space remained a pressing concern and an ongoing site of activism for African American women.

Reformers and clubwomen from across the racial and ethnic spectrum had generally been advancing women's interests and their right to respectful and fair treatment in an accessible public sphere, but these efforts had particular significance for women of color. For them, gender and race were deeply intertwined and mutually reinforcing identities. Writing in 1936, African American educator Mary McLeod Bethune expressed this sentiment succinctly: "I suffer the greatest known handicap, a Negro—a Negro woman."[9] African American civil rights lawyer and feminist activist Pauli Murray continued the thread in 1964, when she noted that, "as the civil rights struggle gathers momentum, [African American women] began to recognize the similarities between paternalism and racial arrogance."[10] In 1970, pan-Africanist Dara Abubakari raised the entwined nature of race and gender again: "Now the black woman has been independent, but still she hasn't been able to make any decisions [since] the whole country still oppresses her as a woman. Women must be free to choose what they want."[11] This long-standing recognition of the entangled nature of race and gender in African American women's lives supported a similarly long-lived campaign for rights, recognition, and respect in public by and for Black women.

As these Black leaders recognized, the harassment and humiliation of Black women, even assaults on them, played a particular role in enforcing and perpetuating a discriminatory racial hierarchy. The Mississippi-based civil rights leader Fannie Lou Hamer explained the system this way: "A black woman's body was never hers alone."[12] Consequently, African American women's continuing claims to the rights and privileges of "women" came up against a society that cast them, culturally and institutionally, as something other than proper women because of their race. In their responses, African American women often claimed the gendered status and identity of "respectable woman" as a means of challenging their racialized treatment in public. In making this claim, they challenged the meaning of "Negro" in white American society.

By the middle decades of the twentieth century, the location of these challenges followed shifts in urban transportation practices and moved from streetcars to buses. As historian Robin D. G. Kelley eloquently reminds us, "Dark bodies standing in the aisles of half-empty busses, were daily . . . reminders of the semi-colonial status Black people occupied in the Jim Crow South."[13] The nation's racism found expression in the denial of gender privileges embedded in the laws and customs of public space. The accommodations that were provided for white women but routinely denied to women of color—courtesies of address, preferred seating, doors being held open, others making way for them, and respect for their bodies—communicated second-class status as much as signs saying "WHITES ONLY." Black women also suffered more than indignities when in public. Historian Danielle McGuire uncovered numerous cases of Black women in the South being accosted and raped by white men as they walked along city streets. In one particularly notable case from 1955, Gertrude Perkins was pulled off a Montgomery street and raped by white police officers. All were charged, but then acquitted.[14] Rather than face the open and uncontrolled environment of the street, Black women frequently chose to make their stands on public conveyances, where the demeaning impositions and conditions of Jim Crow intertwined with a methodical denial of any gender protections afforded to white women.[15] In these spaces, African American women invoked their rights as both paying customers and women.

Streetcars and buses served as complicated terrains for racial interactions. Not only did they move through the racialized geography of cities, but also, as riders got off and on at each stop, there was a near-constant spatial negotiation between passengers, employees, and, at times, police. When more whites entered a bus or streetcar, African Americans had to cede their seats and even space in the aisle.[16] Thus, on a busy line a Black person might need to move several times over the course of a trip, depending on changes in ridership and the whims of the driver. On a crowded Atlanta streetcar in the spring of 1943, a white man demanded that a seated Black woman move to the back of the car. When she refused, explaining that hers was the next stop, he struck her, breaking her nose. He landed in criminal court.[17] Gender threaded through the court's investigation of the incident, with the man defending his actions by claiming that white women were standing at the time. The victim and a witness testified that there were no empty seats to which the victim might have moved, asserting her right to retain her seat and offering up a challenge to the racialized gender customs embedded in Jim Crow. The Atlanta woman's refusal to cede her seat and her willingness to testify in court about the assault was not an isolated incident in the 1940s; other Black women in cities across the South also filed charges and demanded restitution for ill treatment on transit.

A particularly clear indication of just how deeply gender segregation was tied to racial segregation came in 1956, when an Alabama state legislator, a white man, sponsored a bill that would allow white women the "choice or election to the entire seat on a bus, streetcar or train" so that they could exclude "an undesirable person from sitting beside [them]." Although the proposed law did not mention race in its attempt to "preserve the dignity, safety and security of women and protect them from embarrassment on public conveyances," its intent was clearly racialized. The representative introducing the bill argued that the "prospect of a Negro man taking a seat beside a white woman" would "disturb southerners" and would be "the most likely to create strife and tension," including "riots or bloodshed."[18] He threatened that, without such "protections," white women would stop riding the bus. The bill—and its sponsor's arguments—carried multiple messages: one needed to be white to be a woman, and white women faced danger from Black men in public space. Black women were invisible, neither included in the category of women who needed protection nor thought of as facing any threat like the threat to white womanhood that required exclusion.

Using white women as the cornerstone on which Jim Crow segregation was built, as this bill and many laws did, sent messages to white women: they were vulnerable and needed to be on guard; public space was dangerous; and in the face of pressure from the civil rights movement, (white) laws and society could not necessarily protect them. Overall, these messages communicated that it would be safer for white women to stay home. Some white women in the South internalized these arguments. Perceiving Black men as a threat, Southern white women were too often quick to accuse them of harassment or rape. Such accusations could even deflect harsh judgment from white women, if they were discovered to have transgressed the social code prohibiting consensual relationships across the color line.

Others, such as Georgia reformer Rebecca Latimer Felton, adopted the ideology as a political weapon to expand the political sway of white women. The white supremacist Felton invoked the vulnerability of white women to strengthen her calls for women's suffrage, while also arguing for prison and educational reform.[19] Even white suffrage leaders in the North, including some who had worked to abolish slavery, avoided situations and arguments that would raise the specter of the unprotected white woman and thereby perpetuate the ideologies and practices of gender segregation that cast white women as victims and Black men as predators, while erasing Black women.

African American women, however, often refused to remain invisible. They proved remarkably dedicated to disrupting Jim Crow in the 1940s and 1950s, particularly through their insistence on accessing women's gender privileges on public conveyances.[20] With the emergence of the mass-based Southern civil rights movement in the mid-1950s, cases of African American women resisting Jim Crow when using public transportation became even more visible and more likely to make it into the historical record, especially if they were arrested or filed formal complaints against the transit companies. National Association for the Advancement of Colored People (NAACP) files from Birmingham, Alabama, contain numerous accounts of women being harassed on public transportation by drivers, police, and white patrons. These records reveal women's confrontational and sometimes even violent responses through loud talking, cursing, umbrella battles, spitting, and shoving matches.[21] Robin D. G. Kelley classifies these skirmishes as "acts of defiance," but we might first consider them as acts of defense on the part of women denied what they deemed fair and respectful treatment.[22] In some Southern cities, African American women's resistance became the rallying cry for mass-based protest, the most famous of which was prompted by Rosa Parks's arrest on a Montgomery bus in December 1955.[23]

When Rosa Parks refused to give up her seat on a segregated bus, she challenged Jim Crow racial segregation on both racial and gender grounds, though popular lore and scholarly research have generally acknowledged only the racial component. The bus driver who ordered Parks to vacate her seat sought to preserve a clear line of segregation by removing this African

Rosa Parks on a Montgomery, Alabama, bus in 1956 after the yearlong bus boycott and successful court case challenging the city's racial segregation ordinance. In initially refusing to vacate a seat in 1955, she used gender conventions to challenge racial segregation. (Bettmann Archive via Getty Images)

American individual from a row of seats where a white man wanted to sit. Parks chose not to move, challenging the race-based law the driver sought to enforce. By not moving, she also challenged informal racial codes by asserting her status as a respectable woman entitled to a seat. As Reverend Edgar French explained to the press in the midst of the bus boycott that followed Parks's arrest, "Mrs. Parks was a lady and any gentleman would allow a lady to have a seat."[24] The gendered dictates of public behavior actually offered her a modicum of protection (or at least the moral high ground) for her actions.

The sexual anxiety surrounding Black men in public and the "threat" they posed to white women made it particularly dangerous for men to challenge Jim Crow segregation laws. Rosa Parks's challenge was powerful because she was less likely to spark violent retaliation, but also because she challenged Jim Crow's denial of her respectable womanhood. Aurelia Browder, another Montgomery native and the lead plaintiff in the court case that worked alongside the bus boycott to overturn the city's segregation statute, had a similar encounter. A driver demanded in April 1955 that Browder vacate her seat to allow a "white man and a white lady to sit down," privileging their race over her gender. When the bus boycott started later that year, she immediately joined, explaining, "I wanted better treatment."[25] Lurking behind Browder's comment, but rarely made explicit in the newspaper accounts and court records, was the "insidious trauma" of segregation, to use the words of historian LaKisha Simmons.[26] It was trauma accumulated from the "small violences of the spirit" Black women encountered daily as they negotiated the insults, harassment, and exclusion of public space under racial segregation.[27]

With gender conventions from earlier eras lingering on into the 1950s (and beyond), it continued to be assumed that a respectable woman would never be expected to give up her seat for the convenience of a man. In recounting the incident that led to Rosa Parks's arrest, one observer stated, "She was a woman and the person waiting was a man."[28] No further explanation was offered. The speaker obviously assumed her audience would understand the gender dynamics of this situation. Claiming even these slightly archaic privileges of womanhood challenged the justifications for racial segregation and discrimination. Asserting this gendered privilege (admittedly one that had been somewhat embattled since the early twentieth century) allowed Parks to defy the racial expectations and claim gendered respectability in doing so.

The yearlong bus boycott that followed—a boycott led by men but planned and executed on the ground primarily by women—inspired similar actions in other cities against the long-standing "bus abuse" that was such a common experience in Black women's lives.[29] In Birmingham, Alabama, Black women bus riders suffered curses and punches from both drivers and white passengers. Focusing specifically on the women who fought back, historians have argued that these "daily guerrilla skirmishes" provided a crucial foundation for the civil rights movement of the 1950s and 1960s.[30] Viewing these "skirmishes" as precursors to that movement, however, erases the gendered nature of Black women's experiences, as well as the dailiness of the slights, insults, and humiliations women of color faced at the hands of men of any race. In a rare moment of recognition, the editor of a Black newspaper in South Carolina referenced the "commonplace experience" of women's harassment, saying, "You can pick up accounts of these at a dime a dozen in almost any community."[31] Black women's history reveals most starkly—but not uniquely—the tie between mobility and autonomy.[32] Their history on public conveyances and their willingness to challenge the strictures of race, class, and gender they encountered there suggests something of what was at stake when women sought to access public space.

Having to fight to be recognized as women set Black women on a different path from the one taken by their white counterparts. White women eventually questioned how some of the "privileges" of womanhood confined and undermined their autonomy. Black women, however, had a very different history, having been generally denied the status of respectable womanhood. Not surprisingly, they were somewhat hesitant to endorse some of the reforms and protests that white women embraced in the 1970s; their reluctance stemmed from their different prioritization of issues and very different history with the category of "woman." When white women sought to relieve themselves of the restricting "protections" society foisted on them as women, Black women had to fight to be recognized as women at all, especially when the privileges white women enjoyed (such as bathroom facilities) functioned as tools to oppress and control African Americans. A Black woman might have few recourses against the advances of a white employer in a private home, but on a train, streetcar, or bus she was a patron, and in these spaces a number of Black women took a stand. And out of what Pauli Murray referred to in 1964 as "their struggle for human dignity," African American women "developed a tradition of independence and self-reliance."[33] They generally did so, however, within the narrow notions of gender propriety that prevailed at midcentury and required them to wage their battles for autonomy while dressed "modestly" and looking "as if you were going to church."[34] In these decades, African American activists accepted this equation, perhaps even strengthening gender segregation in their efforts to challenge racial segregation.

"While They Are Waiting for Their Ideal Man": Single Women in the Era of the Nuclear Family

Of the women who lived in American cities during the middle decades of the twentieth century, those who were young and single often drew the most attention. During World War II, Americans manifested a minor obsession with the freewheeling behavior of the nation's young women.[35] These "victory girls" flooded the nation's cities, particularly those that were home to substantial war production industries and military installations, and raised alarm over what appeared to be not just their willingness but their eagerness to engage in sexual relationships with soldiers. Military staff and local officials, fearing outbreaks of venereal diseases, increased efforts to tamp down more overt liaisons, often by surveilling or restricting women's access to dance halls, taverns, and other sites of public leisure. At the same time these officials encouraged single women to "provide respectable companionship" through more domesticated activities associated with home spaces, such as writing letters or playing cards.[36] The anxiety of the war years clearly contained both gendered and spatialized elements as women's presence in public spaces renewed alarm over promiscuity and moral chaos. By the 1950s, narratives of women in the city shifted to more celebratory treatments of the single girl, though warnings of the harm that might befall a woman who did not follow the gendered rules of public space remained firmly embedded in these stories.

By midcentury, etiquette and advice manuals stopped including chapters that addressed specific geographic locations and public accommodations. Instead, the manners and behaviors associated with public transportation, downtowns, and restaurants appeared throughout the books. While public space had become ubiquitous, so much so that it was no longer worthy of separate consideration, women's presence there had not. While books aimed at *The Single Woman* and *The Woman Alone* often poked fun at older forms of etiquette and offered guidelines rather than strict rules, the advice they dispensed appears remarkably similar to that of earlier books. Margaret Fishback's *Safe Conduct: When to Behave and Why* scoffed at older advice to women on "traveling beautifully, casually, and with distinction" as completely unrealistic (and by implication out-of-date) when one was "coming home on a crowded subway after a long day's work and burdened with packages."[37] But the advice she offered was the same as that given thirty years earlier: keep to yourself and expect no assistance from those around you. Although some of the scenarios in the "modern" *No Nice Girl Swears* did seem new (such as what to do when "your escort passes out in a public place"), the advice drew on the familiar theme that women should be responsible for themselves in public and avoid relying on others: "Get up and leave quickly; take a taxi and go home."[38] Even after the war, the *Vogue Book of Etiquette* continued to advise women to "put a kind, generous interpretation on the actions of others" in the interest of promoting the good of all and avoiding confrontation when out in public space.[39] Authors issued warnings to women that their behavior in public was being observed and judged. "Don't think for a moment," advised Elinor Ames, "that you can do silly things in a big city, and do them with impunity . . . any large city is made up of sections—and each section is a small town, with its small-town characters, gossip, and grape-vine telegraph."[40]

The popular press of the mid–twentieth century certainly reinforced the message that lone women were being watched. *Look* magazine's 1960 article "Women without Men" investigated how women learned to "adjust" to their singleness. Although the author, Eleanor Harris, gave a nod to women's independence in work and socializing, the majority of her piece focused on the strategies women used to "search for companionship." In this pursuit, she excused the "relaxation of moral standards" she had observed on the part of women who frequented neighborhood bars, joined singles clubs, or "pick[ed] up partners on the nearby beach" by pointing out the challenges women faced in the "headlong hunt" for a man: "unattached women outnumber the unattached men by 3,696,000."[41] Stories such as these shifted the narrative surrounding urban women. Unlike her early twentieth-century counterpart who came to the city for work, "the mating instinct" supposedly drove "the single girl to the Big City in search of Mr. Right" by the middle of the century.[42] This image of the single girl invoked pity and erased any aspects of her behavior that might have troubled prevailing social norms. Women's presence in public spaces could also be managed through this narrative: their lone presence was unfortunate but, if they were lucky, temporary, and therefore not something that needed to be accommodated.

Themes of danger and desperation often emerged from these midcentury depictions of the singles scene, further undermining women's independence. An exploration of the "Bachelor Girl" that appeared in the glossy African American magazine *Ebony* highlighted the pressure created by "competing young females" and speculated that it might lead the "aging single 'girl' who realizes that all her efforts were in vain . . . to numb her feeling of loneliness and growing hysteria with tranquilizers and liquor."[43] Commentators also hinted at the dangers of lonely single women becoming prey for married men. Using the work of urban planner Charles Abrams, *Newsweek* declared that one reason why cities were declining by the 1960s was that women did not think that they could come there to find husbands anymore. Abrams attributed population loss in big American cities specifically to "losing the confidence of the female." Abrams blamed the situation on restrictions that limited "casual interchanges" coming from the likes of etiquette advocates such as Emily Post. Advice to women who had moved to a city to offer a smile but then "continue on" might "protect the newcomer's privacy," but such behavior prevented any opportunity, Abrams claimed, for social "convergence" between singles. Abrams's suggested solution was for urban planners to turn their attention to creating spaces conducive to social interaction and spaces with appropriate lighting and policing to make women feel comfortable.[44] Urban planners largely ignored Abrams's recommendations, but entrepreneurs seized on the opportunity to profit from desires for socializing. A crowded "singles scene" emerged in many cities, although reporters declared that, since "men want to date and women are looking to mate," the experience was unsatisfying for many patrons.[45] Regardless of this tension, singles bars became a common institution in American cities by the 1960s.

However, coverage of the emerging singles market, even when lavishly demonstrating the money to be made, failed to erase the negative messages going out to women. Regularly portrayed as a lonely and pitiful figure on an unrealistic quest to find a husband, the single girl might find herself "disenchanted," at best, if she came to a city alone.[46] The single girl of the midcentury appeared incomplete and unfulfilled, an image that pressured women to couple up to achieve social acceptance. Articles touched on the challenges faced by young women who would likely make risky choices to alleviate their loneliness. Some would end up pregnant and then either seek a dangerous and illegal abortion or bear an illegitimate child.[47] Others, "while they are waiting for their ideal man," would find themselves turning to same-sex relationships to alleviate the loneliness.[48] These were not organized challenges to social mores, but women who embraced careers over family, chose roommates over husbands, engaged in sexual exploration outside monogamy and heterosexuality, and built deep and sustaining friendships with other women blurred the contours of acceptable behavior and weakened the credibility of social norms.[49] Despite the warnings and the social pity directed at single women, women did not necessarily behave as they were told.

"Out on the Street We Were Fair Game": Lesbian Visibility

The supposed loneliness of single life offered an appealing, nonthreatening explanation to heterosexual Americans for the emerging visibility of lesbians in the mid–twentieth century. Lesbians could be seen as young women who were too immature to fulfill the roles expected of them by society. Many experts—sexologists, sociologists, and psychologists—also suggested that the pressures on women to date, find a husband, and create a successful family might be overwhelming, causing some women to seek relationships with other women.[50] Historian Marc Stein, studying Philadelphia, noted that an ability to blend in as merely "single women" in the midcentury city "allowed lesbians to avoid adding to the considerable dangers that they already faced as women in public space."[51] With the attention to single women that reached ascendency in the 1950s, urban America adopted an explanatory framework for women who moved through public space on their own or in the company of other women, and this allowed some lesbians to fly under the radar of public scrutiny.

For lesbians, these decades represented a curious mix of opportunity and persecution. The heightened focus on the image of "the single girl" allowed some lesbians to function more independently in public space, especially those who were young and appeared conventionally feminine in their presentation. World War II disrupted traditional social patterns, and mobilization offered many young women reasons to leave home. With opportunities to work, recreate, and live with other women, they could explore "possibilities for sexual self-discovery, including homosexuality," under the guise of serving the nation in a time of crisis.[52]

During the middle decades of the century, bars, restaurants, and clubs catering to gay men and lesbians became key social institutions for the gay community. In the 1950s especially, "the lesbian subculture grew and defined itself more clearly than ever before," notes historian Lillian Faderman, and the gay bars of the era served as crucial spaces to build group identity among a population that had little sense of a collective history and no "safe turf" on which to meet one another.[53] Scholars have recently begun to explore a more diverse set of sites in which lesbians built homosocial and erotic connections, but bars clearly played a pivotal role in creating viable lesbian subcultures, particularly for white, working-class lesbians.[54] The bars functioned as a tonic to the stresses of lives lived in a society that privileged a narrow definition of acceptable sexuality and gendered appearance. In these spaces, gay people found or created sites of "publicity," to use Stein's term, where they could make themselves visible to others in the community and "reterritorialize" small corners of an otherwise heteronormative urban public space.[55] Although lesbians and lesbian-identified spaces may not have been as overtly political as those of gay men, lesbian bars still signaled what historian Nan Boyd deems "a form of cultural politics and collective resistance" among women living outside normative sexuality.[56] In this way, the mid–twentieth century represented a unique moment for women who sought emotional and erotic relationships with other women, providing both a sense of identity and community rooted in particular urban spaces.

As important as the gay bars of the 1950s were to growing lesbian communities in many cities, they were never entirely safe spaces. Women in bars risked activating the stigma against women drinking in public without a male escort. In establishments shared by gay men and lesbians, this danger could be mitigated by quick changes in partners at the bar or on the dance floor when

Bars known for hosting lesbians offered rare but valued opportunities for socializing, particularly during the mid-twentieth century. While still at risk for harassment and police raids, patrons at these establishments were often safer than in other public spaces. Women posing for a picture at the Green Door in North Hollywood, California, 1955. (June L. Mazer Lesbian Archives)

outsiders entered the space. Bars that drew a crowd of primarily women did not have such defensive options. Police also targeted bar patrons for harassment and raided gay bars regularly. Periodic campaigns to "clean up" cities often led police to the barrooms and backrooms of gay clubs to look for same-sex couples. Sometimes undercover police officers sought to entice patrons into "inappropriate" behavior that might lead to a disorderly conduct arrest. Gay men were more likely to be targets, but women did not escape police harassment. For example, patrons of a Greenwich Village bar, the Sea Colony, reported that police officers put their hands down women's pants after pushing them up against a wall.[57] Leslie Feinberg's autobiographical novel *Stone Butch Blues* recounts raids, detentions, arrests, and beatings. "The cops always pulled the police van right up to the bar door and left snarling dogs inside so we couldn't get out," Feinberg wrote. "We were trapped alright." Once at the police station, those detained could hear the abuse and humiliation heaped on the others, knowing that "the next time the cell door opens it will be me they drag out and chain spread-eagle to the bars," or subject to beatings or rape. Those who came to bail them out had to face the hostility of the police—"their leers, their taunts, their threats"—while they "strained to hear from back in the cells" what was happening to their companions.[58]

The hostility of police dovetailed with negative media and mainstream cultural attention to lesbians in the 1950s. Women who demonstrated a lesbian identity on the streets found themselves subjected to a host of harassments. "Butches," or "studs," often wearing men's clothing and short haircuts, drew particularly negative attention in public from police and many straight people.[59] As Lillian Faderman and Stuart Timmons explain, these women "were a visible emblem of how some females refused to assume their traditional roles" and therefore "the forces of reaction came down upon them."[60] Joan Nestle, a self-identified femme from this era, agreed; butch women "did announce themselves as tabooed women who were willing to identify their passion for other women by wearing clothes that symbolized the taking of responsibility."[61] As philosopher Judith Butler notes, mainstream society will "regularly punish those who fail to do their gender right."[62] Similarly, two women presenting themselves visibly as a couple in public "provoked anger on the streets." "The sight of us," Nestle recalls, "was enraging" to some straight people who understood visible lesbians, particularly butches, to be "a symbol of women's erotic autonomy. . . . The physical attacks were a direct attempt to break into this self-sufficient erotic partnership." While they might have appeared to be "courting violence," Nestle explains, "we . . . knew the political implications of how we were courting each other and chose not to sacrifice our need to their anger."[63]

Whether or not butches and the femmes who appeared with them in public ascribed such overtly political intentions to their appearances and actions, they certainly knew the dangers they faced and developed strategies to mitigate them. Extensive interviews conducted by Elizabeth Lapovsky Kennedy and Madeline Davis with a midcentury lesbian community in Buffalo, New York, revealed this cognizance and the toll on many of the threat of harassment. "Out on the street," one interview subject explained, "you were fair game."[64] As a woman named Matty recalled: "I actually had walked down the street with some friends not doing anything and had people spit at me, or spit at us, it was really bad."[65] For some, "it was easier to walk down the street if at first glance people thought you were a man. . . . You might feel safer if you went out dressed more like a guy so people wouldn't hassle you late at night."[66] For others, the solution was to not wear pants or other clothing that might call attention to themselves except when in friendly spaces, such as gay bars.

While the butch-femme social code and the gay bar scene played a powerful role in organizing the public and social life for some, queer social life varied markedly based on class and race. Semipublic house parties offered women the opportunity to explore queer desires and sociability without the class stigma of the bar scene.[67] The location, dates, and times changed, lessening the potential for police intrusion but also making parties harder to find. Many new arrivals and teens lacked access to the house party networks and had to try the bars first. While there were lesbian bars for whites in Detroit, most of the city's African American lesbians socialized in people's homes. Generally considered private spaces, homes clearly served a "public" function as sites of connecting and socializing that protected the city's Black lesbians from both "racial prejudice from white lesbians and homophobic reaction from their black communities," according to scholar Rochella Thorpe.[68] Some middle-class lesbians rejected the butch-femme roles associated with the working class and tended toward assimilation in their appearance. *The Ladder*, the first lesbian newspaper, advised its readers to adopt a "mode of behavior and dress acceptable to society."[69] The editors and the organizers of the larger homophile movement (gay and lesbian civil rights) from which the newspaper sprang hoped that "integration" would limit harassment and encourage acceptance of lesbians. Dee, another Buffalo resident, endorsed "passing" as straight when she admonished, "When we're out in public we should sort of not flaunt gaiety."[70] Hoping to avoid conflict and promote acceptance, a Minneapolis woman explained, "At the time we wanted to look, in appearance, as non-threatening as we could."[71] Socializing in less public spaces, accommodating, and passing all functioned as lesbian strategies for survival in the decades before an organized, overtly political movement for gay rights emerged in the 1970s.

As Sherrie Inness argues, passing, or at least "partial passing," was (and remains) "an unavoidable part of a lesbian's life" and was never an uncomplicated experience. Butches, whose stature within working-class lesbian communities grew the more masculine they made their appearance, faced extreme prejudice when trying to find an apartment, hold down a job, or move through "straight" public space. Some of the butches at the heart of Buffalo's lesbian bar scene, for example, often relied on femmes to support them financially, which allowed them to choose more extreme personal appearances, especially closely cropped hair. Even these women, however, walked a fine line. They might wear a skirt to ride a bus or at home if they lived with their parents, but they lost status if they were spotted by other lesbians from the community when they did so.

By the 1970s, when the gay rights movement emerged, the popularity of the strict social roles of the 1950s and 1960s, particularly that of the "butch," came under scrutiny by lesbian feminists, who often sought to undo the gender differences they saw re-created in those roles. At the same time, however, these politicized lesbian communities strengthened their condemnation of women passing as heterosexuals. Poet and activist Adrienne Rich, for example, advocated for lesbian visibility and referred to "assimilation" as "the most passive and debilitating of responses to political repression, economic insecurity, and a renewed open season on difference."[72] That visible identity, however, was not strictly tied to sexual activity or desire, but also depended on a kind of "surface identity" constructed through "dress and mannerisms," particularly the 1970s "dyke uniform" of flannel shirts and jeans.[73] But as Arlene Stein writes of this time in *Becoming Lesbian*, "Lesbians tend to be members of, or at least travelers through, heterosexual as well as homosexual worlds," and they therefore must "satisfy the requirements of both" or face being targeted by heterosexuals or excluded by homosexuals.[74] So, while the definition of what it meant for a lesbian to pass as a heterosexual shifted over the decades, the tension and dangers embedded in public presentation for gender-nonconforming and "sexual-deviant" women remained. There were also clear tensions during the middle decades of the twentieth century between the opportunities afforded to build visible communities and the persecution that identifiable lesbians faced in an era of narrowly defined gender roles and sexual identities.

"Everything in the Culture Militated toward Pleasing Men": Girl Watching and Midcentury Surveillance

In 1954, Don Sauers, a New York advertising copywriter, wrote a short book entitled *The Girl Watcher's Guide*. The breezy and often tongue-in-cheek tone of the book captured the beginning of a trend that lasted well into the 1970s. Girl watching, he explained, was quite different from looking. To merely look was to insult beautiful girls who deserved to be watched—and appreciated—because "they are there."[75] *Life* magazine announced the arrival of "girl watching" with a four-page spread in 1956. Popular music in the 1950s and 1960s picked up on the trend as well. White harmonizers The Four Lads praised "the harem parading for me" in their hit "Standing on the Corner," while the O'Kaysions had many Americans singing "I'm a Girl Watcher" and several record labels put out collections of music "to watch girls by." The girl-watching phenomenon of the mid–twentieth century was part of the backlash that followed the expansion of women's roles earlier in the century. The "working girl" from an earlier era had gained cultural acceptance, but her "celebration" at midcentury promoted a normative image of youth, whiteness, heterosexuality, and availability for marriage. And real women, whatever their age or background, were measured by these norms.

Girl watching lay at the intersection of 1950s cultural ideals and anxieties, but it also adapted well to the changing cultural milieu of the 1960s. When girdles and crew cuts gave way to miniskirts and mop tops, girl watching got a makeover as well, courtesy of the sexual revolution and eager advertising agencies. Girl watching became a phenomenon in the mid–twentieth century in large part because it fit within the emerging etiquette governing public behavior, complemented Americans' beliefs about their cities, and reinforced Cold War gender norms that privileged both whiteness and heterosexuality. The girl-watching fad rapidly became fodder for newspaper columnists' lighthearted assessments of changes in the weather, fashions, and television programs. Girl-watching clubs—even national and international associations—formed in the 1960s. Advertisers cashed in on the "harmless" fun of girl watching to promote a host of products, including Diet Pepsi, which began advertising itself as the drink of "girls that girl watchers watched." Urban boosters promoted their cities with girl-watching contests, and Don Sauers published two more editions of *The Girl Watcher's Guide* by 1972. For women, the popularity of this fad signaled yet another shift in the gendered terrain of the city. Rather than hide their presence in public by wearing dark and demure clothes and behaving quietly, women—at least those who fit the norms of "watchability"—were now to present themselves for men's enjoyment and be grateful for the responses they received.

As articulated by Sauers, girl watching was a noble pastime practiced by virtually all men. "Any male is eligible, although most girl watchers are over ten and under one hundred and four," he joked. And virtually all women were potential subjects. "It is impossible to make a hobby," noted Sauers, "of watching [only] one girl." Advocates of girl watching in the 1950s and early 1960s portrayed the practice as an innocent, harmless hobby that was rewarding for all involved. Men watched women because it made them "feel *good*." "And there is even less doubt that the girls have ever minded," Sauers explained.[76] Popular media picked up on these themes, declaring girl watching a "masculine sport," "high art," and "quite relaxing."[77] A men's magazine dedicated to girl watching declared that it had become an "accepted social pastime . . . most men indulge in to some extent." "Some don't," the editors acknowledged, "but they're dead."[78]

Girl watching further entangled white supremacy with gender segregation. Race appeared only implicitly in these popular renditions of girl watching, but images suggested that the "new" craze specifically gave permission to white men to more boldly watch white women. Crafted within the racial norms of midcentury America, men of color received no such license to engage in the practice, and any attention they might direct toward white women continued to hold deadly consequences. When the Black teenager Emmett Till was accused of whistling at a white woman in 1955, he was beaten and drowned by white men. Deeply embedded prohibitions for men of color against watching white women remained not just intact but reinforced by extralegal violence. The coexistence of breezy renditions of the innocence of girl watching alongside brutal race crimes clearly demarcated the racial boundaries of girl watching. White men had long taken the prerogative to focus their attention on women of color, whenever they chose, although that remained a taboo topic among most whites. Girl watching was a phenomenon with a long cultural reach in the ways it embedded racialized male privileges and restrained women's behavior.

The girl-watching phenomenon of the 1950s actually challenged basic tenets of an established system of etiquette in which men and women were to be both independent and innocuous, drawing little attention to themselves and asking nothing, not even attention, from those around them.[79] In the nineteenth century, men who violated these standards by staring at women were labeled "jackanapes" and "cads," and they were to be "hissed down, thrown out, or even arrested."[80] At least until the mid–twentieth century, men who wished to appear well mannered could not offer an arm, tip a hat, make a comment, or even let their eyes meet the gaze of a woman— even a woman they knew—without her invitation. That men talked about the "sport" of watching women in the 1950s suggests a remarkable departure from established manners. But in a nod to those older conventions, popular descriptions of girl watching emphasized that the actual watching needed to be subtle and discreet. In other words, the idea of girl watching could be fodder for discussion, but in practice the watchee was not to know that she was being watched. The Girl Watcher's Guide discouraged direct conversation or any attempt to "pick up" a woman, practices generally associated with the crass behavior of the working classes. "Respect the rights of the watched," the author cautioned. "A girl watcher who asks for name and telephone number is like a bird watcher who steals eggs."[81] A popular song from 1956 reminded listeners that internal thoughts should remain private: "Brother you can't go to jail for what you're thinking."[82]

To keep girl watching on the side of good taste, men also needed to honor the long-standing middle-class value put on practicing individual restraint in public and appearing both respectful and respectable. The appearance of middle-class respectability, in clothing and behavior, became men's defense against suspicion of having breached good manners. Keep moving, girl-watching men were told, dress "*conservatively*," and "appear to be *going somewhere*."[83] Men who had perfected "the half-lidded, unobtrusive or veiled appraisal" of women were praised, and ridicule was heaped on unsubtle "swivel heads."[84] With so high a value placed on subtlety, ultimately women in public had to assume that even if they could not detect it, they were being scrutinized—for their dress, behavior, and ability to attract men's attention: "The real, live girl is only and always the object of his quest, the subject of his contemplation. Standards must be kept high."[85] All women might be the objects of male scrutiny, and they would have few visual clues as to when and by whom they were being observed.

A product of its time, girl watching was both a component of and a complement to the suburbanized domesticity at the heart of American culture in the decades following the end of World War II.[86] Even when Americans did not or could not fully embody the era's ideal, they still had to negotiate a culture infused with it. As described by sociologist Winifred Breines, the "white, affluent, and suburbanized" 1950s, however "familiar and reassuring," also contained a "contrasting underside" that was "alienated, disoriented, and discontent[ed]." A consistent theme in the scholarly literature of the postwar period traces the anxieties produced by a powerful, yet unattainable, ideal. Highly privileged young white middle-class women, for example, looked uneasily at the path laid before them in a time when, according to Breines, "liberating possibilities were masked by restrictive norms; they grew up and came of age in a time when new lives beckoned while prohibitions against exploring them multiplied."[87] For men, anxieties emerged from the pressure to be what sociologist Michael Kimmel has called the "impossible synthesis of sober responsible breadwinner, imperviously stoic master of his fate, and swashbuckling hero."[88] In addition to these gender (and gendered) tensions of the era, Americans believed that the conformity and technology of the modern age was undermining the differences in the sexes and feminizing society. Blame for these changes often fell on American women, who were accused of coddling their sons ("momism") and emasculating their spouses through the demands of home and family.[89] While domesticity prove more an ideal than a lived reality, the mythology carried significant weight.

The act of girl watching soothed some of these anxieties and tensions, particularly those of men. Girl watching invited men to see themselves as successful, confident, and at ease in the world. A similar ethos drove the success of *Playboy* magazine, launched in late 1953, just months before the publication of *The Girl Watcher's Guide*. *Playboy* promoted a "masculine world of racy consumption, narcissism and leisure" and reassured men that they need not be a slave to the mind-numbing conformity or emasculating forces of the 1950s.[90] Girl watching, coming from the same cultural stew as *Playboy*, shored up a sense of manliness perceived to be damaged by suburban domesticity, but it did so without fully negating older forms of masculinity that stressed self-discipline and hard work. Girl watching was a "playboy" practice, rather than a whole lifestyle, in which the man in the gray flannel suit might indulge while away from the suburbs but still earning the money that supported his family. "Much of our sense of social order and continuity," argues Barbara Ehrenreich in *The Hearts of Men*, "has depended on the willingness of men to succumb in the battle of the sexes: to marry, to become wage earners and to reliably share their wages with their dependents."[91] Girl watching offered a reward for men who had "succumbed" to their assigned domestic roles.

For both men and women, girl watching served as a public version of the sexual scripts and "extreme stereotypes" attached to the gender roles of the 1950s.[92] Men needed to demonstrate their sexuality in a "masculine" way, through control and dominance. Women, however, were to attract men's attention and lure them in, but hold the line with chaste behavior, to "captivate without capturing."[93] In courtship women were expected to entice men with the promise of erotic fulfillment, but without engaging in intercourse. This script required that women in public demonstrate passive and submissive sexuality.[94] Girl-watching practices fit these narratives by encouraging women to attract men without seeming to do so intentionally and to also maintain sexual propriety by not responding to any overtures from strangers.

As much as the deeper themes of girl watching may have derived from the tensions over sexual propriety and gender roles in Cold War American culture, the practice either denied that those tensions even existed or made light of them. Discussions of girl watching consistently treated the practice in a playful manner. The *Washington Post* suggested that female office workers be required to wear unattractive bloomers so as to recover the productivity lost to girl watching, noting that "40 million American men spend a half hour on the job each day staring at a pretty working girl. This means that 20 million hours—or 228 years—are frittered away every single working day."[95] Sauers and other girl-watching advocates continued in the comical vein, reminding men engaged in the hobby of basic safety precautions: Don't watch girls while driving, pouring hot coffee, or clipping hedges. And "don't let less important matters interfere. If you find that girl watching is taking more of your time than your lunch hour allows, quit your job."[96]

Humor was always near the surface in portrayals of girl watching—usually a silly sort of humor that worked largely because of assumptions that women were "prey" and therefore not threats to the power of "hunters." Playing off the hobby of bird-watching, *The Girl Watcher's Guide* offered an amusing typology for women that ranged from the "Well-Preserved Fortyplus" to the "Horn-Rimmed Booklugger." A beautiful woman might appear on a sidewalk and draw the eye of a driver or stop a conversation, but she was only a momentary distraction and nothing more. After proclaiming that all members of the Ardent Girl-Watchers' Association could "appraise, classify and give the true zoological name for each . . . species [of girls] at twenty paces," the club president defended their practice by arguing, "You'd be stretching a tired bra to claim that collecting retina imprints of passing females is any less a salutary hobby than, say, saving stamps or strings, G or otherwise."[97] The naturalizing of girl watching through references to birds and habitats and its equation with hobbies contrasted the practice to the complexity of other social interactions, particularly those associated with marriage, as men were encouraged to "savor the tidbit without the wed bit."[98]

Humor, whether self-deprecating or mildly racy, softened the violence of the predator-prey imagery, but it did not diminish the message to men and women about who controlled the space or held the social power. Scholars widely agree that gender roles in the postwar era "were by no means unified despite the enabling myth of domestic, heterosexual normalcy."[99] Girl watching did at least some of the cultural work needed to maintain that image, feeding the mystique that contributed to what one scholar called an "apparent and cheerful stability" in the 1950s and early 1960s.[100] Keeping it funny also helped girl watching appear harmless and morally safe. In a period that relied heavily on sexual innuendo rather than explicitly eroticized public interactions, girl watching both suggested heterosexual desire and muted it at the same time.

Girl watching contained an inherently urban component and in postwar urban (and urbane) culture, watchable "girls" served as a glittering accessory to the gleaming office towers and general glamour of American downtowns during their "moment of grace."[101] Columnist Dick Kidson noted in the *Los*

Angeles Times in the late 1950s that there were "more girls than birds around the city."[102] Girl watching was particularly rooted in the mythology of "down-town" and mid-twentieth-century office culture. It relied heavily on the crowds and anonymity of these spaces. "The sidewalks of our city streets are the most popular" spots for girl watching, Don Sauers declared, particularly the sidewalks of the business districts and particularly at lunchtime, when legions of female office workers poured out of their buildings.[103] A reporter for the *Los Angeles Times* praised the urban designers who produced Century City in LA for creating "the best theater in the country for girl-watching," though he admitted that it might not be "exactly what the dreamers had in mind, but it is certainly a fringe benefit."[104] *The Girl Watcher's Guide* stressed the role of the imagination, advising that "total strangers make the best subjects," while Frank Loesser's lyrics for the 1956 musical *The Most Happy Fella* encouraged "brothers" to use their "rich imagination" in selecting their "imaginary dish."[105] Business districts, where people passed quickly, rarely encountered others they knew, and often traveled alone, proved the most popular sites among enthusiasts, as girl watching relied on anonymity.

Girl watching of the 1950s reflected and reinforced a changing culture deeply influenced by an expanding middle class and the domestic impact of rising Cold War tensions. Americans embraced domesticity—family and home—as a "buffer" against the uncertainties of the post–World War II world.[106] But someone had to work for the money it would take to outfit suburban retreats, and not all Americans had formed the families that would live in these ideal homes. It was these populations that could be found on the streets of America's downtowns, and it was here—away from the domesticity of the suburbs—that girl watching flourished. As early as 1950, and in clear contrast to express beliefs that women should be homemakers, half of all married women worked for wages, and that number would continue to climb. This trend potentially threatened men's role as the family provider and the secure masculinity offered by that identity. Girl watching earnestly and enthusiastically managed this threat by imagining the working women on the sidewalks of American cities as single women who were available for male appraisal. Women to be found downtown at 9:00 a.m., noon, or 5:00 p.m. could be assumed to be single "business girls" and not someone's wife or mother. Women might abound in the suburbs and shopping malls, but those seen in such venues were assumed to be safely married, probably even mothers—they were not girls. It was the young, single, self-supporting women who most needed to prove their femininity in Cold War America, and girl watching of the 1950s encouraged precisely this. While management practices and office design reinforced a gendered hierarchy in the world of business, girl watching did very similar work in the anonymous spaces of American cities.[107]

Girl watching required a performance from both genders, but the lessons for women—instructions on how and where to be available, alluring, cheerful, receptive, and accommodating—were particularly strong. "It cannot be said often enough," recalled one woman, "that for a young woman in 1953 everything in the culture militated toward pleasing men."[108] A magazine published briefly in the late 1950s, *Girl Watcher*, amply demonstrated the highly sexual—and particularly white and heterosexual—messages of girl watching. This rather explicit rendition of girl watching featured images of women seeking the male gaze by wearing provocative clothes and striking alluring stances. Female models in tight skirts vamped for the camera on city sidewalks, looking much like the public space counterparts of the women who appeared in contemporary *Playboy* issues. One model, June Wilkinson, even appeared in both magazines in 1959. Articles declared men "the Hunter" and women "the Hunted" while offering men tips on bagging their prey.[109] Young women romped half-clothed through parks in pictorial spreads. Whether in the tame *Girl Watcher's Guide* or the more sexually explicit *Girl Watcher* magazine, men were supposed to watch and women were supposed to perform. These scripted displays of gender roles reinforced heteronormativity for both men and women. Girl watching and acting as if one were being watched were ways to prove that one was following the rules. Cold War domesticity rendered asexual and deviantly sexual individuals as threatening to a culture that prided itself on the nuclear family.[110] Girl watching was a performance of sexual pursuit for men and sexual availability for women that reinforced a heteronormatized public sphere in which men watched women for sexual gratification and women performed to garner the approval of the watchers.

Girl watching says much about constructions of gender, but these were racialized constructions in that they conceived of cross-gender desire as not just "not interracial" but wholly white. Girl watching imagined a city in which the stage was clear for whites to play out their sporting games as much as it envisioned masculine dominance. The absence of any discussion of race suggests both the assumptions of privilege on the part of those who wrote about or otherwise codified girl watching and their need for a simple narrative of desire and control that any direct mention of race would have destabilized. The whiteness of girl watching was unmistakable, though precisely because of the privilege of whiteness, it did not need to be explicitly made so. Girl watching was inherently dangerous for men of color, both because of its connection to sexuality and its location in the "white" business districts of urban America. Mythologies surrounding men of color, particularly Black men, as hypersexed and the long history of extralegal violence against men of color for the "eye rape" of white women made looking at them a dangerous act.[111] Jim Crow segregation of the South and de facto segregation in the North marked American downtowns as white. The privilege of looking at white women was clearly reserved for white men, and the masculinity enacted through girl watching represented the intertwined nature of racial and gender roles in the postwar United States.

As much as girl watching was a product of the particularities and proclivities of the 1950s, it proved remarkably adaptable to many of the changes brought by the 1960s. The practice lost some of its purported innocence but retained a humorous take on the power of women's beauty. In the 1960s, men cheered on the women adopting the liberating trends of the decade, such as rising hemlines. Girl watching of this era meshed seamlessly with the culture of youth, sexual liberation, and heterosexual expressiveness.[112] Montreal embraced these attitudes by adding a "girl watching week" to Expo '67 and emblazoning billboards with the message to "KEEP MONTREAL BEAUTIFUL. WEAR A MINISKIRT."[113]

With the evolution of girl watching in the 1960s, its basic tenets shifted. Men's appraisal of women became more blatant, even more public in a sense. Press coverage of new trends in women's fashion routinely included a note on whether or not the "girl watchers" would approve. A shift toward boots in 1963 was "expected to bring jeers from veteran girl watchers," while the rise of the miniskirt proved "good news . . . for girl watchers" in 1970.[114] Watching became stock-in-trade for "local color" stories and celebrity coverage, including boxer George Foreman posing with a Playboy Bunny to receive the title "Champion Girl Watcher."[115] The Girl Scouts of Chicago exploited the phenomenon to fundraise by holding a "Girl Watchers' Tea." Attendees were given dark sunglasses—standard equipment for all serious girl watchers—and "music to watch girls by" played in the background while the GSC encouraged wealthy Chicagoans to watch over the actual girls of the city through financial contributions.[116]

The humor of the girl-watching fad communicated cultural norms and reinforced power structures. As was the case with much of the press attention to the phenomenon, the founding of the International Society of Girl Watchers in 1960 in San Francisco was certainly meant to be in jest. By the end of the decade, the organization claimed fifteen thousand members whose goal was to move girl watching from a "furtive, amateur pastime" to something receiving "open recognition and employ[ing] the most sophisticated methods of eyeballing" in order to "glorify the American Girl." Society members received credentials that they presented to likely women in order to buy the watcher time to evaluate and rank the women from "um-m-m-m-m, lovely," to "cold." A positive appraisal allowed the watcher, in contrast to the 1950s dictates of subtlety, to present a woman with a "watching eyeballs lapel sticker" so that she and all others would know that she was a "watchable" girl.[117]

The most obvious explanation for the shift from a secretive, subtle style of watching to a much more flamboyant, aggressive, public style of watching was the commercialization of the fad. Companies selling cigarettes (Pall Mall), soda (Diet Pepsi), alcohol (Seagram's), and even airlines (Transworld) picked up on the phenomenon. In the re-creations of these 1960s and early 1970s advertisements, girl watching was much more active and obvious than what Sauers had described in the 1950s. By the late 1960s, advertisers began to use girl watching not only as a tool to reach men, but also as a means to attract women as well. Diet Pepsi launched a new campaign in 1967, for example, declaring that "every girl wants to be a girl girl watchers watch. Diet Pepsicola helps keep it that way."[118] Refrigerator magnets, sweatshirts, drinking glasses, and cocktail napkins declared one a "girl watcher." Classified advertisements listed apartments as "girl watcher" specials.[119] Eye drops promised to soothe the eyes after "too much girl watching."[120] Folding binoculars, promised the manufacturer, would be "perfect" for girl watching.[121] Promotional events also institutionalized girl watching with contests for the "most watchable girl." City officials and businesses capitalized on girl watching precisely because of the fun and playful image of the city it helped to craft.

With the commercialization of girl watching, women were now urged, not to hide their presence in public, but to present themselves for male enjoyment and be grateful for the responses they received. In 1969, *Glamour* magazine counseled women to "act like a beauty" when "a workman whistles appreciatively."[122] Advertisers encouraged women to draw attention to themselves while in public, seeking validation and perhaps even justifying their presence on city streets. Gimbels department store advertised clothing lines as "the most watchable dresses," promising women they would be "driving every guy mini-mad" as they walked down the street.[123] Popular music captured the image of women noticing and even cultivating attention. In "I'm a Girl Watcher," for example, the blue-eyed soul group the O'Kaysions admired the women "putting on a show." Paralleling the narrative of the newly emerging sexual revolution of the 1960s, girl watchers and the girls they watched no longer needed to hide their participation in this activity.

While girl watching resembled other, older manifestations of the urban spectacle, its appearance in the 1950s and commercialization in the 1960s tell us much more about the evolution of constructions of privilege and power for these decades. Girl watching both reflected and reinforced constructions of heterosexuality, whiteness, masculinity, and femininity in the postwar period. Girl watching was every bit as much a privilege of whiteness and straightness as being served first or exclusively at a soda fountain or sales counter, sitting in the front of a bus, or entering through the front door of a theater. Girl watching was also a male privilege, and just as much a privilege as being able to dine in a restaurant alone, stay in a hotel without an escort, or order a drink at a bar. Race and heterosexuality were both conspicuous and invisible in the postwar practice of girl watching, which was thoroughly, yet not explicitly, white. In this way, it reflected myths of American democracy that assumed difference to be invisible while holding out norms that were clearly white, male, and straight.

Conclusion

In many ways, the paradoxes of the mid–twentieth century do much to reveal the significance of organized movements for social change in the history of women and public space. With the memory of the Progressive Era all but erased by the Great Depression in the 1930s and World War II in the 1940s, the reform-oriented organizations supporting women's access to public space had largely disappeared or shifted their identity away from activism around gender segregation. The Cold War push for Americans to demonstrate a high degree of conformity in order to win the cultural competition between the United States and the Soviet Union drove narrow definitions of womanhood and appropriate sexuality. These definitions often neatly mapped onto the imagined space of American cities in which married women occupied the suburbs and young single women who had not yet married (but surely would, in the mainstream imagination) were found in downtown offices. Women's ability to function independently often tracked with their similarity to these images of what women should be doing and where they should be doing it. Although girl watching seemed to praise women, relatively narrow definitions of "watchability" reinscribed aspects of gender segregation's complicated behavioral codes for who belonged where and what characteristics entitled women access to public space. The phenomenon's playful and commercialized portrayal supported a culture of surveillance and opened the door to harassment or exclusion for those who did not fit its narrow ideal.

In many ways the girl-watching phenomenon was the explicit, even positive, acknowledgment of a trend in urban life that critics had been noting since the nineteenth century—the pleasure of the urban spectacle. In the industrial metropolis of twentieth-century America, an individual's presentation in public was all that others might have to judge them by. Girl watching played on that reality, while also helping structure interactions in public space, but it did so in a way that reinforced gender as one of the most significant markers of identity. The practice offered tacit acceptance of women in public spaces, particularly white women, but also reinforced the expectation that in those spaces they would be women first and also under surveillance. Real women had to fit themselves around these images or bear the consequences of being different. For African American women, these decades represented a renewed push to be included in the definitions of respectable womanhood and the protections it offered, and their actions helped to spark the modern mass based civil rights movement. For lesbians, the prosperous postwar city opened up opportunities to build community, but taking advantage of them could expose women whose appearance revealed their sexual identity to harassment and violence. During these years, questions over the right of women to be in and use the city that emerged in the early decades of the century seemed to have been resolved into acceptance of their presence in public. The expectations for women's appearance and behavior, however, remained constrained and even narrowed. Some women, particularly those from marginalized social groups, pushed on these boundaries. In the decades that followed, many more women, particularly white middle-class women, would rejoin efforts to challenge the limitations imposed on them by the norms of public space.

4

When Girls Became Women

Confronting Exclusion and Harassment in the Long 1960s

"It is difficult for a woman to walk down the street without being weighed, measured, and judged," explained a woman from Lawrence, Kansas.[1] Author, activist, and longtime New York City resident Susan Brownmiller, in recalling uncomfortable and intrusive encounters on crowded subway cars and sidewalks, explained that these daily occurrences were "a part of life," something to be expected and endured.[2] Two women shopping in downtown Syracuse stopped at the city's fanciest hotel for a drink only to find themselves turned away for being "unescorted" by a man. Reinforced by the girl-watching craze and rampant consumerism, American culture and cities carried an image as playful, prosperous, and fun in the 1960s. But as these women's experiences suggested, the reality of urban life for women often felt quite different.

Etiquette did not offer women a way to challenge the cultural restrictions on or appraisals of their presence in public space without appearing rude, paranoid, or less than respectable. Women were told to believe that the attention they received from strangers was a positive reinforcement of their gender identity and that policies excluding them from certain public accommodations protected them. They were taught that being confrontational, making a scene, or going into a bar unescorted was unladylike.[3] Challenging a man for "merely admiring" her or "accidentally" bumping her on a crowded street would put a woman in the awkward position of being rude if she rejected his compliments or claims of innocence.[4] To enter the masculine domain of a bar was to risk even more harassment. In the words of novelist Marge Piercy, such harassment left women to be "stalked like the tame pheasants who are hand-raised and then turned loose for hunters to shoot, an activity called sport."[5] As individuals, women had little recourse when so treated and were left feeling humiliated and vulnerable.

The context in which these behaviors occurred also started to shift as Americans began to see cities as increasingly menacing by the late 1960s and 1970s. This sense of urban menace—which stemmed in part from inner-city race rebellions that surprised and terrified so many whites, subsequent white flight from cities, and the growing equation of urban problems such as crime, drugs, and poverty with people of color—seemed particularly pronounced to white women. As one woman who lived through the period said, "It was not just edgy in some places . . . it seemed very dangerous all of the sudden."[6] Susan Brownmiller recounted, "If you took the train in the morning, it seems there was a molester in every car."[7] The atmosphere of hostility and guardedness suggested by Brownmiller reflected both a politicization of women and emerging perceptions of urban America as particularly dangerous. Journalist Betsy Israel labeled these years "the days of mace," a reference to the precautions women needed to take to protect themselves.[8] A growing litany of "self-defense" books instructed women to fear the city and to honor their suspicions when they encountered men in public space. As the author of one such book confirmed for her women readers, "In today's world danger is an unfortunate reality."[9] Authorities echoed this message, as when the head of the New York City rape squad announced, "Single women should avoid being alone in any part of the city, at any time."[10]

New York led the way in the early 1970s, but other cities soon followed, becoming what historian Peter Braunstein has labeled the "erotic city"—a place where public pornography, promiscuity, and prostitution "effectively closed off" large sections of the city to families and lone women.[11] The "sexualized climate" of the 1970s was one that *Playboy*, girl watching, and the larger "playboy ethic" of the 1960s had helped create by focusing on men's leisure, consumption, and sexual permissiveness, but bunny costumes held little power next to strip shows.[12] Peep shows, hard-core porn movies, and the general eroticization of public space created a vastly different streetscape in the 1970s city. Women negotiated and interpreted the streets of this decade very differently than they had in the "graceful" 1950s, and this change in approach, in turn, led to a new interpretation of girl watching and uninvited encounters with strangers on the street and other public places as threatening rather than benign.

The feminist movement that emerged in the late 1960s and 1970s offered new tools for at least some women to use in examining the social structures under which they lived. While dominated by white women, at least initially, the movement redefined many "personal" issues as social and political problems, including harassment and exclusion. Early organizing on the part of many liberal and radical feminist groups often focused on collective challenges to the humiliation and unease that women had experienced in public spaces from practices that allegedly complimented or protected them. Women did not come into the feminist movement because they had been whistled at on the street or embarrassed by being turned away from a bar or restaurant, but once they were in the movement and hearing these issues raised, women quickly tapped into the hurt from "a lifetime's accumulation of these petty assaults."[13] They eagerly added public harassment to the growing list of grievances that fueled feminism of the 1960s and early 1970s. Although these early campaigns did little to illuminate or challenge the ways in which gender segregation reinforced heterosexuality and white supremacy, they did bring new language and ideas about the harm of exclusion and segregation into mainstream culture, laying bare the illusion that gender segregation protected women.

"The Most Insidious Forms of Discrimination": Gendered Public Accommodations and Exclusion

In the 1960s, many eating and drinking establishments in cities around the country excluded women altogether or served them only if escorted by a man. Women could not lunch in the Oak Room of the Plaza Hotel in New York City. Nor could they drink at the bar of the famous Russian Tea Room. Common assumptions—lingering from the previous century—equated lone women in public with prostitution or at least questionable morals and justified policies and laws that kept women out of many public accommodations that served alcohol or catered to a male clientele. These policies in turn reinforced a male-privileged, heterosexual public space to which women had limited access and in which they needed to perform an appropriate role in relation to men (as girlfriend, wife, or mother) to avoid negative labels. Etiquette manuals, popular magazines, teachers, parents, and society at large approached exclusionary laws and policies as a form of "protection"—both of vulnerable women from men and of society from predatory women. These attitudes communicated to all women young and old who had any "common sense" that it was not safe—morally or physically—for a woman to venture into the male domain of a bar or any establishment whose primary business included selling alcohol or supporting male socializing.[14] This exclusion of women from certain types of common public accommodations etched male supremacy and heteronormativity even more deeply onto the social, physical, and economic landscape of American cities.

Beginning in the late 1960s, however, feminists successfully confronted this type of urban gender segregation through sit-ins, pickets, demonstrations, media campaigns, legislative pressure, and lawsuits. These attacks on the legal and social restrictions on women in public accommodations fit well with other goals of the feminist movement when it emerged in the late 1960s.[15] For many coming to feminism in this moment, policies that excluded women altogether or required women to have a male escort represented an obvious and intolerable indignity and was indicative of many more subtle indignities faced by women every day. Public accommodations attracted the efforts of a wide range of mostly white feminist activists and organizations because it so readily connected with their other priorities and with emerging theories concerning the social limitations placed on women.

Two main types of public accommodations practiced gender discrimination in US cities by the 1960s. The first included bars, grills, downtown clubs, and many restaurants that catered to local and traveling white middle-class businessmen. Restaurants such as Stouffer's in Pittsburgh, Schroder's Café in San Francisco, Whyte's in the Wall Street area of Manhattan, the Russian Tea Room, Sardi's, and P. J. Clarke's in New York City, the London Chop House in Detroit, the aptly named The Retreat in Washington, DC, the Bull and Bear in Chicago, and the Clam Broth House in Hoboken, New Jersey, banned women during lunch hours, restricted them to isolated and sometimes more expensive second-floor dining rooms, or kept them away from the bar area. In many major hotels, including the William Penn in Pittsburgh, the Monteleone in New Orleans, the Continental Plaza in Chicago, the Minneapolis Radisson, and the Beverly Hills Hilton, women were excluded from "men's bars" and banned during "executive" lunch hours.[16] These institutions self-consciously cultivated their masculine atmosphere and reputation— "splendidly stag until 3 pm," declared the Oak Room of New York's Plaza Hotel—in offering businessmen a place to unwind or work the social side of a deal.

The second type of public accommodations that kept women out or opened only their back doors and backrooms to them were the working-class neighborhood pubs. An emerging male culture in American cities at the turn of the twentieth century resulted in an explosion of bars where men, according to historian Howard Chudacoff, "could escape from the pressures of both their work and domestic lives . . . and reinforce class, ethnic, and, perhaps most importantly, gender identities."[17] Massachusetts, Rhode Island, New Jersey, and Montana all restricted tavern licenses to male-only establishments, as did several cities. Where statutory prohibitions did not exist, lingering social and cultural practices from the nineteenth and early twentieth centuries excluded women from most neighborhood bars and taverns.[18] Some Progressive reformers endorsed these restrictions in order to protect women's virtue and reputations, but most middle-class urbanites and public officials supported restrictions in order to protect men from predatory women, particularly when fears of venereal disease spiked during both world wars.[19] Even as Americans' relationship to drinking began to change after the end of World War I, these male-only institutions continued to flourish. Proscriptions against some public drinking for women loosened.[20] While new establishments such as speakeasies and nightclubs welcomed heterosexual couples, these did not replace traditionally male establishments.[21] The bars and restaurants that restricted the presence of women held strong into the 1970s, reinforcing masculine identities, in part, through the exclusion of women.

Most activists in the emerging women's movement of the late 1960s had encountered male-only bars, but few had applied a political interpretation to their exclusion from them.[22] By 1968, however, the burgeoning women's movement started to raise questions about such gendered practices, and the issue began showing up in both local and national feminist groups. Karen DeCrow, a newly minted lawyer and founder of the Syracuse chapter of the National Organization for Women (NOW), had not given restrictions on women in public accommodations a second thought until an acquaintance reported being turned away.[23] DeCrow immediately knew this "was discrimination from the racial analogy," having worked with African Americans to challenge racial barriers to public accommodations in her native Chicago. She bristled at the "escorted women only" policy and its implication that women were incomplete or immoral without a man. Finding these assumptions "nonsense" and "insulting," she took the issue to her fledgling NOW chapter and set about challenging the bar's policy through complaints, pickets, and, finally, a lawsuit.

DeCrow's epiphany proved not to be an isolated incident; the issue spread quickly amid the earnest feminist organizing taking place in 1968. That spring NOW board members realized that the hotel where they were meeting contained a men-only restaurant. They immediately set up a picket of the bar and adopted the issue as a priority for the year. DeCrow ran a workshop on it at the national NOW conference later that year.[24] Initially, members thought little of the new issue, but once DeCrow framed exclusionary practices as a denial of civil rights, the room exploded in discussion.[25] Everyone seemed to know of an establishment with such policies, and many had moving stories of being embarrassed when they were turned away for being a woman, or a woman alone. Some recognized the implication embedded in these encounters that they might be prostitutes, and they struggled with the stigma.[26] NOW formally added open access to public accommodations to its list of goals and declared February 9–15, 1969, "Public Accommodations Week." Fledgling local chapters organized dozens of "eat-ins" and "drink-ins" in cities across the country; when Betty Friedan and thirty or so other NOW activists visited the Oak Room of the Plaza Hotel, they received national press coverage.[27]

The issue of gender-restricted public accommodations fit well with the resurgence of explicit organizing around women's rights taking place at the end of the 1960s. NOW formed in 1966 to create "a new movement toward true equality for all women in America." NOW's liberal orientation promised to tackle "the conditions that now prevent women from enjoying the equality of opportunity and freedom of choice which is their right, as individual Americans, and as human beings."[28] Policies that explicitly excluded women clearly violated the equal opportunity focus of the organization. Representative of liberal feminism's focus on women's economic opportunities, Friedan, NOW's president from 1966 to 1970, kept her public pronouncements on the issue confined to a business-oriented argument. Men-only policies excluded "women from the communication network and decision-making process by denying access for women to important business contacts during the lunch hour."[29] Because these places were where business was conducted, the exclusion equated to employment discrimination.

For other feminists, particularly those from more radical feminist groups, men-only establishments symbolized patriarchy's domination of the landscape of American society. The work of the African American civil rights movement in challenging voter discrimination and racial segregation in schools and public accommodations inspired a younger generation of mostly white women to organize for gender equality. Others were politicized by their involvement in the antiwar movement building against the US war in Vietnam, but found themselves relegated to second-class status in organizations dominated by men.[30] Members of women's liberation groups defined themselves as more radical than the women of NOW, explicitly focusing on women's autonomy more than equality. For these feminists, men-only policies

represented both the day-to-day discrimination women faced and the symbolic place of women in American society.

Whatever their path to activism, white feminists from across the ideological spectrum of the emerging movement understood policies against women
in public accommodations as "outright segregation" and symbolic of women's
treatment "as second-class citizens."[31] "Exclusion has always been one of the
most insidious forms of discrimination," one activist explained.[32] In language
penned by DeCrow but used verbatim by activists in Connecticut, Chicago,
Los Angeles, and elsewhere, "It means the right to human dignity, the right to
be free from humiliation and insult, and the right to refuse to wear a badge of
inferiority at any time or place."[33] They felt direct action against these policies
was deeply symbolic, a means of "fighting all discrimination."[34] Although some
women of color joined the early "second-wave" feminist organizations and participated in public accommodation protests, white women predominated in
the feminist organizations of the late 1960s and early 1970s.[35] The feminist
organizations created by and for women of color that emerged in the mid-
1970s greatly expanded the ideological reach of feminism, but they appeared
well after the public accommodations issue had largely been won. African
American women, of course, had a long history of demanding access to public
accommodations. One is left to wonder, had the timing been different, how
Black feminist organizations in particular might have tackled the issue.

Seeing a practice that was justified as a measure to protect "respectable"
women from immorality, the harsher side of men, and the corrupting world
of business as a form of discrimination was the kind of questioning of convention that was central to the women's movement of the late 1960s and early
1970s. Compared to wage inequality, sexual harassment, rape, poverty, and
lack of health care, insisting on getting served your martini at a particular
bar—especially when there might be three other bars in the immediate area
that would serve you—could appear frivolous. But when feminists stepped
back to survey the landscape of the cities in which they lived, restricted public accommodations were obvious symbols of the ways in which women's
lives were circumscribed and the language of protection had limited wom-
en's opportunities. Here were actual signs that said women were different
and could be treated that way: "NO UNESCORTED LADIES WILL BE SERVED,"
"LADIES' ENTRANCE AT THE REAR," "MEN ONLY." The signs proclaimed wom-
en's exclusion from the public sphere—the realm in which public opinion
and the interests of the "public body" developed and spread and where the
body politic, those with power in society, gathered to discuss and debate

the issues of the day.[36] In a consumer-oriented society where, according to historian Lizabeth Cohen, "much of public life transpired in commercial venues," exclusion from public accommodations omitted women from vital public spaces and practices and symbolized the vulnerabilities and indignities women experienced every day.[37]

The issue also struck a deeper and more emotional nerve with many women. The newly developing tactic of consciousness raising—in which feminists explored what had formerly been thought of as private or personal issues in a political and societal context—also encouraged women to name the harm that restrictions they had encountered in supposedly public places had caused them. In legal cases, women reported that being turned away from bars and restaurants caused them "severe mental anguish and embarrassment."[38] This language could easily be dismissed as mere legalese, but as oral histories and private documents attest, women did feel embarrassed, flustered, ashamed, and disgraced when refused service in a bar or restaurant because of their gender. More was at stake in these encounters than the quandary of what to do with yourself while waiting for your date, or for a table; the experience brought home the realization that society thought, in the words of DeCrow, "women don't belong in the outside world."[39] Feminists described the experience of being turned away as "unfair and humiliating," "an unconscionable embarrassment," "insulting," "depressing," "demoralizing," "immoral," and "demeaning."[40] The feminist movement gave women the support, the numbers, the community, and the language to do what women generally could or would not do as individuals: challenge the exclusion and the assumptions that supported it.

In tackling the arguments that bar owners and patrons used to keep women out of certain public accommodations, feminists encountered a number of obstacles internal to the movement and to themselves relating to respectability, class, and race. The reluctance of many women, especially those who identified as feminist, to take up the issue completely blindsided those who saw its merit as self-evident. But for many women both in and outside the movement, women alone in public and women in bars still raised the specter of sexual impropriety. "Proper" women needed to perform a dependent gender role and demonstrate their heterosexuality by either staying out of public spaces or being escorted through them by a man. Women who did not follow these norms ran the risk of being harassed or labeled a prostitute. Most male-only establishments used the woman-as-prostitute image as their first line of defense for women's exclusion. Any woman who challenged these policies, then, might be labeled immoral. Women repeatedly signaled awareness of the risk. Newspaper coverage of feminist demonstrations routinely quoted a woman questioning why any woman would want the "degrading" experience of sitting at a bar.[41]

Reflecting the power of the threat of being labeled immoral in maintaining gender hierarchies, even some of the most committed activists periodically lost their focus on equal access as a civil right in order to make claims for their own—and fairly traditionally defined—respectability. The Miami NOW chapter, for example, called its campaign against the men's grills in department stores "Operation Friendly Persuasion" and wore "respectable" middle-class costumes, including tailored outfits, hats, and white gloves, when they tried to integrate establishments. DeCrow counseled NOW chapters to try to avoid the respectability question by dressing "conservatively" so as not to "give [the press] anything to attack you for."[42] Many leaders, including Friedan, carefully stressed the argument about opening business opportunities to women, indirectly challenging the assumption that women went to bars only to solicit men.

White feminists also ran aground on the issues of their own class and race privilege. Those involved with the bar protests tended to be white, middle-class activists who favored establishments where only their gender set them apart from other white, middle-class patrons. Activists demonstrated little cognizance of this pattern.[43] Most defended their targets as "famous," or they focused on the symbolic nature of the policies, suggesting that the choice of establishments to challenge did not really matter and implying that women of all races, classes, and sexualities would benefit from victories in this realm. As a white feminist told an African American waitress who tried to enforce the men-only policy in a Yonkers, New York, lounge, "We're fighting all discrimination by this action." The skeptical waitress, perhaps more concerned with keeping her job than "fighting all discrimination," still declined to serve them.[44] White, middle-class feminists' tendency to adopt universalistic language and avoid questions about class privilege and lingering racial discrimination became a larger issue for a movement whose members' hopes for inclusiveness never fully materialized.

Feminists, many of whom had cut their activist teeth on public accommodation protests in the civil rights movement, saw compelling similarities between the exclusion of Blacks and the exclusion of women. Pauli Murray, a NOW founding member, had seen the analogy years earlier and dubbed discrimination against women "Jane Crow."[45] The members of the New York City NOW chapter announced that "no public accommodation in the US could maintain a policy of 'Whites Only' or 'No Jews Allowed.'" "A 'Men

Only' policy," they argued, "is an equal violation of the civil rights of women" and should not be tolerated "in a nation made so conscious by the black movement of the consequences of denying individual dignity and rights."[46] When two white women asked the maitre d' of Cleveland's Gazette Lounge—which hosted a "Stag Buffet" for lunch—"Do you admit Negroes?," he answered, "Everyone is welcome." "How come women aren't?" they replied. "You'll have to ask the management" went the response.[47] As this confrontation suggested, protests against gender exclusion could not ride the coattails of the civil rights movement. Federal law might prohibit signs excluding potential patrons on the basis of race, but a host of other informal factors, including residential racial segregation and hostile reactions by white patrons, certainly kept many African Americans out of a great number of bars in the late 1960s and 1970s. Owners and managers not yet wholly convinced of the need for racial equality remained even more skeptical about gender equality.

Despite a weak racial analogy and the class biases of the activists, the focus on access as an issue of women's civil rights spread, and more protests followed NOW's Public Accommodations Week actions in 1969 and 1970. Typical actions saw small groups of women touring multiple establishments in a single outing. Following the model of civil rights sit-ins, women sat at bars, demanded service, interrogated bartenders and owners, and sometimes even "liberated" the bathroom. When confronted by groups of feminists and the curious press, a few establishments immediately changed their policies regarding women. Some even hoped to salvage good press from the incidents and made a show of opening their facilities to women, offering free rounds and, in at least one case, breaking out the champagne.[48] The Polo Lounge in the Beverly Hills Hotel affirmed its policy of men only at the bar, but when protesters from the local NOW chapter arrived with the press in February 1969, the maître d' claimed no such policy existed. Further needling the activists, he made the sycophantic comment to reporters, "The more girls I have, the more sunshine in my heart."[49] Most policies against women did not fall so easily.

More commonly, managers resolutely refused to admit or serve the vocal activists who appeared in their establishments. Some barred or locked the door, while others allowed the women to sit but ordered staff to ignore them.[50] All the while, bar and restaurant staff unapologetically defended their restrictive policies. Some asserted that since they had not "had trouble with women" before, the activists who challenged it could be dismissed as "just a bunch of troublemakers."[51] The manager of the Biltmore's bar offered little defense of the exclusionary policy and merely declared, "The men come here for business lunches; their conversation is not for women. Here they can relax and be themselves."[52] Those in charge of more upscale establishments expressed disdain for women's ability to handle the check and tipping. Others raised "the bathroom defense," hoping to delay opening to women by pointing to the lack of restroom facilities for women or the sorry state of the facilities for men that women would be forced to use.[53] Those in charge of taverns claimed that business would suffer as men refused to drink alongside women, or that their patrons' wives would not let them come to the bar if other women were there. A few trotted out old protection arguments, claiming their crowd too "rough" for women, and others expressed fears that the presence of women would lead men to start fighting.

The male patrons of these establishments showed similar hostility, at least in talking to the press. A seventy-five-year-old man in South Boston's L Street Tavern declared women "are a nuisance."[54] Some hoped to scare women off using the same arguments that would be later deployed by those opposing the Equal Rights Amendment: if men only laws and traditions fell, they claimed, women would have to pay their own way, be drafted, share bath rooms with men, and change their own tires and light bulbs. Feminist protesters were often most surprised by the resistance they encountered in the fanciest venues, having mistakenly assumed that their class and race privilege would afford them a warmer welcome.[55] Confrontations between protesters and patrons got heated, and a few turned physical; in addition to engaging in shouting matches, women had beer poured on their heads and their blouses unbuttoned, some were shoved, and sometimes they were bodily barred or removed from the establishment.

In most cases, however, male patrons seem to have resisted women's "intrusion" by calling up "the code": the rules of respectability and safety that governed women's behavior in America. The code contained clear spatial elements. Statements that "this ain't no place for a woman!" made blatant the gendered geography that women challenged in their protests.[56] Women's presence in male space opened the door to questioning their right to "public" space, their character, and, of course, their respectability. The manager of the Brown Derby in Los Angeles hinted at protesters' ulterior motives when he commented to the press, "I can't imagine why any women would want to sit unescorted at the bar."[57] Men drinking in bars proved far less subtle. Leering and suggestive comments impugned protesters' motives with speculation and peppered them with come-ons: "I'd say it's because she's looking for something," and, "Sit at the bar, Baby . . . I'll sit with [you]." For women, patrons' reactions were not wholly surprising, but still rather frightening. After facing "a murmured session of group misogyny," one activist found herself "wondering how many more men there were like these, walking the streets—more than my feminist imagination would dare to imagine."[58] These exchanges reminded all who witnessed them that women had violated the code by entering the bar and demanding service and therefore had forfeited their right to be treated civilly or with respect. They also reveal the hostility with which American society greeted the early feminist movement and the ways in which gender segregation was deployed against it—particularly through policing women's behavior with appraisals of their appearance and withholding hollow promises of protection when women appeared in certain spaces.

As the momentum of the women's movement grew in the early 1970s, so did reactions against it. Resistance to women in bars shifted from questions of women's morality to a desire to protect men from women. For some men, the traditionally masculine space of bars seemed to be the last stronghold of masculinity, and male patrons raised dire predictions for the state of American society if these establishments disappeared. Just as gender discrimination in public accommodations came to signify for feminists a broader set of restrictions placed on women by American society, institutions that embraced these practices came to be seen as the "last hope" for embattled men.[59] "In this troubled world," lamented a New York City Council member in 1970, "there has to be an oasis in the desert for men. . . . If they take this away from us, what have we left?"[60] The irony of this lament, of course, was that it was raised well before some of the most stunning victories of the women's movement occurred, and the opposition only strengthened feminist sentiments that the tradition had to go: "It is the last place they are going to let you in so, of course, it is the place you have to get in."[61]

Doing their best to act as the last bastion of masculinity, some establishments stubbornly refused to serve women, even as late as 1972. The New Hotel Monteleone in New Orleans even incorporated the changing tide into its advertisements, proudly proclaiming its masculine, heterosexual identity: "Lunch for the liberated male. Women. Bless them. They're the most delightful creatures on earth. But there are times when a Man prefers the company of other men. To discuss business for instance, politics, sports, or, of course . . . women."[62] Tom Brown's restaurant in Midtown Manhattan declared itself a "masculine bar."[63] The Biltmore Hotel tried to retain the name of its bar after a local antidiscrimination ban went into effect, claiming that "Men's Grill" did not imply that women were not welcome. The chairman of New York's Commission on Human Rights, Eleanor Holmes Norton, flatly rejected the argument and ordered a name change.[64] The William Penn Hotel in Pittsburgh opened its barroom to women according to that city's new law, but refused to take down the old "MEN'S BAR" sign until the local NOW chapter threatened legal action.[65] In Chicago, a "confrontation" between local NOW members and the manager of Berghoff's restaurant over his refusal to remove the "MEN ONLY" sign garnered national TV coverage and led the women to file a formal complaint.[66]

Not surprisingly, these confrontations had great media appeal. Many columnists used the issue as an excuse to rant. Andrew Tully opened one piece with this comment: "I keep trying not to notice the more idiotic activities of Women's Lib, but just when I'm about to decide that the fringe nuts are also people something comes up like the case of the Biltmore Hotel's Men's Bar."[67] William F. Buckley Jr. also used the public accommodations issue to complain about "the lengths that Women's Lib is nowadays going."[68] Articles often made bewildered or skeptical references to the "zealots" of "the new women's liberation movement" or were overtly hostile.[69] Most editors found humor in the issue and adorned their pages with cute headlines such as "Women's Liberation Gone Bar Hopping," and "Lib Wins Another Round." Dismissive coverage from reporters included references to the "NOW girls" and the "spokesgal" or a focus on activists' outfits more than on their messages.[70] Lurking behind the hostility and much of the humor lay contempt for the basic idea of women's equality. Certainly some press coverage was quite good and offered explanations of the larger issues at stake. In noting a particularly important victory, for example, *Newsweek* pointed out that "the 'ladies' weren't all that interested in lunching on Liederkranz-cheese-and-onion sandwiches in . . . scruffy, sawdust-sprinkled ambience—it was really the principle of the thing."[71] Even though the breadth and depth of the message did not always get through to the press, the amount of coverage generally pleased the activists and helped keep up momentum on the issue.[72]

Although many activists had high hopes for forcing change in the public accommodations arena through the courts, the legal system presented serious obstacles to this strategy. In New Jersey, women fared well when a state court ruled that access to public accommodations was a civil right for all persons.[73] In Syracuse, New York, however, where the Hotel Syracuse had a "no unescorted ladies" policy for its bar, women from the local NOW chapter met with much more resistance in the court system. Faith Seidenberg, a founding NOW chapter member, veteran civil rights activist, and lawyer, filed unsuccessful suits in federal and state courts challenging the hotel's policy.[74] Seidenberg and her plaintiff in those first cases, DeCrow, decided it was time to find a new bar and a new legal approach to challenging discrimination in public accommodations.

They finally settled on McSorley's Old Ale House, a storied bar in New York City's East Village that carried a proud reputation of not serving women. The bar's original owner, an Irish immigrant, according to the lore of the saloon, "believed it impossible for men to drink with tranquility in the presence of women," and he would personally escort out any who strayed into the establishment.[75] Over the years the "manly" culture of the bar grew and a large bell behind the bar would be rung loudly if ever a woman crossed the threshold, cueing the bar's patrons to drive the interloper away with jeers and shouts.[76] Fans of McSorley's cherished the coarse reputation of the bar as a workingman's retreat. When Seidenberg and DeCrow entered McSorley's, they were not bodily thrown out or arrested, but patrons hounded them and beat up a young man who showed them some sympathy.[77] Terrified, the women fled and opted to file a civil suit against the bar in federal court.

Seidenberg v. McSorley's Old Ale House, Inc. (1970) resulted in a stunningly good decision for the feminists. Judge Charles Tenney acknowledged that "the vast majority of bars or taverns cater to both men and women without occasioning . . . moral or social problems."[78] Adopting the argument of the feminists, Tenney continued: "To adhere to practices supported by ancient chivalristic concepts . . . may only serve to isolate women from the realities of everyday life, and to perpetuate, as a matter of law, economic and sexual exploitation."[79] Ultimately, the decision in the McSorley's case broke new legal ground. It found that the liquor license held by the bar indicated sufficient state involvement to merit the application of the Fourteenth Amendment's equal protection clause, a legal argument that had been unsuccessfully tried by civil rights lawyers working on racial discrimination in public accommodations.[80] Lawyers around the country widely cited the McSorley's case, but it would prove less than definitive. In *Millenson v. The New Hotel Monteleone* (1973), lawyers for the American Civil Liberties Union (including Brenda Feigen Fasteau and future Supreme Court justice Ruth Bader Ginsburg) used Seidenberg's argument from the McSorley's case against a hotel bar, only to be denied.[81] The favorable ruling in one district and an opposite ruling in another left the meaning of the Fourteenth Amendment for gender discrimination in public accommodations unsettled.

Feminists ultimately did win clearer victories on the public accommodations issue, not by mounting legal challenges in the courts, although the publicity they generated undoubtedly helped pave the way, but by amending laws at the local and state levels. Many cities had antidiscrimination ordinances on the books from the late nineteenth century, and activists set about getting "sex" added to the language that already forbade discrimination on the basis of race, creed, color, or national origin. In the summer of 1970, New York City and Pittsburgh led the way, amending existing laws concerning public accommodations to include sex. Most state legislatures followed the municipal examples and added sex to human rights ordinances over the course of the next two years.

New local and state laws, a few favorable court decisions, and heightened public awareness of the issue created an impressive change in the laws and conventions governing public accommodations in urban America by 1973. Feminists used this momentum. With language, tactics, and some laws built around public accommodations, feminists began questioning dress codes (many bars and restaurants refused to serve women in pants), restrictions against women working as bartenders, and discrimination in supposedly "private" clubs. Legislation banning gender discrimination in public accommodations often led to similar initiatives to eliminate gender discrimination in municipal housing and employment. Victories on the public accommodations issue served as "proof that the women's revolution is indeed being won in the '70s," stated the *New York Times*, and became something "we built on," according to one activist.[82] The issue had been so dramatically successful in enough cities that NOW removed it from its agenda by 1972, channeling many of the arguments brought to bear on the issue into campaigns for improved educational opportunities for women and support for the Equal Rights Amendment. Other feminist organizations, particularly those on the West Coast and in New York and Boston, took a different route by translating their broadest understandings of the significance of discrimination in public accommodations into campaigns against prostitution, rape, pornography, and street harassment.

"We Don't Want to Be Sexual Objects Anymore": Feminists Confront Street Harassment

In 1970, a small group of Chicago women organized a protest outside the city's convention center. Concerned that their actions might draw a hostile response if they targeted male strangers, they enlisted a friend to help them with their street theater. He stuffed his pants with a balloon and strolled casually down the sidewalk while the women shouted assessments of his physique. Others ran through the crowds handing out flyers explaining to startled observers that they meant to draw attention to the unwelcome encounters women had on the streets every day. Rather than treat these experiences as complimentary, as women's magazines generally recommended, the Chicago activists interpreted them as intrusions into women's personal space, threats of violence, and indications of women's second-class status in society. What had once been called "girl watching" was given a new name by these activists, "street harassment," and it became just one of many aspects of women's lived experiences in cities scrutinized by feminists in the latter decades of the twentieth century.

Feminists of the 1970s treated girl watching and street comments as something more than isolated events. They problematized men's visual evaluations of women in public space and the furtive touching that often accompanied them, reframing these ubiquitous practices as part of larger cultural patterns that reinforced women's inferiority. They sought to change the rules of the game that governed social order. The issue surfaced frequently in the 1970s in informal feminist discussions and appeared regularly in the poetry, art, and essays of the myriad feminist newsletters of the period. For many women, harassment emerged when discussions turned to their daily lives. A Boston woman noted that traveling the city making deliveries for her job subjected her to near-constant and unwanted attention from men.[83] During a feminist consciousness-raising session dedicated to discussing rape, she realized these experiences left her fearful, not flattered, and this fear was more than concern about being delayed or inconvenienced. The fear became central to analyses of the function of street culture as a form of social control over women and the connections between harassment and larger patterns of violence toward women.

Through discussions of street harassment, activists honed their ability to name the harm these practices inflicted on women's psyches. One Venice Beach resident described being approached on the street by men: "It's knowing you have to prepare for the on-slaught [sic] that ruins the whole idea of going out."[84] The possibility of harassment and rape, argued Chicago feminists, "makes us consider, in ways that men never have to, where we go at night, with whom, how late we'll be and when and how we'll get home." Common threads of "suspicion and mistrust" run throughout descriptions such as these, and through them women came to understand that they were not alone in their fears of public spaces.[85] "Our oppression and suppression are institutionalized," argued Boston feminist Roxanne Dunbar. "All women suffer the 'petty' forms of oppression. Therefore, they are not petty or personal, but rather constitute a widespread, deeply rooted social disease. They are the things that keep us tied down day to day, and do not allow us to act."[86] Women quickly came to realize that the roles society expected them to act out in public—roles scripted by practices such as girl watching—often elicited shame, stigma, embarrassment, and unease, feelings that signaled inferiority and a lack of power. As was the case with exclusion from public accommodations, women often found that these exchanges tapped into great wells of anger, which they expressed as "rage" at the unwanted attention they received from men in public spaces.[87] This sense of exposure, vulnerability, and anger often shaped women's responses to encounters on the street as they became more decisive, aggressive, and confrontational in the 1970s, having come to recognize how these "incidents . . . make women feel powerless and dehumanized."[88]

From examinations of the individual toll paid by women to be in public, feminists of the 1970s developed a three-pronged analysis of the issue. First, they declared that practices such as girl watching, particularly the girl-watching contests and festivals, objectified women. The act of looking, feminist film critic Laura Mulvey theorized in 1973, placed the spectator in a masculine position, compelling those they observed to "[bear] the burden of sexual objectification."[89] The dominant perspective of the spectator reinforced the "to-be-looked-at-ness" of women. Second, feminists spoke to how street harassment curtailed women's autonomy by forcing them to "choose your neighborhoods and choose the hours, and choose the circumstances that you can be out."[90] The implication behind this point being that limited geographic mobility in turn restricted women's political, social, and economic mobility and their ability to function as autonomous members of society.

Finally, feminists placed girl watching and street harassment on a continuum of men's violence toward women, with rape and murder at the other end. This third line of reasoning resonated heavily within feminist circles— women readily recounted in the pages of movement newsletters the fear they felt when a man stared at them or spoke to them on the street. In making this connection to rape, the movement to end violence against women named the source of harassment and violence as a society that tolerated and even encouraged the subjugation of women, what today we call rape culture. The "mutual enjoyment" narrative that characterized girl watching as harmless and enjoyable for men and women alike sometimes blocked recognition of this idea in mainstream society during the 1970s and 1980s.

Recognizing both the individual harm of harassment and the larger societal underpinnings of the phenomenon, feminists encouraged women to reject the behavior outright rather than avoid or minimize its existence—or worse, internalize it and blame themselves. Feminists advocated a crowd-level public response to stop harassers and support victims. Radical feminists from

Boston's Cell 16 took matters into their own hands after a series of attacks on women drew little attention from the police. The women, proponents of teaching women martial arts for self-defense, mounted their own nighttime street patrols around the city.[91] In a scene from the 1983 feminist utopian film *Born in Flames*, a woman emerging from the subway is "checked out" by two men, who then start making comments to her and eventually push her to the ground, presumably to rape her. The woman is rescued by a group of whistle-blowing, bicycling feminists who surround and drive off the perpetrators and then comfort the woman who has been attacked. The scene is earnestly feminist in its portrayal of how a verbal confrontation can lead to physical violence, but it also demonstrates how an aware and activated society can successfully intervene in the moment to save someone from victimization.

By challenging watching, touching, lewd and suggestive, evaluative, or even just uninvited comments that women often received in public space, feminists asserted their right to privacy—to be left alone—as they traveled the city. One Boston feminist, for example, expressed "fury" at men for "intruding upon my privacy on the street." She yelled at one man, "Who the hell do you think you are, talking to us uninvited?"[92] By the early 1970s, comfort, safety, and privacy on the street had come to symbolize basic human dignity, particularly for white feminists. These activists declared their right to choose their activities in public based on their perceived needs and not on the moral judgments of others or the prospect of feeling unsafe as they traversed the city.

It is tempting to think feminists might also have been challenging the class and race privilege embedded in girl watching, especially considering their background in the New Left and the civil rights movement, but there is little evidence that they applied this level of theorizing. Research by scholars into the experiences of women in different locations in the social structure, however, suggests just how much the age, marital status, and race and class privilege of these activists may have shaped their interpretation of girl watching and street harassment. The mostly white, single, childless, middle-class feminists who took up the issue believed that if they successfully challenged the objectification of women in public, all women would be able to travel through the city unmolested. Sociologist Esther Madriz found, however, that African American women generally expressed more fear of hate crimes based on their race than fear of what are generally considered gender-based harassments or crimes, such as rape. Women of color also showed more concern for the safety and treatment of their children than for themselves, and older women of all races feared crimes against their personal property.[93] Madriz's findings suggest that ending the social sanctioning of girl watching and other practices that singled out women as women in public would have far less impact on many women's fears concerning public space than was anticipated by the feminists of the 1970s.

Despite their race and class biases, these activists did recognize that space was more than just one's physical surroundings; space was infused with social meaning and organized by and around domination and subordination.[94] It both reflected and enacted social hierarchies.[95] Girl watching dictated that women act as the objects of male gaze, the subjects of male hobbies, and the stock of advertisers—all roles that reinforced women's lack of control over the perception and treatment of their bodies in public spaces. Key to shifting women's place in public space was feminists' claim for their "competency" to participate in the public sphere.[96] Asserting competency challenged urban practices such as girl watching, touching, and commentary that rendered women passive subjects rather than autonomous actors. In this sense, feminist challenges to street harassment also challenged the ways in which commercialization and objectification tended to stifle and exclude women from political debate and action.[97]

The first steps in this challenge came in the form of organized "ogle-ins," during which women harassed men on the streets; feminist self-defense classes; and handbooks that empowered women to individually resist and demand better treatment. To invade men's privacy and claim power to define space, feminists often chose tactics that turned the tables on men and appropriated the privilege of watching. In 1970 and 1971, activists in Los Angeles, New York, and Chicago staged very public demonstrations opposing girl watching and street harassment. At these ogle-ins, women verbally assessed the physical assets and flaws of men on the street in an effort to "make men understand how degrading their flattery is."[98] In Los Angeles, a group calling itself Sisters Against Sexual Slavery (SASS) conducted a "boywatching" session to protest the Century City Chamber of Commerce's "Girl Watching Week," which included a "watchable girl" contest, in the fall of 1970. Blatantly and successfully co-opting the media attention generated by the Chamber of Commerce's event, the protesters carried signs asking "WHY GIVE AN AWARD FOR BIGOTRY?" and explained to men who saw girl watching as harmless that "being accosted by total strangers on the street is not an honor." "Women don't welcome these invasions of their dignity and privacy," they declared.[99]

Feminists challenged the roots of girl watching when they took their protests to America's first and most masculine downtown in the spring of 1970:

First L.A. Ogle-in

Against
n ogle-in
ad hoc
ned the
protest
26 Girl
ry City
nning a
ring the
ciety of
l women
and to

oywatch
irlwatch
nphasize
men are
erlooked
ly.
dresses,
at 11:30.
e media
w began
ws were
of their
r totally
s began

n in as
g. They
oh!" at
it "Hey
with me?"
d to find
ld they
nbers of
ften the
rters.
m mild
women
ons and

d more
young
ed older
women
d some
m. One
a tape
by,she
ts, and
nished

Ann Forfreet

sympathet
men were
the group
pinched,
out. NBC
selectively
One m
oglers, re:
the boyw:
out men
exasperat
he tried t
an outs
evaded h
head with
her and h
warning
One
the wom
equally
they do
so decer
talk so
talk."
And
toward
tense. T
the gro
overtly
Some
street
quickly
behave
of ogl
Boyw:
innoce
S.A
oglein
disrup
mean
Bi
the (
over
their
had
He
des

Patricia T. Rosa

are of children." Men interviewed

wo

Los Angeles feminists used street theater to challenge gender-based public harassment with an "ogle-in." Everywoman, September 11, 1970. (Labadie Collection, University of Michigan)

Wall Street. New York women performed guerrilla theater on the sidewalks of the Financial District during a busy lunch hour with an ABC News camera crew in tow. Relying heavily on the protective power of humor, these activists carried signs announcing "OGLE DAY" while they shouted comments to the bewildered men they passed on the crowded sidewalk: "Oh they're so beautiful, all of them"; "Look at the legs on that one"; "Keep your best leg forward, sweetie"; and "Sweetie, you're old but I like you." In a post-demonstration interview, one of the participants explained in all seriousness, "We're trying to point out what it feels like to be [smooched] at, whistled at, and put down constantly, sexually, every time we walk down the street. They tell us that it's supposed to be a compliment. We're supposed to dig it because we're supposed to dig that we're sexual objects, and we don't want to be sexual objects anymore."[100] Although feminists had used the ogle-in tactic to oppose the street harassment of women, their intent was not to fight for equal opportunity to "boy watch." Instead, they strove to make streets more physically and psychologically safe for women by invoking women's right to maintain their privacy and the right to be left alone while in public.

As the 1970s continued, feminists argued for women's right to safe and unfettered access to public space with increasing frequency. Groups of women in cities around the country flocked to self-defense courses and held public rallies to challenge harassment, public pornography, and the violence faced by women. A group of women in New York organized themselves as the "Bod Squad" to "follow a decoy down the street and execute a citizen's arrest on the first guy to tongue-type her."[101] Radical feminists in Detroit decried the loss of "a basic civil liberty—the right to be on the street," and suggested "reinstating the evening walk" by gathering small groups of women to essentially patrol the streets together, offering women escorts in their travels and confronting men who acted suspiciously.[102] By the 1980s and into the 1990s, feminist scholars, mostly sociologists and legal scholars, began to research the issue. Their studies documented women's experiences, analyzed the perceptions of both the harassers and the harassed, and interrogated the culture of fear that street harassment fueled among women. The resulting studies assessed the ramifications of the "sexual terrorism" that street harassment created and maintained a focus on the macro-level impact of these practices in producing a "ghettoization of women" in American society.[103]

When the issue crept into the popular press in the 1980s and early 1990s, however, feminists' critique of a culture of violence toward women was co-opted by a focus on the individual. *Glamour*, the glossy publication aimed at young adult women, had instructed its readership in 1969 to "smile in friendly acknowledgement" when favorably appraised on the street. In the 1980s, the magazine's editors continued to include pieces that reflected this older ideology by suggesting that attention on the street might "sometimes give you a nice ego boost," but they also began to call for "an hour on the jogging path without men's catcalls" and offered women suggestions for "how to talk back."[104] *Vogue* began to question old assumptions that "all men like to girl watch and girls don't mind it," and *Mademoiselle* recognized the negative impact of street harassment, offering women advice in 1984 on "putting up with put downs."[105] Women were being told by magazines not to tolerate harassment anymore and, instead, to challenge it. "Don't 'Hey, Baby' Me," announced *Glamour* magazine in 1992.[106] Lost in the advice was the feminist message that society's dismissive attitude toward harassment revealed a larger structural inequality women faced as a result of their gender.

At least some of the feminist messages about the nature and impact of street remarks did filter through to the broader American society. Reporters in the mainstream press, for example, started regularly using the feminist term "street harassment" (though often in quotation marks, at least through the early 1980s).[107] Drawing a line between occasional "jokes or flirting" and "serious attempts at intimidation and the degradation of women" emerged as a common theme in discussions of street harassment aimed at women by the late 1980s.[108] It was almost as if women became willing to concede the point that watching could indeed be harmless (as girl watchers always maintained), as long as society would discuss the more violent behaviors women encountered on the street. Elizabeth Kuster, a women's self-defense teacher, argued in the pages of *Glamour* that women needed to "reach a consensus about what constitutes harassment" and then challenge it on a daily basis. She suggested that "discreetly checking someone out" or a comment such as "nice dress" were "okay," but that "continuously staring . . . in a sexual way" or making a comment on a woman's clothes and then turning to watch her walk down the street constituted harassment.[109] African American commentators, who had been remarkably absent from earlier discussion, finally joined the conversation in the late 1980s to offer firm opposition to obvious visual assessments. They reminded readers that girl watching was "the kind of violation of Black womanhood that Black men once died to prevent," and they admonished Black men for practicing it.[110]

Feminist challenges to the patriarchal control embedded in girl watching and gender-based public harassment did more than question the objectification of women in public spaces. These challenges suggested that a new set of rules was needed for interaction in public space, and they also pointed to changing conceptions of gender roles and the urban environment in which they needed to function. Moving the issue into scholarly and popular conversations represented some progress on the issue, but it was far less definitive than the gains made on public accommodations. Don Sauers, author of the kitschy *Girl Watcher's Guide*, reflected on the "death of girl watching" in a 2001 essay. Bemoaning the "loss of the lovely word 'girl'" and his hobby of girl watching, he blamed the "landslide victories of indignant feminists" in the 1970s and 1980s. "All I feel is a bewildered sadness," he continued, "that an occasional and usually spontaneous pastime I considered pleasurable and innocent has been declared uncouth and offensive, not just by card-carrying feminists but by a depressing number of ordinarily tolerant women."[111] Die-hard girl watchers, however, never ceded the argument that the practice was anything other than "innocent" and "flattering" to women, yet the critiques raised by feminists apparently had some impact, for even girl watching's most ardent supporters came to recognize, if not to understand, that even "ordinarily tolerant women" preferred not to perform their gender before a panel of catcalling strangers.

Conclusion

The feminist movement of the 1960s and 1970s had deep connections to the cities in which it grew and flourished. Urban conditions and women's experiences in cities became significant items on the larger feminist agenda in these years. As both the public accommodations and street harassment issues suggest, much of the feminist movement's work of the 1970s and beyond lay in challenging gendered practices and institutions of urban living. Both issues provided a way for women to understand and confront some of the humiliating and potentially dangerous experiences of urban living. They provided a way for women to declare their right to function in the city as autonomous beings. For feminists, at issue was women's right to move through allegedly public space without having their presence excluded, evaluated, controlled, impeded, or commented upon.

Public accommodations and street harassment were some of the earlier and more tangible challenges to gender segregation to emerge from 1970s feminism. As such, they showed how a dedicated group of activists led a generation of women to reject the restrictions placed on their lives by reforming legal and societal conceptions of rape, undoing discriminatory housing practices, challenging gender-based violence, questioning the dangers of public transportation, and tackling the sex-segregated labor market. Taken together, both issues provided a resounding critique of "chivalry" and "respectability" and called into question laws, practices, and actions that restrained women's choices. The exclusion from some public accommodations and the harassment of women by strangers on the street made the gender hierarchy of cities explicit. If we ask, as feminists in the late 1960s and 1970s did, what it meant that women did not have access to some bars and restaurants, or what it meant that their personal space might be intruded upon whenever they left their homes, then we begin to understand how differently women experienced urban space compared to men—even men of the same class, ethnicity, or race. As ubiquitous practices, both segregated public accommodations and gender-based harassment represented women's truncated presence in the public sphere, so challenging them held both practical and symbolic appeal.

5

The Public Is Political

Demanding Safe Streets and Neighborhoods

Carol Hanisch, writing in 1969, coined what would become the slogan for many feminists: "The personal is political."[1] Betty Friedan, founder of the National Organization for Women, expressed a similar sentiment a year later: "This is not a bedroom war, this is a political movement."[2] By the 1970s, much feminist organizing focused on addressing what had often been dismissed as the individual or ubiquitous experiences of women as collective social problems instead. This approach echoed through issues ranging from women's relationships with their doctors to dealing with lecherous supervisors at work. Although these efforts looked to some outside observers like an agenda to make changes only in the private realm, feminists actually aimed to undermine the association of "personal" with "private" and blur the lines dividing "public" and "private" as well. Activists tackled both the daily experiences of women and the structural forces that constrained their options by pointing to the connections between the two arenas. Feminists raised a host of issues dealing specifically with public spaces and institutions. This generation of feminists questioned the source of the hostility and violence women experienced and developed collective strategies to demand more open and safe access. The public, in other words, was also political.

The collective and coalition-based efforts of feminists in the late 1970s and 1980s, in seeking to shift the politics and boundaries of the public realm, revealed a deep commitment to challenging narratives of victimhood and danger foisted on women. Activists built an antiviolence movement against a backdrop of national concerns over escalating rates of serious urban crime and clear messages to women that they were not safe in public. They challenged the image of danger coming from the individual stranger lurking in the dark alley by bringing attention to the far greater likelihood that women would be sexually assaulted in their own homes by their intimate partners. They also challenged the increasing sexualization of American culture and the threatening atmosphere it lent to some public spaces. Antiviolence feminists, many of whom were young and white, also learned to partner with activists of color and other community groups to question the priorities of politicians and police in allowing dark alleys and other threatening spaces in the urban environment to continue to exist.

Recalling the early 1970s in New York, Susan Brownmiller observed the "explosion of porn" firsthand and offered an explanation of the impact of its public display:

The four-block walk from Forty-second Street and Eighth Avenue, my subway exit, to the New York Public Library on Fifth . . . transmogrified during those years from a familiar landscape of tacky souvenir shops, fast-food joints, and Kung Fu movie houses into a hostile gauntlet of Girls! Live Girls!, XXX, Hot Nude Combos, and illegal massage parlors one flight above the twenty-five-cent peeps. It wasn't just the visual assault that was inimical to my dignity and peace of mind. The new grunge seemed to embolden a surly army of thugs, pimps, handbag snatchers, pickpockets, drug sellers, and brazen loiterers whose murmured propositions could not be construed as friendly.[3]

Historian Carolyn Bronstein calls the increasing availability and visibility of sexually explicit material Brownmiller described as "the democratization of pornography," and many feminists of the 1970s saw violent implications for women in this trend.[4] Campaigns critiquing the mass media, antipornography efforts, and a multifaceted campaign to reconceptualize rape as an act of violence were central to this phase of the feminist antiviolence movement. Alongside these better-known campaigns, however, feminists also built remarkably successful coalitions with community and neighborhood groups to reclaim city streets from unsavory and criminal elements, control public pornography, improve police protection, and assert neighborhood autonomy. It was in these initiatives that feminists' vision of a livable city, one that would feel safe for women from many backgrounds, became most apparent.

"Practice Being Brave": The Urban Crisis and Narratives of Danger

"Strolling by the lake. It sounds lovely, doesn't it?" asked a 1979 manual purporting to offer women "commonsense" advice for negotiating their everyday lives. "But," the author continued, "what if you are walking down by a lakefront in a city like Chicago and someone attacks you?" The advice offered in this case was that "your best escape route might be the water. Jump in and swim underneath the surface as far out as possible."[5] The book containing this pearl of wisdom was part of a genre of publishing aimed at women that emerged in the 1970s. This mainstream "self-defense" literature hit the market in force at precisely the same time as second-wave feminism opened new opportunities for women. Advice to women had changed drastically from the emphasis on civility and etiquette that dominated in the self-help literature early in the century. These new manuals stressed self-defense over manners, and authors promised women that the information contained in their pages could "save your life!"[6] They told women in no uncertain terms that "violent crimes—from purse snatchings and muggings to beatings, rapes, and other brutal assaults—happen every day. And they happen to women."[7] The city, as imagined by these authors, was fragmented and disintegrating. Physical danger lurked around every corner, particularly for women who through "ignorance and carelessness" allowed themselves to be victims of "rapists, muggers, molesters or purse-snatchers."[8] What women needed, according to this genre of advice literature, was to learn "how to avoid danger."[9]

Reflecting an increasingly negative view of urban life in the latter twentieth century, the self-defense movement that began in earnest in the 1970s proclaimed itself the answer to women's fears of public space. That such an answer was needed suggests that apprehension and suspicion came to play a far greater role in women's lives in the late twentieth century than had been the case earlier in the century. Although the self-defense phenomenon acknowledged and accepted women's presence in public spaces, it placed the responsibility for how women fared on individual women themselves. Most self-defense literature validated and propagated women's fears. These messages reflected anxieties over cities as well as women's rapidly shifting roles in the late twentieth century.

By the 1960s, Americans were beginning to lose their optimism about cities. Where earlier generations had seen potential, many now saw hostile and competitive populations and dangerous spaces. Neglect during the years of the Great Depression and World War II had taken its toll. Urban renewal projects razed swaths of inner-city districts in an attempt to overhaul the urban infrastructure. Sports stadiums, convention centers, and parking lots replaced neighborhoods, further displacing already stressed populations that were disproportionately poor and people of color. New expressways cordoned off downtown office districts from surrounding neighborhoods and provided easy escape routes, for those with resources, to flee to the suburbs. Employers and merchants followed, taking advantage of new transportation opportunities on the expressways, cheaper land, and an accessible white-collar workforce. Those left behind saw their opportunities for both housing and jobs decline dramatically. Riots erupted from Newark to Los Angeles to Detroit and other cities in the 1960s. The violent crime rate started to climb. An epidemic of drug addiction and mounting homelessness joined the growing list of urban ills. Cutbacks in social services funding and programs for the mentally ill exacerbated these problems in the 1980s. Urban crime rates, particularly the rate of violent crime, soared in the 1960s and 1970s and would not peak until 1990.

At the same time as America found itself in the midst of this "urban crisis," women's lives were undergoing significant changes. By 1960, there were one million more female-headed households than there had been in 1950, and by 1975, one of every four households was headed by a woman.[10] Employment rates for women increased sharply, rising from 30 percent of women working for wages in 1960 to 67 percent of women holding paid positions by 1990.[11] While women became more likely to support themselves or to contribute to the financial support of a family, cautionary tales and media fascination with horrific crimes kept up a countermessage that lone women were in danger. In 1964, newspapers splashed across their front pages the fate of Kitty Genovese, a New York City woman who was attacked and murdered as she walked home alone late one night, while neighbors all around heard her cries and reportedly did nothing.[12] Movies such as *Taxi Driver* (1976), *Looking for Mr. Goodbar* (1977), and *The Accused* (1988) amplified fears of lone women's exposure to the worst elements of the city, providing disturbing images of women's vulnerability to prostitution, murder, and rape.

The suddenly dangerous conditions of American cities seemed to demand a "new set of rules" for women to follow, and publishers answered this need with a new genre: the self-defense manual.[13] The guiding principles of these tomes stressed the preservation of self over concern for others in what the authors now agreed was a dangerous world. The great bulk of self-defense manuals that started appearing in the 1970s and 1980s focused their advice on how women might "behave" their way out of frightening or dangerous situations. Authors warned women away from defending themselves physically, assuming they would rarely be successful. "It would be foolish," announced a 1979 handbook, "to fight back and perhaps aggravate the offender into doing something worse."[14] Most stressed "the safety precautions [women] should take . . . in any of the routines of daily life to avoid becoming the victim of a crime."[15] They were instructed that "a little paranoia is really good for every woman."[16] According to these manuals, public space was inherently dangerous to women, it was something to be avoided, and women needed to honor their fears, suspicions, and instincts when out in it. As a 1975 author confirmed, "in today's world danger is an unfortunate reality" for women.[17] Women now feared for their lives, not their reputations, when they ventured out alone.

In the 1970s and 1980s, women were told again and again by the media, by men who watched them or directed comments at them on the street, by judges, by the press, by police officers, and even by self-defense instructors that they, as individual women, were ultimately responsible for what happened to them in public space. In an extreme example of this message, one author of a manual claiming to help women declared, "A woman who sexually excites a man and then stops him, claiming she's 'not that kind of girl,' deserves to be raped and sometimes is."[18] It was women's responsibility, then, to avoid or avert the dangerous consequences of their presence, not society's obligation to lessen the dangers of public space.

Although the manuals promised to teach women "self-defense," chapter after chapter reinforced the message that the only viable defense was avoidance. Women were instructed to avoid men, but also to avoid being alone. Most of all, they were told to avoid places where they might encounter strangers. Don't go into a cocktail lounge. Steer clear of public lavatories. Get off a bus if you're being hassled, or sit near the driver in the first place. "Walk near the edge of the curb and away from doorways, alley entrances, large bushes, or trees, which provide hiding places for criminals," women were advised.[19] Women with blond hair were instructed to wear a scarf because they were "more obvious at night than brunettes."[20] Women needed to be ready to flee at all times by planning escape routes, never letting their attention be distracted from the street, carrying only one bag, and wearing flat shoes so they could run. "As you walk," one author instructed, "anticipate trouble spots and plan how you will react in each situation in which trouble might develop."[21] Women were told to avoid drawing attention to themselves, take up less space, and become invisible lest they draw the criminal element to them.

These mainstream self-defense manuals did recognize that despite all the

Advice to women from Attitude *(1986) by Lisa Sliwa. (Used by permission of Crown Books, an imprint of Random House, a division of Penguin Random House LLC. All rights reserved.)*

precautions that a woman might take, she was bound to be out in public at some point. Self-defense advocates instructed women that others around them were not to be trusted or relied upon, so women needed to shift their attitude. Some self-defense manuals claimed that exhibiting passivity and timidity (what might have been read as appropriately quiet reserve early in the century) made them more likely to be victims. What this approach overlooked was that society's perception of women as vulnerable ultimately made women more vulnerable. Behind the calls for women to "act as if you own the street," to "show no fear," and to "display a little more bravado" was the assumption that women really were melting from "inward fright" and that any bravado they might muster would be manufactured rather than genuine.[22] "Practice being brave," women were told.[23]

The timing for the appearance of this conservative self-defense literature is significant. As the feminist movement of the 1970s crested, bringing with it unprecedented opportunities for women in education, employment, politics, sports, and recreation, mainstream advice told women it was dangerous for them to step through the door and out into the world to take advantage of these changes. Society turned women's problems—such as safety in public space—back on feminism, implying that if women had not pushed for greater opportunities, they would be safe and secure in marriages and a family home.[24] Journalist Susan Faludi explained in her 1991 book *Backlash*, this "counter assault on women's rights" was not formally organized or overtly political, and that was precisely the source of its strength. "It is most powerful," she argued, "when it goes private, when it lodges inside a woman's mind and turns her vision inward, until she imagines the pressure is all in her head, until she begins to enforce the backlash, too—on herself."[25] Scholarly studies of crime and "victimology" in the closing decades of the century indicated that the message of danger and fear had taken strong root. Sociologists confirmed that even though women were *less* likely than men to experience crime in a public place, they were consistently *more* fearful of the possibility. Esther Madriz concluded, "Fear of crime teaches women that some rights are reserved for men, such as the right to use public places."[26] Telling women to be wary, to stay home, to never be alone, and to obey their fears certainly encouraged them to internalize the backlash and believe that the opportunities opened by second-wave feminism actually put women at great physical risk.

Couched as it was in the language of "common sense"—of what any rational woman would do to stay safe—the self-defense literature's view of lone women in public as potential victims inviting violence proved hard to challenge, though some feminists tried. One group of activists in the late 1960s and early 1970s concluded, "It's about time that we as women got strong in order to defend ourselves."[27] A small body of self-defense literature from the 1980s also challenged the "commonsense" advice of fear and avoidance by offering a feminist perspective. Susan Smith published her book *Fear or Freedom* with the feminist Mother Courage Press in 1986. "Self-defense training is a powerful experience for women," Smith explained, "because it confronts fears, exposes the inner depth of femininity training . . . and provides an experience of relief" from the powerlessness that such training cultivated.[28] Smith promised her readers that by overcoming their "learned helplessness and socialized weakness," they would find "increased freedom, control, and self-discovery."[29] Historian Martha McCaughey labels this argument for self-defense "physical feminism" and locates its roots both in a handful of self-defense manuals and in the more prolific trend of self-defense classes for women. Physical feminists approached the body "as a political construct, invested with ideologies, and as such as worth defending."[30] Feminists conceived of self-defense as more than a set of tactics available to individual women, explained Py Bateman's 1978 manual *Fear into Anger*, and instead saw it as "a way of improving all our lives by freeing us from the lurking fear that has become so much a part of us" and "recognizing women's need for self-defense is a positive sign of social progress."[31] These authors distinguished themselves from nonfeminist self-defense advice and its "avoidance rules which encourage women to perform bizarre rituals to 'avoid' attack," and they criticized the way that literature had "preserved the image of women as passive beings" in need of protection.[32] The feminist self-defense movement responded directly and primarily to messages of vulnerability and danger that women faced as gendered individuals in public space.

"We Are Marching to Take Back Our Streets": Feminist Organizing against a Hostile Urban Environment

As part of a larger movement to end violence against women, feminists also organized collective challenges to urban spaces and cultures that seemed to support the objectification and victimization of women, including the prevalence of sexually explicit material. Highly sexualized and violent images of women in advertisements and popular culture drew particular ire from activists, but so did an increasingly sexualized urban landscape where stores, theaters, and advertising brought sex into the public realm in pervasive and visible ways. Feminists called attention to the violent images of women in public advertising. A billboard featuring a bound and bruised woman and the text, "I'm Black and Blue from the Rolling Stones and I Love It," went up in Los Angeles to promote the Rolling Stones' 1976 album *Black and Blue*. In response, feminists demanded that Atlantic Records cancel the ad campaign and they organized a boycott of Warner Communications, which owned the label.[33] Antiviolence feminists picketed movie openings for high-profile X-rated films that were receiving significant coverage in the mainstream media, such as *Deep Throat* and *Snuff*, a film that ended with the gruesome murder and evisceration of a woman. Feminist antiviolence groups organized boycotts and letter-writing campaigns against the corporations that funded magazines and films that featured the sexual exploitation of women in their story lines.

In the 1970s, feminists also banded together, often with other activist allies, to reclaim the streets, sidewalks, and neighborhoods of their cities. These activists countered the images of dangerous men (often men of color preying on lone white women) that appeared in the self defense literature and broader popular culture. They pointed instead to physical spaces and the socialization of men that encouraged objectification, harassment, and violence toward women. Feminists targeted the propagation and display of violent sexualized images of women that pervaded the public sphere, particularly in the "sex districts" that started appearing in most big cities in the 1970s. They also called attention to the vulnerability of working-class and racial minority neighborhoods to invasions of "adult" businesses, since these areas often lacked the resources to counter this trend. Feminists raised concerns about the atmosphere created in these areas where public pornography tended to concentrate, highlighting its impact on the women who had to live, work, or pass through these districts. Take Back the Night (TBN) marches, which grew out of the multifaceted antiviolence movement of the 1970s, embodied many of these aspects of feminist interventions in public, geographic, and cultural landscapes. The protests served as a collective expression of women's frustration with violent American culture and with particular aspects of the urban environment, and they reveal the multi-issue, coalition-based political change efforts in which some feminists engaged in the 1970s and 1980s.

Although it is clear that the movement began in the 1970s, the exact roots of Take Back the Night marches are contested. Some activists' recollections of TBN's origins reference a 1973 march in San Francisco. Others point to the 1975 Philadelphia vigil for a woman who was stabbed while walking home one night. Still others cite the "Reclaim the Night" marches in Belgium and Rome in 1976 as the start. At a rally in Pittsburgh in 1977, the title of a memorial poem for a murdered woman became the moniker—as well as the slogan—for these events organized to "Take Back the Night."[34] Activists attending a feminist antipornography conference in San Francisco in 1978 organized the first national Take Back the Night march. Demonstrators took to the streets of North Beach to protest the degrading atmosphere women experienced near adult bookstores, theaters, and strip clubs.[35] As one of the organizers explained, "For an hour, [the street] belonged not to the barkers, the pimps, the pornographers, or to the theater owners, not to potential rapists, not to whistles, hassles or catcalls. It belonged instead to the songs, voices, rage, vision, strength, and presence of the 5,000 women who took back the night."[36] The San Francisco march drew activists from around the country, but most TBN marches flourished over the years as local, grassroots events. By the mid-1980s, these nighttime rallies and marches demonstrating the unwillingness of some women to accept "the fear of going out after dark" had become annual events in many cities and on college campuses.[37] "We are marching," they proclaimed, "to take back our streets."[38]

Particularly in the 1970s and 1980s, TBN shed light on hostile urban conditions and patriarchal entitlements embedded in public space, while connecting to a long tradition of violence against women—and women challenging that violence.[39] As one participant during these early years recalled, "The marches were a response to the carefully drilled messages with which we grew up—a woman should never go out at night without the protection of a man. So the idea was that if women marched as a group they could be out at night (in the street, in fact) all by themselves."[40] Feminist folk singer Holly Near's song "Fight Back" captured the tone of the protests, particularly the rejection of the ways in which women were socially conditioned to be victims:

> But my fear is turning to anger
> And my anger's turning to rage
> And I won't live my life in a cage, no![41]

Marches challenged "rape, sexual harassment on the streets and blaming the woman for violence," explained novelist and activist Marge Piercy. The demonstrations also encouraged women to "fight back" against "the idea . . . that women had been trained to be afraid to go out at night without male protection, and together we would demand to have the right to use the streets

Women's First March against Pornography, at Broadway and Columbus Avenue, San Francisco, c. 1977. (Photo by Mary Anne Kramer, courtesy of San Francisco History Center, San Francisco Public Library)

at night," continued Piercy.[42] The common theme in these observations was that society—not women themselves—needed to change.

As much as TBN challenged the fear many women experienced in public space, the marches, rallies, speakouts, and candlelight vigils also reflected the composition, goals, and conditions of the individual cities and local organizations that spawned them. In Los Angeles, for example, the 1980 march drew five thousand supporters to Hollywood to charge purveyors of pornography and business owners with "profiting off women's bodies." At the rally that followed, however, speakers from a variety of local organizations raised a host of related issues, including rape, domestic violence, child abuse, and police harassment of prostitutes.[43]

The variety of issues raised by Take Back the Night marches in the 1970s and 1980s also reveals the connection between feminist perceptions of safety and broader community priorities, particularly those espoused by residents of the neighborhoods where adult businesses flourished. TBN events enabled coalitions to form across racial boundaries through a shared interest in ending violence. "Violence," explained a Pittsburgh march organizer, "is used to keep not only women in place but all oppressed groups, especially Third World people, seniors, and children." African American newspapers in New York and Atlanta published detailed and sympathetic announcements of TBN marches in those cities. In Los Angeles, women's and anti-violence groups in communities of color collaborated in TBN organizing through the mid-1980s. LA feminists joined the Black Coalition Fighting Back Serial Murders to call for immediate police accountability for failing to protect African American women. This alliance also embraced a broader agenda that included challenging all violence against women as well as abuses against immigrant refugees.[44] "Because we believe that sexism, racism, and classism are inextricably linked," Boston's TBN organizers explained, "we will continue to concentrate our efforts in low income areas and racially mixed communities."[45]

Self-identified feminists, many of them white and middle class, who embraced a broader trend of coalition activism across social justice organizations and issues in the 1970s are only recently receiving focused attention from scholars.[46] In Boston, for example, activists used TBN to advocate for what they saw as the interrelated and international needs of the elderly, women of color, poor women, women being released from prison, domestic violence and rape survivors, and inmates of mental institutions and prisons. They allied themselves with women's shelters, prostitutes' rights groups, tenants' organizations, unions, abortion advocates, victims' rights groups, prison reformers, and welfare rights advocates. Boston's TBN march in the spring of 1978 emerged from a coalition of nine separate organizations and a group of diverse, unallied individuals.[47]

TBN was a key strategy that feminists deployed to "put the anti-rape ideology that had been developing since 1970 into action," according to historian Maria Bevacqua.[48] This ideology rejected the idea that rape was an individual experience and one that could be avoided by any properly cautious woman. A march in Santa Ana, California, in 1983 drew attention to rising rates of rape in suburban, affluent Orange County, once thought to be a sanctuary from the crimes of the city. As one coalition member explained, "There are no 'safe' communities. Safety is an illusion." Sounding much like her urban colleagues, one of the organizers proclaimed that this march "symbolize[d] women's right to be out in the world without the fear of sexual assault and without the protection of men."[49] In Washington, DC, marchers called for the city to become a "hassle free zone," which they felt was desperately needed because "women's human rights are being violated when we are denied the right to walk down the street or sit in the park or ride the bus or run in the park or drive our cars without being verbally raped and verbally molested by disrespectful men and boys."[50] In ways that self-defense classes, individual action, and feminist writing could not, Take Back the Night events offered the opportunity for bringing media attention to the problem of violence against women and for coalitions to engage in shared direct action.

TBN marches empowered people interested in claiming urban space for women and other oppressed groups. In the minds of many activists, the marches represented not only a strike against the violence women experienced, but also, in the words of Holly Near, "our commitment to secure our neighborhood."[51] Participating in the marches offered individual women the opportunity to feel empowered by community support in urban spaces. A Chicago marcher expanded on Near's sentiment: "I'm here," she declared in 1980, "because I'm sick of being hassled. I'm afraid of coming home at night." She continued, "I'm here to show the city it bothers me," and explained, "I think it shows more that it's bothering you if you're in a group."[52] In San Francisco, TBN marches were billed as "a NON-violent show of strength." Women marched "for streets that are safe for women to walk on" as well as "to protest the rise in pornography, women-battering, rape, and sexual harassment that have kept women off the streets for centuries," and they often included in these actions communities of color, working-class neighbors, survivors of institutional and personal violence, and activists from a range of backgrounds. Responding to the Reagan administration's shift in funding away from social services in favor of Cold War foreign policy spending, a TBN marcher bluntly told a reporter, "I'm not afraid to be nuked. I'm afraid of being raped on the way to the supermarket."[53] These annual marches created a spectacle and thereby created opportunities for women and their allies to critique social policy and articulate their priorities for the cities and cultures in which they lived.

A range of issues came together in nighttime marches along city streets, revealing just how fundamental women's access to public space was to feminists of the 1970s and 1980s. In Boston, the broad and painstakingly developed list of demands for the 1978 march suggests the breadth of issues raised under the call for women to "reclaim the night." "We march together at night to protest the many kinds of violent attacks directed against women every day," the organizers announced. "While physical attack on the street is most obvious," they continued, "the same system of male power over women operates in other forms of violence against women—specifically violence within the home and within institutions." Under the TBN banner, women called for everything from publicly funded lighting improvements and women's self-defense classes to federal compensation for victims of sexual assault, housing for domestic violence survivors, prison reforms, and new legislation to protect rape victims from interrogation about their sexual history. "We demand these reforms because they are our rights and have been our rights all along," they proclaimed. "It is important to work for these changes because they may offer us some protections and make our space more livable."[54]

Taking over the streets en masse represented more than just creating a moment and a situation in which women could feel safe in spaces usually perceived as dangerous to women. As the Boston group's members explained on their two-year anniversary, the marches provided "an opportunity for people to experience feeling safe and feeling powerful by acting together."[55] Take Back the Night marches were meant to encourage in women a feeling that they were entitled to safety at all times and in all aspects of their lives and to make a statement about the needs of communities and the rights of the disempowered to live their lives free of violence.

"Confront Those Responsible": Challenging Public Pornography

Alongside the feminist organizing of TBN, coalitional feminist antiviolence work also emerged in the 1970s and 1980s from residents of urban neighborhoods—women and men—who began sustained battles with the owners and patrons of adult businesses in order to challenge the sale and display of sexually explicit material. These ultimately successful efforts to rid certain neighborhoods of adult businesses—peep shows, theaters featuring women dancing topless, shops selling sex toys and pornography, X-rated movie houses, and massage parlors—intertwined community and municipal politics, economic revitalization, and women's rights to create a productive "neighborhood feminism" unique to this era. These neighborhood and antiviolence activists echoed many of the same themes about women's right to be and feel safe in public spaces, but they couched their work in community efforts to reclaim neighborhoods, challenge urban decline, and guide urban renewal in vulnerable areas of the city where adult businesses had begun to flourish. What began as sporadic protests grew into multiyear campaigns against businesses dealing in sexually explicit materials by existing neighborhood associations, newly forming radical feminist organizations, and local officials. The activists who came together to oppose these bookstores and theaters organized, picketed, politicked, lobbied, testified, and allied their way toward a vision of neighborhood commercial districts that would serve the needs of the surrounding community, discourage crime, and make the area safe.

In the late 1970s, feminists in Los Angeles, San Francisco, Philadelphia, Boston, and New York City called for regulation of what they called "public pornography." These feminists objected to the images of naked or bound women on marquees and posters lining sidewalks. They gave voice to women's discomfort at having to encounter the patrons of adult businesses and theater barkers who offered vivid descriptions of the sexual entertainments the establishment had to offer as women passed along the sidewalks. Although sometimes accused of sexual prudery (even by other feminists), antipornography feminists' objections to sex shops and districts sprang from deeply held beliefs that the explicit materials and encounters to be found in and around these places encouraged violence toward women. Many feminists came to believe that pornography was inherently a form of violence against women. Driven by the emerging sexual revolution in America, Supreme Court decisions that undermined obscenity laws, and new technologies that made video production widely accessible, pornography became increasingly available and visible beginning in the 1970s. These conditions led some feminists to seek allies and new tools in curbing the spread of what they saw as the dangerous aspects of an increasingly sexualized culture that was coming to occupy very real physical spaces in American cities at a time when violent crime rates were soaring.

Playing off some of the tactics and ideology behind Take Back the Night and building on the larger antiviolence movement within feminism, activists focused their efforts on areas where profit was made off violent and highly sexualized images of women. Antipornography activists created guided tours through urban sex districts around the country to bring attention to the economy that profited off these images of women and supported the larger culture of violence permeating American society in the 1970s and 1980s. Groups embracing these tactics hoped "to confront those responsible for perpetuating media violence: producers, distributors, store owners, porn consumers, and consumers of other media" in a way that would also help them "educate ourselves and others about what porn really is, get media coverage, [and] make porn-viewers uncomfortable."[56]

Times Square was one of the earliest targets of antipornography feminists. After a march from Columbus Circle to Times Square in the fall of 1979, Women Against Pornography (WAP) gave tours of the area into the early 1980s. One of the organizers, Dolores Alexander, recalled that the tours "were very popular. [The tactic] was not really a fundraiser, but God, it was an amazing consciousness raiser."[57] After the successful 1978 march during the antipornography conference, feminists in the San Francisco Bay Area organized themselves as Women Against Violence in Pornography and Media (WAVPM). They expressed alarm over the "hostile climate" of commercialized sex districts and chose to confront the sexualized and masculine atmosphere of San Francisco's Tenderloin and North Beach districts directly by giving "porn tours," beginning in 1980.[58] North Beach was also becoming the center of gay male life during these years. When some members of San Francisco's municipal government wanted to regulate the adult businesses in this district, outspoken members of the gay community accused them of homophobia for targeting some of the few public spaces where gays could meet up. Straight feminists tended to either sidestep or stay ignorant about the issue of how restrictions on adult businesses could put them in conflict with the gay community. Some lesbians, however, launched their own efforts to challenge the "masculine" atmosphere of gay neighborhoods and increase lesbian visibility in the district, with events they dubbed "Castro on the Rag."

Like many feminist organizations involved in antipornography work, the antiviolence groups held the owners of "pornography" bookstores and theaters responsible, as well as the "politicians who give out permits for 'live shows'" for the "hatred of women expressed in pornography and other media-violence to women."[59] Tours were held on a regular basis, and attendees paid a small fee to participate. The tours usually began with a slide show that included statistics on violence against women and the growth of the porn industry; then the group set off to see the peep shows, dirty bookstores, and theaters of the districts. By the 1980s, porn tours were a familiar tactic. One was even organized for the 1985 NOW conference in New Orleans to take delegates through Bourbon Street's sex shops and theaters in order to build support among members for the antipornography resolutions on the agenda for the national meeting.

Porn tours were not tourist events, and participants tended to be local politicians and other community and antiviolence activists. Sometimes the only participants were members of the groups that organized them; they may have been curious to see the districts from the "safe" vantage point of a group, or just interested in maintaining a visible feminist presence to put business owners and their patrons on notice that they were being watched. These spaces and women's experiences in them were concentrated representations of broader concerns with violence and women's vulnerability. Challenges to sex districts, then, were both literal—in their objections to the commercialization of sexualized and violent images of women—and symbolic in the questions they raised about women's place and vulnerability to violence in American society. Much as Take Back the Night marches did, the porn tours used protests against particular landscapes perceived as especially hostile toward women as a means of pointing to the larger dangers faced by women in a heteronormative, patriarchal culture.

Some critics, however, charged porn tour organizers with promoting censorship or sensationalizing the issue. "They are simply a different form of sexual tourism," one writer quipped about the New York City antipornography tours, "a voyeurism one step removed from that of the peepshow customer, the enjoyment resulting from aroused indignation rather than aroused passion."[60] Activists vehemently objected. They wanted to expose the content and culture of the districts to politicians and, in particular, to the media in order to build support to take action against the businesses. In their eagerness to create a counterpresence in the heavily masculine and patriarchal arena of these sex districts, however, they left themselves open to serving the political and economic agendas of others. Those with designs on these areas sometimes exploited the work of the feminists to create opportunities for their own projects. In New York City, a group of commercial developers provided WAP with free office space in Times Square. Historian Whitney Strub deemed this move "a successful attempt to enlist feminism in [a] corporate rehabilitation" of the area that drove most of the sex shops out of business.[61] Politicians also used the rhetoric and experience of feminists and other grassroots movements to band together with developers and stop further development of pornography districts through the use of zoning ordinances. In San Francisco, Dianne Feinstein led this charge—first as an elected representative to the Board of Supervisors and then later as mayor—supporting legal measures designed to prohibit adult businesses from clustering together. She led her own porn tours of what she called the "smut capital of the United States" to bring media attention to the issue, as well as to her political platform during her unsuccessful bid for mayor in 1971. In 1973, she succeeded in pushing through an ordinance prohibiting public display of nude images. When pushing for legal tools to limit the expansion of adult businesses, Feinstein relied heavily on research into zoning laws done by Laura Lederer, the director of WAVPM, while also partnering more publicly with a local developer and the head of the San Francisco Police Department vice squad.[62]

"We Have to Change These Things for All of Us": Feminist
Neighborhood Organizing

The activists running porn tours in several American cities by the early 1980s generally came to the issue of public pornography through their antiviolence work. For residents of urban areas filled with adult businesses, however, the motivation to challenge public pornography could be found in their daily experiences. Neighborhood residents provided some of the earliest and most sustained opposition to the presence of adult businesses and the kind of neighborhood decline they seemed to represent. In response, they created a movement driven by a unique alliance of feminism and neighborhood activism in the 1970s and early 1980s that reveals key pieces of feminists' visions for the city. They demonstrated that feminism could and did make meaningful contributions to neighborhood movements and local politics through both ideology and direct action. Beyond this, neighborhood activism provided a useful avenue for feminists to further their goal of ensuring women's autonomy on the city streets and sidewalks women traversed daily. This autonomy began with the right to move freely through their own neighborhoods without feeling objectified or harassed.

This activism, what I call "neighborhood feminism," emerged in full force in neighborhoods surrounding the commercial district along Lake Street in South Minneapolis. The formerly stable working- and middle-class area began a steep decline when a freeway bypassed them to connect the suburbs and downtown Minneapolis.[63] Aging housing stock, outdated schools, declining homeownership rates, and a loss of professional businesses followed. Residents and many business owners began describing Lake Street as "tough."[64] Poverty and crime rates rose in the 1960s and 1970s. Businesses serving the neighborhoods—hardware stores, small movie houses, laundry services, and grocery stores—closed, and adult bookstores and theaters moved in to replace them. By 1983, twelve such shops could be found along the twenty-five-block Lake Street corridor.[65] A committed core of well-educated and long-term residents—including many homeowners but increasingly many renters as well—and area business owners steadily fought the decline of this area.[66]

The move to reclaim the Lake Street commercial strip for the neighborhoods of South Minneapolis grew, like much grassroots activism, out of informal discussions on sidewalks and across kitchen tables. When an adult bookstore opened in a corner building that had once housed a pharmacy, neighbors "got the effort going."[67] These businesses drew the ire of residents for occupying storefronts that stood between neighbors and the goods and services offered mere blocks from their homes. A trip to Sears, the shoe store, or the market increasingly entailed passing darkened windows and "ADULTS ONLY" signs. Encounters with bookstore patrons while waiting on the corner for the Lake Street bus too often led to sexually suggestive comments, propositions, and unwelcome touches being thrown at neighborhood women. "Look at me, I'm short. I'm fat," one local woman told a reporter, and still she received taunts such as "Lean on me" while waiting at the corner and "Hey, baby, I like my meat well-seasoned."[68] It was this harassment of women and girls in particular on which the neighborhood came to focus. Residents complained of store patrons "hustling women in the neighborhood."[69] Both men and women began to speak of the "detriment" these stores represented to the area: they brought unwanted businesses and displaced needed ones, encouraged prostitution, and attracted patrons from other parts of the city who harassed residents on the sidewalk.[70]

The treatment of women on the street served as a primary measure of whether residents deemed a business useful to or good for the neighborhoods. Whether or not pornography was "moral" or "right" rarely entered the dialogue. Residents accepted the existence of pornography, but objected to it being peddled in their "backyards" because it was "bringing people into the neighborhood that we didn't want."[71] As a local politician characterized their argument, "We're here to say we have civil rights, too. We're not stopping their right to sell pornography but we're saying 'Not in our neighborhood.'"[72] "I don't like the attitude I see from the people coming in and out of the porn establishments," one area homeowner explained to a reporter. "Women on the street corners and at bus stops are being harassed. I don't care what happens inside the bookstores and theaters. What happens out on the streets is what bothers me."[73] Although local residents perceived women (and girls) as the ones who suffered most directly, the issue was never thought to be women's alone. The safety of women served as the primary indicator for whether these were good neighborhoods.

Even though it was clearly perceived as a neighborhood issue, not solely as a women's issue, it was women who actually conducted the direct action protests that began in 1979. Older African American community organizers brought experience to the table, while white women brought their energy, their respect for the work of the civil rights activists, and their gender. These activists started confronting adult businesses and raising the issue in neighborhood organizations, business associations, and with local politicians. A group formed to conduct sidewalk demonstrations and hold pickets outside the objectionable businesses, adopting the tongue-in-cheek name South Side Sewing Circle.[74] The Circle's women played off the image invoked by their name and dressed in the traditional feminine garb of an earlier era when they picketed the adult bookstores and theaters.[75] "On Friday afternoons," one of the activists recalled, "we would put on gloves and walk around the store like we were shopping, but what we were trying to do was intimidate the customers" and drive away business.[76] As intended, their hyperfeminine garb helped create a contrast with both the patrons and the merchandise of the adult businesses. By putting women on street corners without obvious male protectors, they also created an opportunity to elicit a sympathetic response from passersby and the media. The more traditional conceptions of women as vulnerable and in need of protection that were on display, however, had to coexist with the obvious assertion of the activists that all women had a right to be in public space—and to be there without courting harassment and without being escorted by a man.

Even though only women tended to be responsible for the direct action part of the local antipornography movement, the three formal neighborhood organizations in the area adopted ousting the adult businesses as a top priority for the area—not just for its women—in the late 1970s and early 1980s. Residents recalled that these neighborhood associations and the neighborhoods themselves were good places for women because of the large number of "strong women" who were active there.[77] The neighborhood organizations also took "women's issues" seriously—on the theory that what was good for women would be good for the neighborhoods—and challenges to adult businesses predominated in their political lobbying efforts. These districts also elected Sharon Sayles Belton, a founder of a local domestic violence shelter, to represent the south-side neighborhoods on the city council, yet another example of the fruitful cross-pollination of feminism and neighborhood activism in the 1980s.

The neighborhoods' demands for action on this issue resulted in multiple zoning ordinances. The city moved to use zoning to restrict adult businesses from locating near residences, churches, and schools. Reflecting an approach that did not engage with pornography as a moral issue, activists continued to insist that they would not dictate whether pornography should be legal, only that it should not be sold and displayed in a neighborhood where residents did not want it. When courts struck down the first ordinance, neighborhood activists took local officials on tours of local adult businesses. The chief of police conceded, "Rubbing our noses in it helps us understand the problem from the neighborhood's point of view."[78] The city passed new zoning laws in 1983 and 1986.[79]

For some activists, the city moved too slowly and zoning seemed an insufficient tool for combating the adult businesses. They turned to Catharine MacKinnon, a pioneer sexual harassment litigator, and Andrea Dworkin, a fiery writer and activist opposing violence against women, for help. MacKinnon and Dworkin taught a class at the University of Minnesota in which they advanced the argument that pornography was "a systematic practice of exploitation and subordination based on sex which differentially harms women." Local activist Wizard Marks captured the reaction of many in the neighborhoods when she recalled thinking, *Dworkin has an idea? Is it a good one? Who knows? Let's see.*[80] Neighborhood activists introduced MacKinnon and Dworkin to local politicians, and the city council hired the pair as consultants to write an amendment to the city's civil rights code to include pornography as a form of discrimination, allowing civil suits against those involved in its production or sale.[81]

Unlike neighborhood activists whose challenges to pornography had all been place-based, MacKinnon and Dworkin's radical political feminism attacked pornography itself as "central in creating and maintaining the civil inequality of the sexes."[82] Some gay male activists, who had been quiet during discussions of zoning laws, raised oppositions to the ordinance, fearing that it would lead to increased police harassment of gay men.[83] Despite rushed hearings, objections from gay men, and opposition from the Minnesota Civil Liberties Union, the ordinance was passed twice by the city council, only to be twice vetoed by a liberal mayor who believed it violated the right to free speech.[84]

Some Minneapolis activists embraced the emerging national feminist antiporn movement, but most neighborhood association members and local politicians returned to a place-based approach after the failure of the civil rights ordinance. The city council appointed a task force, which recommended zoning, better policing, and opaque covers on explicit materials. The task force also endorsed novel and more extensive approaches, such as using nuisance abatement laws, eminent domain rights, and limited buyouts of adult theaters as part of larger economic redevelopment plans. At this point the alliance of feminism and neighborhood activism splintered. Antipornography feminists accused the city council of wanting "to push us into back rooms of bookstores with gags in our mouths and under opaque covers." Neighborhood activists, however, responded positively to the task force recommendations and began to focus more on broad neighborhood revitalization.[85] From the late 1980s on, the neighborhood associations followed national trends and focused more on working with public officials, the police department, private developers, and the local business community to foster economic redevelopment plans and broader anticrime initiatives.[86] They assumed that if the local economy improved, quality-of-life issues (which was where they tended to place public pornography) would take care of themselves. This development did not represent a rejection of women's safety or the goal of women's autonomy as a meaningful issue, though radical feminists often characterized it this way, but rather a maturation of the neighborhood movement, which was coming to better understand the structural factors that had made the area susceptible to deterioration in the first place.[87]

The case of South Minneapolis in the late 1970s and early 1980s reveals that a practical, on-the-ground brand of feminism could work well on the neighborhood level. Neighborhood feminism animated areas where residents saw both women's sense of safety and lowered crime rates as positive trends that reinforced each other and where what was good for women was believed to be good for the neighborhood. Although neighborhood and feminist interests became more distinct with the failure of the pornography ordinance, the connections between them did not disappear entirely. The Eighth Ward reelected Sharon Sayles Belton, who next went on to serve two terms as the city's first African American and woman mayor, beginning in 1993. Well into the 1990s, South Minneapolis continued to host the largest Take Back the Night rally in the country, and the city council continued to zealously defend its 1986 zoning law and cooperated with federal officials to successfully prosecute one of the city's "porn kings" on obscenity and racketeering charges.[88]

Although the "pornography as a violation of women's civil rights" ordinance failed to become law in Minneapolis, it did become a model for antipornography legislation in locales across the country, from Cambridge, Massachusetts, and Suffolk County, New York, to Bellingham, Washington, and Los Angeles County in California. These campaigns relied on the work of newly emerging antipornography organizations around the country: Women Against Pornography (New York City), Women Against Violence Against Women (Los Angeles), Women Against Violence in Pornography and Media (San Francisco), Women Organizing Against Pornography and Prostitution (Oakland), Organizing Against Pornography (Minneapolis), and Women Alliance Against Pornography.[89] Such an ordinance proved particularly controversial in Indianapolis, where Dworkin and MacKinnon cooperated with conservative politicians to get it passed and signed into law. Even though the Indianapolis ordinance was ruled unconstitutional in 1985, the idea behind these laws—that the very existence of pornography violated women's civil rights—had taken firm root in the feminist movement and shifted discussions of pornography away from the earlier focus on public displays of sexually explicit materials.[90] The national debate over pornography moved away from the realm of "rights to free enterprise" and "neighborhood integrity" to the arena of free speech and civil rights. The theory behind the Minneapolis ordinance—a proposal that had never even become law in the city— essentially hijacked the issue on the national scene and within the feminist movement of the 1980s. The national movement to end violence against women, of which this opposition to all pornography was now a central part, turned rancorous.

The increasingly hardline approach of "antiporn" feminists, with MacKinnon and Dworkin at the helm, created extreme discord within the feminist movement. Cognizant that censorship and "protection" had been used in the past to "oppress sexually active women, including those who sought birth control, abortions, or sex information, lesbians and bisexual women, prostitutes, and workers in the sex industry, as well as those who sought to make information about sexuality available to others," anti-censorship feminists feared that these ordinances and expanded censorship laws would be "empowering the state in ways that will reduce rather than increase women's control over their lives."[91] They criticized anti-porn feminists' use of porn tours and slideshows for their "shock-value" to emotionally manipulate elected officials and the media.[92] MacKinnon and Dworkin would continue to spread their message of pornography's inherent violence toward women, but the issue became too toxic for many feminists in the 1980s, and fallout from the debates derailed the mass movement to challenge violence against women for many years.

Conclusion

In the 1970s and 1980s, America declared that it was in the midst of an urban crisis, and popular culture messages told women that whatever new opportunities the feminist movement had created, it was too dangerous for women to step out the door and take advantage of them. These messages revealed the backlash against movements for greater empowerment on the part of African Americans and women. Images of Black men expanded from angry to dangerous, and white women became victims rather than individuals. To challenge this backlash, feminists had to battle not just traditional notions about the risks to reputation that women invited when they appeared in public but also a perception that physical violence inevitably awaited women who attempted to function independently. While some feminists tried to confront the narratives of fear and danger embedded in the advice offered to women, the uncertainty and chaos Americans increasingly saw all about them in late twentieth-century cities found expression in messages that women should rather jump in a lake than risk an encounter on a sidewalk with a stranger.

In the activism of the late 1970s and 1980s, even after the "second wave" had crested, feminists advanced a fairly radical vision for urban America. The activists shaping this vision used women's experiences as a litmus test for the health of neighborhoods, the success of urban infrastructure and policies, and the ability of women to function fully and autonomously in society. They interrupted visual and cultural messages that portrayed women as objects and victims. They challenged the image of the lone male as a threat and instead pointed to the threatening atmosphere created by the public sale and display of explicit materials that featured sexual violence toward women. Very much in line with what activists had been doing in their campaigns against street harassment, feminists in the 1970s and 1980s demanded a safer, cleaner environment for women, access to public space, and a responsive legal system in order to better serve the needs of women. They argued for an improved quality of life in urban America, one that would take women's concerns and experiences seriously, although they had to do so within a culture that was coming to fear cities. Activists had to challenge the narratives of danger that kept white women off the streets, questioned the worthiness of poor women to receive protection, and discounted the worth of the lives of women of color. Summing up the impulse behind the kind of organizing in which feminists and their allies engaged in the late 1970s and 1980s, Nancy Weisman has argued that alleviating women's fear and victimization could stop the slide of urban decline because women's withdrawal from the streets (out of fear) actually "leaves streets open to criminal behavior."[93]

The feminist agenda of this period, an agenda that stressed women's autonomy, access, and safety, has generally been lost in descriptions of 1970s and 1980s urban America. Popular and scholarly attention to what historian Josh Sides calls the "spectacles of sexuality," which seemed to pervade American cities beginning in the 1970s, tends to focus on the pitched political battles between liberals and conservatives, entrepreneurs versus urban boosters, intragroup clashes over neighborhood territory, and morality plays over "family values."[94] The violence and vitriolic language emerging from this history obscure the much more mundane concerns raised by feminist and community groups. In the face of polarizing language about the First Amendment, personal rights, urban renewal, soaring crime rates, and institutionalized racism, women's pleas for regulation and moderation got lost in the noise. In the 1970s and 1980s, however, dedicated groups of feminists in cities across the country took steps to "Reclaim the Night" from the violence of men. They challenged the fear that had become "a part of women's day to day lives" and used that challenge as a "means also to reclaim the rights which have been denied to all women: our rights to self-determination and control over our lives and our bodies."[95] Feminists realized the limitations of self-defense, marches, and temporary takeovers of tenderloin districts in keeping—and making women feel—safe in late twentieth-century urban America. These efforts represented only a piece of a much larger agenda. Activists framed women's experiences as social and collective problems, opened dialogues on policing and urban planning, and joined the conversation over urban renewal and neighborhood revitalization through alliances with community and zoning campaigns. Both the challenges and the solutions offered by feminists in the 1970s and 1980s were aimed at making cities safer for all by making them feel safe to women.

6

Taking Up Space and Making Place

Late-Century Institution Building

In the late 1970s, a group of feminists in the San Francisco area began a fund-raising campaign for the purchase of a large building to house their many activities. The impetus for acquiring their own building emerged after the group failed to find a location to host their conference on images of women in the media. Organizers wanted to make the conference a "safe space" for women by restricting attendance to women only, but no public venue would allow them to do this, and no private venue was large enough. Although the conference came off without incident, the experience convinced members of the Bay Area Women's Center that women needed to have spaces entirely under their control. As feminist folk musician Holly Near, a supporter of the building project, explained, "Sometimes when we borrow other people's space, we also have to borrow their restrictions."[1] The group eventually secured a building and opened The Women's Building, which expanded the ability of the women in the organization to enact meaningful political and social change on their own terms.

This bold endeavor represented a larger set of goals and strategies of self-defined feminist organizations from the 1970s and early 1980s that found expression in the physical environment of cities. In these decades, older traditions of using public space for demonstrations were joined by new demands for space to serve as the physical embodiment of women's belonging, autonomy, and rights. Feminists of the 1970s created public and collective institutions in cities across the country to serve women's needs. They founded and patronized women-centered commercial spaces in record numbers as well.

Building women's centers; opening feminist bookstores, restaurants, and coffeehouses; and establishing crisis centers represented concrete attempts to confront and intervene in the everyday production of meaning, shift women's position in society, and reshape gendered experiences through the use of space. These efforts showed, if sometimes only in a small way, what cities could be like when they had institutions that valued women's autonomy. These initiatives proclaimed that, by virtue of their existence, women mattered enough to have a place. This fresh wave of institution building echoed the work of Progressive Era reformers in both form and function by offering women public spaces that countered the hostility and inadequacies of the mainstream public sphere. These initiatives grounded parts of the feminist movement and made it accessible to a wide range of people and causes, while also offering women access to recreation, financial opportunities, goods and services beyond food and clothing, and a wide range of social services not provided by family, the private marketplace, or government.

Businesses run by and for women and community or service centers serving women reflected a sense among some women that they had enough fundamentally in common with other women to warrant separate spaces defined by gender. In the 1970s, when many ethnic and racial community spaces were being created, these initiatives on the part of feminists were not unique; indeed, sometimes the trends intertwined as women also created women-friendly spaces and programs within their neighborhoods and other communities. The success of these women's institutions reflected a lingering sense that some women, still feeling like second-class participants in the public sphere, needed safe spaces specifically for them. These spaces could serve as a refuge from more public spaces in which they did not yet feel they fully belonged.

"Seize the City": Feminist Building Occupations

The most dramatic demonstrations of feminist connections between space and politics came in the form of occupations of vacant buildings, a practice known as "squatting." Activists used the buildings they occupied as resource centers for women and also as stages on which to make grand political statements on the place of women in society. When feminists in New York City and Boston took over abandoned buildings in 1971, they demonstrated their belief that women needed physical spaces in which to organize, connect, and serve the needs of women. Activists participating in these occupations set up temporary women's centers hosting classes and social services, built feminist and lesbian networks, and issued demands for increased support services, employment, and housing. They justified their actions by arguing that cities had failed to meet women's needs for housing and temporary shelter, health care, childcare, access to affordable and healthy food, and appropriate education. "The city wouldn't dare bust us," one activist explained. "We're only providing the services that they should be providing."[2] The buildings served as important sites to literally house a wide variety of issues important to feminists. These activists also struck a symbolic note by choosing buildings with histories or locations important to women in which to create inclusive (at least for women and other oppressed groups), public, and visible spaces to meet needs that were often dismissed as private or individual issues. In these spaces, activists created collectivist and feminist initiatives around education, housing, health care, community building, political action, sexuality, childcare, food, and self-reliance skills.

Feminists found inspiration in the radical neighborhood-based activism of other 1960s organizations. In the face of neglect, abuse, and exploitation by city officials and landlords, the Black Panthers and the Puerto Rican Young Lords Party had not only created their own safe streets and play spaces, initiated programs for children, and improved health care, but also tackled the worsening housing shortage in New York City. In the summer of 1970, poor families launched Operation Move-In (OMI), during which they claimed their right to affordable housing by occupying vacant apartment buildings. Squatters and the tenants' rights activists who led the actions challenged the right of private property owners to hold badly needed affordable housing off the market in anticipation of razing older rent-controlled structures and constructing new high-rent buildings in their place. Feminists found both encouragement and mentorship in the squatter movement. Here an older generation of seasoned female activists practiced "a model of 'on-the-ground' women's activism, which complemented the more self-conscious women's liberation movement," according to historian Roberta Gold. The close "squatter-sister" relationship between tenant and feminist leaders in New York City proved a foundation for a "web of connections" between the movements and inspired feminist squatting actions in the city.[3] Feminists took tactics from the tenants' rights movement and adopted them to fit their own goals.

In the fall of 1970, a radical women's group, the West Side Women's Center, "liberated" a storefront on the Upper West Side in New York City. Working with activists from Operation Move-In, the feminists identified a boarded-up storefront on Amsterdam Avenue slated for demolition. The location placed their Women's Center alongside thirty or so other squatter-run storefronts that ranged from childcare centers to karate studios, creating what activists called a "liberated zone" where "new communities" worked to "gain control of [their] lives."[4] The Women's Center served as a place in which to "rap, exchange information on various women's issues, exchange clothing, enjoy free dinners, and meet their sisters to organize."[5] By the summer of 1971, reflecting its radical political milieu, the center's name evolved into the Westside Women's Liberation Center. The center began hosting an abortion program—a referral and information service—and formed a housing committee, which supported the work of OMI and the Puerto Rican Young Lords in moving poor families into empty city-owned buildings.

The Westside Women's Liberation Center began with (and maintained) close ties to the community organizations that had formed to resist urban renewal demolition plans that threatened poorer neighborhoods. Despite this connection, the activists behind the center struggled to define their place in the wider tenants' rights movement. Much of the center's work focused on providing referral, counseling, and networking services to women and a venue for consciousness-raising work. Initial appeals stressed that "all women are welcome to come to their center." But as one organizer explained, "I felt that it was especially important for my storefront to relate to the other storefronts and to the squatting families" in the neighborhood.[6] As a result, these activists chose to work primarily with women from the local communities but did attempt to engage the men as well. When the city moved to clear the area in advance of urban renewal demolition, it treated the Women's Center and the other enterprises in the OMI squatter movement the same. All received eviction notices in the summer of 1971.

Another group of New York City feminists, aware of the squatters at the Westside Women's Liberation Center and eager to create a place for women on the Lower East Side, began planning their own action and set a launch date of New Year's Eve 1970. Calling themselves the 330 East Fifth Street Women's Action Committee, they planned to establish a health clinic, lesbian social center, childcare center, feminist school, art workshop, and food co-op in an abandoned building.[7] The building they chose to occupy had been a welfare office and a women's shelter in the past, and this connection to state and public services for women held great symbolic appeal for organizers. The previous owners had relinquished the building to the city three years earlier, leaving it sitting empty and deteriorating. Organizers did not disclose the exact location of the building to be taken over, or even the exact nature of the action, to those they invited to participate. Borrowing tactics from other radical groups, they laid detailed plans for orchestrating the action and sought to minimize the likelihood that law enforcement would be alerted in time to foil their plans.

In the week before the action, organizers cleared out the homeless who had been living in the building, secured it with chains and padlocks, and left inside some weather-proofing supplies they would need if they were to survive in the building for any length of time during a New York City winter.[8] When the women recruited for the action arrived at a local church, they were briefed on the nature of the takeover. Most had no idea that the plan was to occupy a building until this meeting. The activist squatters were also given instructions for what to do if arrested (one helpful hint: "Don't call them pigs"). Lawyers and a "bust line"—an emergency number that activists could call in case of arrest—had been arranged for the first night. After being broken up into "affinity groups" of ten women or so, participants learned one another's names in case of arrest and walked to the target building in waves. Once there, women climbed through a window, the only entrance available. They cleared a large room on the second floor and set up gas heaters and sleeping bags for the night.

The building at 330 East Fifth Street had no heat, electricity, or sanitary facilities when these feminist activists took it over. Nevertheless, activists challenged the city's position that the building should be demolished. They worked hard to clean and repair the building and get rid of rats. They brought in their own workers with the skills to make repairs to the heating and plumbing, often taking advantage of the opportunity to learn to do the work themselves. "We saw the building as a school . . . a feminist school," one participant explained. "Everything that had to be done there was a learning experience."[9] The women enclosed a space on the second floor to make it warm for the children brought along by many of the occupiers. Meanwhile, organizers secured a donation of badly needed glass to repair the windows. As one activist concluded after conceding that the building and the programs they hoped to run in it would require enormous amounts of work, "But you know, we are here and it is ours."[10]

Representatives from the occupying Women's Action Committee and officials from the mayor's office almost immediately began negotiations over the fate of the building and its current occupants. When these talks failed, the city sent in police and officials from the Department of Real Estate to declare the building a hazard and order the women to leave. To the surprise of police and city officials, the women declined to abandon the space they had been repairing and using for twelve days.[11] Police raided the building and removed two dozen or so women by force. When news of the raid spread, upwards of seventy-five supporters quickly assembled at the site to challenge the eviction. When police tried to shut down the demonstration, the activists fought back. As reported in the radical press, "Women were clubbed and arrested randomly in the course of the POLICE RIOT in which once again pigs freaked out and lost control with almost no provocation."[12] Five police officers suffered minor injuries, and twenty-four protesters were arrested.[13] The activists never regained control of the building, and the city quickly tore it down, installing a parking lot for the local police precinct in its place.[14] The women declared their center to be "in exile" and sought other spaces and means to continue the work started there. The food co-op did manage to live on as the Women's Food Conspiracy and eventually found a home inside the Tompkins Square Community Center.

Building occupations, such as those on the Upper West Side and Lower East Side of New York City, reveal both the political impetus and the utopian visions embedded in late twentieth-century feminism. The activists behind these actions were critical of the world in which they lived, sought to make real changes in women's daily lives, and promoted both the collective and individual autonomy of women. Activists explained that they had taken over buildings in order to "dramatize the city's total disregard of the needs of the community (particularly women & children) and to let all women know by our example that they can and must seize things for themselves; and also to set up within a community (ours), and with the community of women themselves, services which are essential to our lives, run the way women know they should be run."[15] Radical feminists appealed to women to support the movement and one another by creating alternative economies: "Sisters please— forego outdated pleasures, abandon decadent poisons, make our own music, read your sisters' books, get your clothes from clothing exchanges, get high on freedom and give that filthy money to the movement." "Every dollar spent on products supports men," they argued. "Every dollar spent here liberates women." Displaying their practical side, they reminded their leftist audience, "World-changing is not cheap."[16] Rejecting the capitalist food system, activists worked directly with farms that produced food and became knowledgeable about nutrition. They also developed an approach to childcare that they hoped would undermine the "sex-role system" and "its penchant for rewarding children for being good little soldiers." Crying, "Seize the city," they allied themselves with other groups to challenge existing power structures based on private property ownership. They offered a free and open space to all women who "are burned out, locked out by capricious men in the middle of the night;

women who want to leave their husbands but have no place to go; women who are jobless & therefore homeless for any reason (often age); street women, runaways, victims of mental institutions, prostitutes, religious fanatics, travelers [sic]—all women are welcome to stay here." The New York City activists promised that, "when the space runs out, other women will take over other buildings."[17] What these urban feminist activists offered was a dramatic and expansive re-visioning of the purposes that city spaces might serve and a full-scale repudiation of urban gender segregation in their rejection of danger narratives and their embrace of community over hollow gender protections.

Feminists in early 1970s Boston settled on a similar set of ideas and tactics, demonstrating once again the proliferation of feminist activism. A core group of activists associated with the Boston Women's Liberation group known as Bread and Roses planned an action to begin on International Women's Day in March 1971. Partway through the day's march, organizers at the head of the parade took an unannounced turn and led hundreds of supporters to a dilapidated building on the Harvard University campus in Cambridge. When the marchers arrived, banners unfurled from the windows proclaiming 888 Memorial Drive to be a "liberated building." As one activist recalled, the takeover was a way of saying to society, "You owe us something."[18] For the next ten days, activists occupied the space, ignoring a court order to vacate. They issued a range of demands for low-income housing, childcare, abortion services, and equal pay. They also called for Harvard to create a permanent women's center. As activists explained, "The struggle to gain control of all aspects of our lives—our bodies, our jobs, our social roles, and our creativity—is the struggle of every woman," and the activists behind this building takeover aimed to give women "liberated territory" in which to wage this struggle.[19] By the time the occupation ended ten days later, Harvard had accepted an anonymous $5,000 donation to cover the down payment for a different building that would become the permanent home of the Cambridge Women's Center.[20] The center hosted a wide range of programs for women, and out of these grew other independent institutions, including services for rape and domestic violence survivors, transitional housing for women, and a feminist school with a strong radical and practical curriculum that taught women everything from auto mechanics to Marxism.

The activists behind these building occupations had a much different agenda than those of the tenants' rights movement and local community groups that pioneered squatting as a political tactic, but feminists drew on the experiences of these organizations and their tradition of female leadership. In Boston, one community organization did go to the press to defend the feminist action, and the feminists ensconced in the Memorial Drive building invited local children to join the happenings in the building. In New York City, squatters and tenants' rights organizations, including the Metropolitan Council on Housing, the Cooper Square Development Committee, and Operation Move-In, lent technical assistance, models of activism, and human resources to the feminist occupations. These groups advised the feminist occupiers on the importance of making repairs, creating an organizational structure for the community occupying the building, spinning the story in the press, and negotiating with police and city officials. The Cooper Square group fed the feminists information on the city's attempts to derail the occupiers by sabotaging the plumbing at the East Fifth Street building. Frances Goldin, vice president for one of the tenants' rights organizations active on the Lower East Side, approached the police on the first night of the occupation. As a figure familiar to the local officers, she was able to keep the women from being immediately removed by reassuring the officer on duty that the women did know how to handle the gas heater. Daughters of two tenants' rights leaders played direct roles in the New York City feminist takeovers. The experience led Goldin's daughter to both come out as a lesbian and pursue education to enter the skilled building trades.

The feminist "squats" of the early 1970s offer a glimpse of the longing on the part of the mostly white feminists to expand beyond their own racial and class positioning and build a more inclusive movement that took seriously the disparate experiences of other oppressed groups. Boston feminists were delighted to have the support of the one organization from the Cambridge Women's Center's predominantly African American neighborhood that championed their efforts, but they remained at a loss as to how to find and communicate with other locals. The East Fifth Street feminists built their actions within the larger squatter movement that was thriving in New York City at the time, aligning their efforts with the poor white, Black, and Hispanic New Yorkers who were challenging the displacement caused by urban renewal projects. They published flyers in English and Spanish in an attempt to reach out to women in the surrounding neighborhood. They eventually shifted their language of solidarity to include all oppressed groups, not just the women of those populations, even as they spoke of the need for self-determination. Working across the boundaries set by gender segregation's ties to racial and class disparities remained challenging.

The building takeovers represented fairly militant tactics not often associated with feminism. Occupations drew on radical political perspectives in their challenge to traditional property ownership and the entitlements associated with private property rights. The feminists who engaged in squats in New York City and Boston were essentially holding buildings hostage in order to gain attention for their cause. "We have been arrested and harassed for making a safety hazard into useful space," declared East Fifth Street activists. But in their view, "the city of New York is the criminal" for "not providing for the needs of the people and when the people try to provide for themselves they are arrested and beaten."[21] The tactics of the feminist occupations proved disruptive and dramatic, but ultimately were unsustainable. Some of the programs they initiated continued, but not in the physical spaces that these women had used to raise their issues and make their claims. Feminists' occupations were unsustainable partly because, unlike the actions of the tenants' rights movements, they did not target spaces that they had traditionally claimed were theirs. The women behind these actions were generally not facing the kind of physical displacement experienced by the low-income communities of color in which the tenants' rights movements were active. Rather, they chose to occupy otherwise vacant or underutilized space as a way of demanding access for women to the wider public sphere.

Even as the occupied buildings functioned as political spaces they also functioned as countercultural spaces within which alternatives to mainstream institutions were created. The women's centers established through building occupations sought to create a "free space" for women, a place where they could explore their identities and community as women free of the weight of patriarchy and heteronormativity that pervaded other public spaces. Women were encouraged to try out traditionally masculine skills in repairing and securing the buildings. All the buildings' programs also included groups that supported lesbian identities. The identification of many of the key occupation leaders as lesbians contributed to the sense that in these women's spaces women were safe to explore their sexual identity, whether it be newly declared or even newly discovered.[22]

Being involved in a squat—the experience of the "collective," of responsibility for a space, of constructing meaning for a physical space through illegal and confrontational tactics—left a profound mark on the activists who participated in these actions.[23] "It was the first time for many of us that we had engaged in a militant struggle so concretely connected to our own needs," one of the Boston activists reflected. "We knew why we needed this building, we could touch, see and feel what we could create. Our defense of the building, were it to come to that, would not be the defense of an abstract ideology, but of an idea concretized and experienced."[24] The "open" nature of the centers feminists crafted—trying to draw in a diverse group of women, issues, and neighbors—represented a very different kind of community-building utopian experiment than the collectivist experiments in housing that some lesbian feminists were trying at the same time.[25] Activists' boundaries, experiences, and assumptions were all tested. Boston feminists, mostly white and middle class, wanted to be allies with the working-class people of color who lived in the area around the building they occupied, but only one neighborhood group would speak with them. Meanwhile, Harvard was willing to discuss all their demands. The activists' negotiations with Harvard led to the opening of a women's center in Cambridge, but any awareness of their own privilege and how it created barriers in building relationships with other oppressed groups and, especially, women of color never fully registered with the core activists. Still, the act of using space—of taking up space—to make political demands and present the issues and constituencies of the movement proved "electrifying" to participants. "What an exhilarating idea," one Boston activist recalled, "that the collective energy of the women marchers could turn into a fighting force demanding that Harvard fulfill its responsibility to its economically and racially diverse neighbors with special attention to the needs of WOMEN."[26] The language feminists used to describe their building actions is telling of the significance of the physical space they occupied. Activists sought to "liberate" buildings in order to liberate women. They acted on the idea that part of the work of feminism was "locating the ground from which to speak with authority as women," as the poet Adrienne Rich later expressed it.[27]

"More than a Restaurant, This Is Part of a Social Movement": Feminist Forays into the For-Profit Marketplace

In contrast to the radical actions of feminist squatters, other feminists of the 1970s created public and quasi-public spaces catering primarily to women through entrepreneurial efforts. Feminist business owners embodied the mission of the feminist movement—and even, at times, some of its more utopian visions—by creating spaces they hoped would be accessible, affordable, welcoming to women, and free of harassment from men. These businesses ran the gamut from being just "women-friendly" to explicitly feminist, lesbian, and/or woman-centric ventures. Feminist restaurants, bars, and coffeehouses had the potential to build community both as social gathering spaces and as purveyors of services and goods to the public. Through an explicitly feminist business model, many created opportunities for women to work in fields that otherwise excluded them, particularly the building trades.[28] Some of these businesses, such as credit unions, offered services that women had been denied in the traditional, androcentric marketplace. Others focused on offering women-created wares or women-specific music and books for sale. Feminist businesses also gave the women who ran them a chance to make a living off work they perceived to have a larger political purpose and greater social reward. Although some owners wanted to make a profit, more wanted to contribute to the movement. The businesses they created existed in a liminal space between idealism, activism, and entrepreneurship. That these businesses were not designed, owned, controlled, or otherwise defined by men or by masculine and heteronormative practices set the ventures apart from the traditional marketplace.

The blossoming of these service and commercial establishments sprang directly from second-wave feminism. Their proliferation demonstrated how extensively women's presence and needs in many traditional institutions and businesses had been neglected. Moreover, women's businesses stood as explicit challenges to the subordinate position in which male-controlled institutions maintained women. Just as YWCA organizers in the early twentieth century sought to demonstrate the viability of a commercial market for serving working women lunches and providing them with decent housing, many women's businesses started in the 1970s also aimed to fill holes in the marketplace for goods and services used by women. The organizations and individuals behind these establishments understood, at least implicitly, that physical space conditioned what was possible and that businesses and services designed, controlled, managed, and patronized by women could expand women's options in a society that often ignored, shunned, or otherwise limited women's possibilities.

One of the best-known feminist businesses to embody these goals was the New York City restaurant called Mother Courage. The idea to open this restaurant emerged during a late-night drive in the summer of 1970. Newly attached romantic partners Jill Ward, one of the major organizers of the Women Strike for Equality march down Fifth Avenue that summer, and Dolores Alexander, the first executive director of NOW, were both struggling to find a way to make a living and pursue their feminist activism. They hoped the restaurant would be a way to support themselves and the movement. They raised funds through loans from friends and family and poured sweat equity into renovating an old luncheonette in Greenwich Village near where many radical feminists lived. Mother Courage opened in the spring of 1971.[29]

From the beginning, the restaurant project was closely associated with feminism, lesbians, and the women's liberation movement. "I think word went out fairly early on," Dolores Alexander recalled, "that we were lesbians and that the clientele would be largely lesbians. The women's movement kept talking about it as a feminist space." High-profile feminists from around the country visited the restaurant, increasing its notoriety. A back-cover article in *Newsday* also raised the restaurant's profile and brought some amount of harassment. Alexander reported being hassled by curiosity seekers from the Securities and Exchange Commission, who had the power to raise questions over their funding model. The owners also encountered seemingly endless red tape in obtaining a liquor license. Suggesting some of the cultural and institutional barriers women faced in opening a small business in 1970s America, Alexander and Ward were repeatedly asked, "'Well, where are the men?' 'Where are your male partners?' 'Who's going to vouch for this?' 'Who's going to be responsible for these bills if anything should go wrong?'" Alexander recalled in a 2004 interview. "They put us through hell."[30]

Once open and in possession of a wine and beer license, however, Mother Courage quickly proved successful. The establishment got good press, and its reputation was bolstered by the prominent feminist patrons it attracted. Kate Millet, author of *Sexual Politics*, was a regular. Susan Brownmiller held the launch party for her book on the history of rape, *Against Our Will*, at the restaurant. *New York Magazine* and the *New York Times* published favorable reviews, and *People* magazine covered the restaurant's third birthday celebration. Various activists from across the feminist political spectrum used the space for their meetings. Feminists from across the country made pilgrimages to Mother Courage during their visits to New York City. "We wanted to be a space for strong, independent women who would be hopefully involved in the women's movement," recalled Alexander, "and that did happen."[31] Alix Kates Shulman, author of *Memoirs of an Ex-Prom Queen*, explained to *People* in 1974, "Just knowing the restaurant is here makes me feel that we can prevail."[32] Mother Courage may have had pragmatic roots in its founders' need to make a living, but it functioned as far more than merely a business.

Balancing the running of a viable business with serving the needs of a social movement, especially when done through decentralized or nonhierarchical decision-making structures, brought both challenges and opportunities. Founded by a feminist collection in the mid-1970s, the Bloodroot Café in Bridgeport, Connecticut, had an even more explicitly feminist mission. Its founders dedicated themselves to creating a "self-sustaining" place for "feminist community for women and men." Consequently, they believed, both the space and the food conveyed important political messages. "Feminism is not a part-time attitude for us," explained the collective members in one of its cookbooks, aptly titled *The Political Palate*. "It is how we live all day, every day. Our choices in furniture, pictures, the music we play, the books we sell, and the food we cook all reflect and express our feminism."[33] As a founding member of the feminist Brick Hut Café in Berkeley recalled, "Struggles at the store were a working-out of feminist principles: The women were strongly committed to a collective model and, perhaps more important, to creating a workspace that was woman-centered and welcoming to lesbians. Although such a space blurred public and private boundaries and increased the potential for conflict, it provided an unprecedented opportunity for lesbian-feminist ideas to be circulated and further developed."[34]

As part of their feminist mission, these businesses challenged heteronormative and patriarchal practices common in the marketplace and central to urban gender segregation, particularly those surrounding eating and drinking in public. At Mother Courage, for example, it was restaurant policy for waitstaff to invite all members of a party to taste the wine, countering the tradition of offering a taste only to a man at the table. At a time when restrictions on women entering a bar alone still lingered (New York City did not pass its law prohibiting the exclusion of women from public accommodations until 1971) and social customs dictated that women should not dine alone in public, Mother Courage offered what one patron called "the one place I can walk into and feel I don't have to be someone else's appendage." "A woman coming to eat here alone," echoed founder Dolores Alexander, "knows she won't feel like a freak and won't get hassled by men." This atmosphere, coupled with a set of intentional "feminist etiquette" practices—such as placing the bill in the middle of the table instead of in front of a man—further disrupted the traditional balance of power between men and women in public.[35] Recognizing the transformative potential of patronizing such establishments, a Los Angeles diner explained, "Eating dinner in a feminist restaurant is a consciousness-raising experience because it makes women realize that headwaiters have treated the woman dining alone as a pariah to be shuffled off to the worst table or as a seductress who has come in search of a man instead of a good dinner."[36] These spaces, in the words of historian Finn Enke, "played a dramatic role in building a culture of activism, constituting a movement, and defining its parameters."[37] Experiences such as these echo the impact of consciousness-raising groups and other more widely recognized forms of movement activism that invited women to see the world differently through a feminist lens.

As was the case with Mother Courage, the goods and services sold in many of these establishments remained secondary to building and nurturing a feminist social movement. Few of the founders of feminist commercial endeavors had much experience in running a business. For women who were inexperienced business owners in an era when banks still rarely lent money to women or collectivist-style groups, traditional funding sources were often hard to secure. Existing financial institutions drastically underserved women in banking and credit services, as was particularly obvious and troubling to feminist entrepreneurs attempting to launch small businesses in the early 1970s. As the founders of Mother Courage did, many turned to their own political, social, and familial networks to overcome this hurdle. The group behind Charis Books & More in Atlanta, opened in 1974, overcame the funding obstacle by first organizing as a nonprofit, thus allowing friends to donate money rather than lend it to the business.[38]

Recognizing that not everyone had networks to leverage, eighteen feminist credit unions opened around the country between 1973 and 1976. These institutions provided the services that traditional banks would not: extending credit to women in their own names rather than their husbands', financing feminist businesses, providing loans for women to get divorced or have abortions, and helping fledgling women's organizations acquire stable spaces in which to do their work. As one California Feminist Credit Union staff member recalled of the 1970s, "It was very personal and we were very proud to be a part of the movement." "We really were performing a service that was needed back then," explained a volunteer for the Seattle credit union. "Times were so different, and you couldn't get help from the police or agencies like you can now."[39] Women seeking to extricate themselves from marriages and retain custody of their children, for example, desperately needed financial help. Lacking in education and work experience and facing the high cost of childcare and limited job prospects, divorcing women in the 1970s often had little means for paying back the loans that had been so crucial to changing their lives. Far more than banks or even traditional credit unions, these feminist ventures waded into risky financial waters.

Feminist credit unions took on that risk as part of their mission. The Equal Credit Opportunity Act, passed by Congress in 1974 and slowly implemented over the course of the decade, helped address some of the most discriminatory lending practices women faced in the traditional banking industry. These laws prohibited discrimination on the basis of sex and marital status, among other things. With their unabashed support of the movement and women's financial autonomy from men, however, the feminist credit unions offered far more than just bland prohibitions against discrimination to the entrepreneurs, individuals, and organizations seeking their services.

Unlike male-only businesses, feminist businesses of the 1970s and 1980s generally made a point of welcoming all who supported the mission at the same time as they declared themselves a woman-positive space. Feminists in these decades generally saw no contradiction between supporting nontraditional businesses specifically designed for women and challenging women's exclusion from male-only spaces, such as bars and restaurants. They understood the feminist businesses as primarily serving the needs of women, but not necessarily serving only women. Owners also argued that the differentials in power underlying "men only" and "women only" in a patriarchal society negated any equivalency. When men excluded women, they preserved a patriarchal power structure. Feminist businesses, by contrast, created spaces that were inclusive, supportive, and empowering for women. The founder of the Susan B. (a reference to suffragist Susan B. Anthony) restaurant on Chicago's North Side—which was typical of feminist restaurants and coffeehouses—explained, "It was a place where being a woman, being a feminist, was the best thing. Other people were okay, and could come in there; a woman could bring her boyfriend in, that wouldn't be a problem. It was just that there, he wasn't going to be as accepted and as 'at home' as she was."[40] And a public accommodation (or even a retail shop that was not a beauty parlor or a dress shop) where a woman felt more at home than a man was still a rarity in these decades. Men came to Mother Courage fairly regularly. The restaurant's manager noted that the atmosphere of an establishment committed to feminist principles could feel quite comfortable to some men who also felt pressured by traditional gender roles: "There are none of the expectations and role playing of the singles scene."[41] Most men, however, were brought by regulars and wanted to support the restaurant and the social movement with which it was associated.[42] One of the founders of the lesbian-feminist Brick Hut Café in Berkeley explained the business model this way: "We welcomed everyone who was an ally in our common cause of social justice and inclusion."[43] In these novel establishments that dotted the landscape of American cities in the 1970s, often showing up in the more left-wing districts or in gay or Latino neighborhoods, women found the rare opportunity to be in public and be relatively sure that they would not be harassed, hassled, or turned away by patrons, owners, or police. It was this point in particular that set the feminist businesses apart from the bars that had welcomed—or at least tolerated—lesbians in the 1950s and 1960s.

Not all the businesses founded by feminists in this era started out with a vision so closely aligned to the movement as Mother Courage, Bloodroot, Susan B., Charis Books, or the Brick Hut. Feminism was "in the air" in the

1970s in most major cities, however, and for white feminists in Detroit the movement found an unintentional home at Detroit's Woodbridge Tavern.[44] The Woodbridge was not a "women-only" business, and it never catered specifically to women. Instead, it was a space owned and run by an outspoken feminist, and consequently it felt comfortable for women all the time and came to feel downright joyous on Friday nights when local feminist and performer Geraldine "Gerry" Barrons sang. Detroit did have a few establishments more along the lines of Mother Courage. The Poor Woman's Paradise Coffeehouse and a feminist bar-restaurant called The Underground were explicitly feminist establishments. The Woodbridge, however, represented a different "spatialization" of the feminist movement. Run by a movement woman who drew heavily on the political network of her activism, the tavern functioned as a feminist mecca every other Friday night for nearly a decade. Marcia Cron, who purchased the bar from her father in 1975, did not set out to do this. Her intent was to reinvent her family's business as a lunch place. But after buying the "beer and a shot" place—not at all a traditional business for a woman entrepreneur at the time—she brought her feminist sensibilities to her business model and dealings.[45]

Cron, a vocal feminist, readily challenged gender conventions that normalized and privileged men in the public sphere: she kept her maiden name after marriage, wrote letters of complaint when not addressed as Ms., and confronted business owners if they assumed that, as a married woman, she did not have a career of her own. She had challenged the exclusion of unescorted women at Detroit's Golden Lion restaurant, bringing a copy of the Michigan public accommodations law with her to justify her right to be served, and she protested coat check policies that reserved the service for men only. When the state refused to issue a liquor license in her name rather than her husband's, she enlisted city council member Maryann Mahaffey in her successful fight against these patriarchal state practices, insisting that since she alone owned the business, the license must be in her name. For Cron, and surely for other women who owned small businesses in the 1970s, taking stands for women's rights in the male-dominated marketplace constituted feminist activism.

When customers pushed her to stay open later and arrange some entertainment, Cron enlisted her friend Gerry Barrons, a fellow Detroit NOW member and a former coworker. Barrons, who had a degree in theater and English, was working full time by the mid-1970s for her own private corporation that helped businesses embrace affirmative action. Her initial response to Cron's request was a slightly indignant, "What? Me sing in a bar?" But when Cron produced a talented piano player named Yolanda Jones to accompany her, Barrons relented.[46] Singing under the name Gerry O'Connor so as to distance herself from her business identity, her powerful contralto voice and penchant for climbing on tables to belt out the feminist anthem "I Am Woman," and her ability to get the crowd singing along quickly led to lines out the door on "Gerry nights." Barrons took requests from the audience—often written on cocktail napkins—and filled in any lyrics she forgot with feminist messages. "The Battle Hymn of the Republic" became a favorite; when Barons sang her own lyric, "Let us live to make women free," the whole room would stand and sing with her, glasses held high and arms wrapped around one another.

Once the popularity of "Gerry nights" at the Woodbridge Tavern was established, some feminists quipped that "the men had the DAC [Detroit Athletic Club] but the women had the Woodbridge."[47] The comparison between these drastically different types of institutions—one a mainstay of the movers and shakers in local politics and the business world and the other a neighborhood bar—highlights the significance of a feeling of belonging and ownership over a space. The "excitement" and "energy" of these evenings had no rival. Nothing else was as popular among the mostly white professionals at the core of the tavern's regular clientele, and celebrities, United Auto Workers officials, and journalists also frequented the tavern on these nights. Cron had not intended to give the movement a home, but she immediately recognized what she called the "value" to the movement (and her business) of "bringing people together." And this business model worked. The Woodbridge Tavern's outsized reputation in Detroit led some to quip that the Renaissance Center (RenCen)—the soon-to-be-iconic complex of four office towers, a seventy-three-story hotel, and a shopping complex then being constructed on the city's riverfront—was "being built in the shadow of the Woodbridge."[48]

The success of feminist businesses, whether short- or long-term, relied heavily on the connection of these establishments to their immediate surroundings. In Atlanta, for example, Charis Books & More survived in large part because of the feminist-lesbian community in the immediate area. As one patron from the early years succinctly explained how the relationship between the store and the community began, "It was in the neighborhood, and women ran it."[49] With a dozen or so lesbian communal households and the headquarters of the Atlanta Lesbian Feminist Alliance in the immediate area, Charis's owners had a ready community and clientele with whom to connect. They ran their business with the philosophy of "be around, be available to the community you are interested in working with, and when they're ready they'll talk to you." They invited the community to meet in their store, and they stocked books on the topics that customers requested. As a result, the store became a hub for communication about social justice movements in the 1970s, as well as a hospitable place for women just beginning to explore feminist or lesbian identities.[50] Filling these roles pulled a store that was not explicitly feminist or lesbian in the beginning solidly into a women's movement that was flourishing in the geographic location in which the store owners had placed themselves.

A familiar pattern appeared in several cities: the concentration of feminist businesses and services in particular geographic areas helped build feminist culture and networks while increasing patronage. In a neighborhood that was heavily gay and lesbian, the Brick Hut Café in Berkeley knit itself into a community of women-owned enterprises, most located within blocks of the restaurant. Although the café moved twice during its twenty-year existence, it stayed close to other commercial ventures with strong feminist and political missions. As one of the founders recalled of the café's final location, "We wanted the new, larger Brick Hut to be an attractive and active space for our community. Other women-owned businesses opened on the same block: Good Vibrations, West Berkeley Women's Books, and It's Her Business. Collectively we were known as Girl Town."[51]

However, the physical location of these establishments also replicated and reinforced some of the weaknesses of the movement.[52] Locating a business in a certain neighborhood had a deep impact on who the clientele would be, while often reproducing the class and race boundaries of organized feminism in the 1970s, and ultimately limited the reach of the business. So while these businesses became important physical locations for the women's movement and functioned as community spaces, their concentration in certain areas could also keep the movement fragmented and sometimes limited their patronage, curtailing their long-term viability.

Like more obviously activist endeavors, the intensity of running a feminist business, even within a supportive community and neighborhood, often took a serious toll on the owners. Burnout claimed Mother Courage founder Dorothy Alexander first; she rotated out after a few years, choosing to work at *Time* and *People* instead. Her partner, Jill Ward, stuck it out for six years, at which point they shuttered and sold the restaurant. During this period, the couple also broke up, though not, according to Alexander, because of the restaurant and its closing. Rather, she explained, there was an "arc" to these kinds of endeavors and Mother Courage had served its purpose. Having reached its zenith in the mid-1970s along with the feminist movement, it continued on for a few years until the owners and patrons moved on.

As both Barrons and Cron attested when recalling the Woodbridge Tavern, supporting women-run businesses was a part of the feminist movement in Detroit in the 1970s, but that support alone could not explain the popularity of "Gerry nights." The sense of camaraderie and fun released on these evenings fed back into the work of the movement as local NOW activists, Cron and Barrons among them, fought for equal accommodations, women's employment rights, and the Equal Rights Amendment. The loss of the ERA in 1982 proved "devastating" to the morale of the movement. As organizing efforts dwindled in the face of this loss, so did the energy at the Woodbridge. Cron would have been pleased to keep "Gerry nights" going, but Barrons called it quits after nine years of belting out tunes about women's empowerment.

A handful of these feminist and lesbian-feminist businesses did persevere beyond the 1970s and 1980s, their life spans often tracking closely to the victories and losses of the larger social movement to which they were connected. For example, the Woodbridge Tavern stayed open for two more decades with Cron at its helm, but it ceased to function as a social arm of an organized feminist movement in the city. Other feminist forays into the commercial marketplace followed a similar trajectory, their success reflecting the strength of the movement. Businesses whose operations were built around an all-woman or predominantly woman clientele often did not survive the loss of the collectivist phase of second-wave feminism. Business models that fused politics and commerce became increasingly rare as the 1980s pressed on, and only a few notable survivors made it into the twenty-first century. The California Feminist Credit Union in San Diego closed in 2011, and the Women's Southwest Federal Credit Union of Dallas followed a year later. Charis Books & More in Atlanta and the Bloodroot Café in Bridgeport, Connecticut, are still in business.

The function of feminist commercial spaces blurred the boundaries between social movement and entrepreneurship, women's centers and small businesses. All were grounded in a commitment to creating positive images of women—as consumers, independent social beings, entrepreneurs, businesspeople, and part of an empowered community. Without the institutionalization through public funding and oversight that some women's service agencies achieved, most feminist businesses begun in the 1970s survived only with the support of an active movement. When that waned, so did the opportunities for these establishments. The closure of most of these businesses—not unique considering the failure rate of small businesses generally—should not overshadow the significance of their existence in helping build communities, model value-driven business practices, and support an alternative vision for urban living that disrupted patriarchal and heteronormative patterns by welcoming and serving women.

"They're a 'Right On' group . . . Pitching to Help Women": Serving Women in the Nonprofit Realm

Complementing efforts undertaken in the for-profit realm, self-identified feminists of the 1970s and 1980s resurrected—and in many cases reconfigured—the kinds of women's spaces built during the Progressive Era, and for some of the same basic reasons, particularly a desire to provide women with the support they needed to live independent lives. Women's centers became invaluable sites where women of the movement could find one another as well as support services.[53] The Women's Action Alliance (WAA), an organization founded in 1971 to support grassroots organizing in the women's movement, called women's centers "the backbone of the movement" because they "often provide[d] the first contact with organized feminist activity for women looking for involvement."[54] The centers served the needs of the communities and neighborhoods in which they were located. They usually hosted a range of activities, referrals, and classes, but even more fundamentally, they functioned as "simply a place for women to get together with other women—to talk, relax, console, plan, meet, laugh and cry in a supportive environment."[55] Women's centers provided some of the key physical spaces in which traditionally domestic or private matters, from childcare to sexuality, could be brought into the public sphere. Often starting in the private spaces of activists' homes or in quasi-public spaces borrowed from sympathetic organizations, the growth of the feminist movement in the 1970s made the need for these centers to find quarters of their own more urgent. The women's centers spawned by second-wave feminism served as important hubs, in the words of Finn Enke, that "interfaced with public institutions to increase women's sexual, economic, and spatial autonomy."[56] Through visible and quasi-public institutions, these centers offered a mix of direct services, education, and outreach on a range of issues pertaining to women's lives.

In many cities, early women's centers found space and organizational support in women's institutions from the early part of the century, particularly YWCAs, a tangible link to a tradition of challenging the constraints placed on women in twentieth-century American society. As Fran Willis of the NOW chapter in Essex County, New Jersey, explained, "The 'Y' isn't just a place to make pottery any more. They're a 'Right On' group, and they're right in there pitching to help women."[57] This center, the product of a coalition of women's groups in the area, offered a staffed phone line to assist women twelve hours a day, a drop-in space open six days a week, and a "headquarters for dispatching information" on the women's movement and social services. The new women's center offered classes on financial and legal issues and workshops on returning to work or school and on racism and sexism. It also kept a referrals list for lawyers, childcare, counseling, doctors, employment agencies, and more. Other YWCAs followed this example. Staff members from the Y framed these developments as a coherent evolution of the institution's mission: "The YWCA has always worked for women and supported them in whatever roles and goals they have chosen to follow. . . . This center speaks to the feminist in all women. . . . We hope the center will help women develop a new awareness of themselves and their potential."[58] As was the case with most women's centers begun in the 1970s, programs served both political and pragmatic ends as they sought to empower women and connect them to resources for support.

Other centers emerged from women's organizations seeking an established and visible space for the movement. In Los Angeles, a coalition of nine women's organizations, including those representing union and working-class women, the local NOW chapter, and several small, radical women's groups, spent four months planning the Women's Center, which opened in January 1970. The founders strongly believed that a stable space would help women new to the movement find it: "We feel (optimistically) that once we get an address—i.e., the actual physical, visible headquarters—that women will start to crawl out from under the woodwork." They expected the storefront center to serve as "visible evidence that 'something is being done' about women's problems and needs."[59] In New York City, funds paid to a coalition of women who wrote a supplement for the *Ladies' Home Journal* covered the rent for a year on a loft on West Twenty-Second Street. This women's center opened in the spring of 1970 and served as a meeting space and an information clearinghouse for the women's movement, which, a reporter rightly noted, "had begun to resemble an epidemic" but was still "largely unstructured."[60]

One of the more direct and lasting ways in which women's social change organizations could achieve a permanency for the women's movement and support a reconception of urban space was by actually owning buildings rather than just renting or borrowing spaces. Being a property owner—a highly vaunted position in American society—gave the organizations that could pull it off a new source of authority for inserting themselves into the public sphere. Just as many women's organizations in the early twentieth century had come to believe, some feminist organizations of the 1970s and 1980s decided that they needed a physical space of their own. As different as these two eras in women's organizing were, owning a building came from a fairly comparable set of broad desires and had a remarkably similar impact on the organizations that undertook it. Just as some reform-oriented groups of the early twentieth century had learned decades earlier, some second-wave feminist organizations came to believe that, in order to further their mission, they needed a space that reflected their values and served the needs of women. By owning a building, however, organizations established a new and long-term relationship with the physical districts in which they located themselves and a new relationship with the political and economic structures of the city and surrounding neighborhoods—relationships that would challenge them to redefine their missions and constituencies. Owning a building shifted the very nature of the work these organizations undertook and did so in ways that made the work of the different generations of activists intriguingly similar. Gendered spaces such as these, to use Daphne Spain's framing, "qualified as both a perceived space of objective bricks and mortar and a conceived space of meaning and symbolism."[61] These buildings announced women's intention to take up visual and physical space over the long term and to thereby claim broad rights for women to exist as autonomous individuals.

The story of The Women's Building (TWB) begins with the founding of an organization called the San Francisco Women's Centers (SFWC) in 1970. During its first decade, the SFWC founded a domestic violence shelter, launched a feminist credit union, and organized the Women's Alcohol Coalition. The SFWC also helped organize the 1976 Conference on Violence against Women. The search for a building to own was prompted by the organizers' inability to find a large public space for this conference that would allow them to exclude men, whose presence they felt would hamper women's dialogue about violence. After a painstaking process of self-examination and coalition building, the SFWC purchased a four-story building on Eighteenth Street in the Mission District in 1979 and named it The Women's Building (TWB). Renovations created offices, meeting rooms, and a large performance space, all of which were made available to organizations and events that advanced gender equity, provided resources for women, or supported multicultural visual and performing arts.

As SFWC members quickly discovered, organizations that bought and developed property had before them an entirely new set of resources to be deployed in the interest of social justice. They could and did reshape properties to reflect the movement's needs, renovating and repurposing to keep pace with evolving goals and also making choices about who could use the space and on what terms. But buildings also took constant tending, requiring staff and maintenance, and they needed updating. For The Women's Building, "the contradiction sharpened," one member reflected, "between SFWC's identity as community organizers par excellence and the need to become building managers and master all the skills required to do this."[62] Members struggled to adapt their collective-consensus-unity model of organization and decision-making to the realities of owning a building, acting as a landlord, and essentially running a business.

Early organizers were continually surprised by the expectations that people had for the building. People "assume that the existence of a physical structure which is larger than any other women's structure in the world (or symbol for women) must be huge and full of resources," one frustrated staff member exclaimed.[63] The cadre of organizers at the heart of the SFWC gradually came to understand that the fact that they had a building at all led many feminist and community groups to assume that TWB "had it made" and did not need money or volunteers' time. Desperate to get a handle on their decision-making structure, define the "publics" they should serve, and decide on a future for the organization and the building, staff and volunteers began a long series of strategic planning meetings in 1982—led by, tellingly, a business professor.[64] This process led the organization to finally unite "around the fact that the Building was both a political and fundraising asset, an important resource in the community's fight for social change and that our role, as political activists, was to master the skills needed to manage this facility, make it self-sufficient financially and preserve and develop the progressive perspective of its politics." By the late 1980s, staff time had shifted away from programming as the organization recognized the need to recruit women with financial planning, personnel, real estate, and building management expertise for the board of directors.[65] Their activism became more about how they used—and let others use—the building and less about the intangible resources of networking, organizing, and planning that were the foundation of what they had done before. "We struggle," one member admitted early in TWB's existence, "about whether we are a neighborhood center or a women's center."[66]

As The Women's Building moved forward, members who initially had little connection to the neighborhood and no sense of historic mission in their work became more integrated into the neighborhood as they became increasingly cognizant of the historic value of the building itself.[67] TWB offered substantial bilingual programming and services and high-quality childcare

A second wave of feminist institution building in the late twentieth century offered women space for classes, meetings, and social services. (Photo by Nathan Voght, The Women's Building, San Francisco, CA)

to a heavily Spanish-speaking neighborhood, while also campaigning for abortion rights for low-income women and women of color, championing immigrant rights, and promoting antiracism groups—all important causes in the Mission District community. Maintaining the building became a way of maintaining the movement and building feminism into a broader set of social justice issues alive in the Mission.

If owning a building pushed San Francisco activists toward providing services, the history of local YWCAs reveals that buildings could also move the traditionally service-oriented organizations created in an earlier era in the opposite direction and politicize them. The San Diego YWCA, like many of its counterparts in the 1970s, found itself saddled with an aging downtown building in an era of suburban growth. Rather than invest in much-needed structural updates, the organization closed the three residential floors in 1971 and tried to sell the whole building. The situation was salvaged in the late 1970s, however, with a community development grant sponsored by the US Department of Housing and Urban Development (HUD) and a new focus emerging from second-wave feminism. Newly renovated with federal funds, the downtown Y reopened in 1980 as a racially desegregated facility, the city's first domestic violence shelter for women, and, later, a shelter for homeless women. YWCAs in other cities similarly re-created their institutions for a new era. Brooklyn and Detroit, for example, both successfully secured federal funds to open their first domestic violence shelters in former YWCA residences.

To follow the history of YWCAs on the local level is to see that urban YWCAs and 1970s feminist organizations, such as the San Francisco Women's Centers, actually had a good deal in common in the late 1970s and early 1980s. At least some of that similarity derived from the fact that both anchored their programs in large, visible urban spaces. These organizations existed in relationship to their cities and made a lasting and visible impact on their neighborhoods through their buildings. Owning a building slowed down any changes these organizations wanted to make—because of the capital needed to make physical changes and the responsibilities of day-to-day operations—but also gave them stability and resources to weather those changes. Rather than volunteers, instigators, critics, or activists, members of these organizations became primarily service providers—albeit providers with a keen sense of social justice and awareness of the discrimination faced by certain groups of urban women. Owning and running a large building was a risky business for social change organizations, but in the end it had a stabilizing effect for these organizations. Over time, physical institutions allowed some women's organizations to become significant and lasting social institutions that adhered to far more inclusive practices than the mainstream commercial society around them.

"New Ones Spring Up to Take Their Place": Institutionalizing Feminism

Although some of the broad-based women's centers created in the 1970s survived the decade, most did not. The fate of women's centers reflects the general trajectory of the women's movement of the late twentieth century but also reveals the institutionalization that many women's organizations, particularly those dedicated to specific causes, underwent as the movement progressed and eventually faded. "The institutionalization of feminist activism," concludes Finn Enke, "entailed building feminist networks and, at the same time, increasing involvement with mainstream social service agencies and funding sources."[68] Although the mass-based feminist movement peaked in the late 1970s and started to dissipate in the 1980s, work on some of the causes and tangible gains of the movement continued in rape crisis centers, domestic violence shelters, and women's health centers. Many of these remain in operation today and receive enough public funding to maintain a stable existence and physical presence in American cities.

The Women's Action Alliance, which was founded specifically to propagate and support feminism on the local level, attempted to connect grassroots efforts across the country beginning in 1971. The high-profile feminists behind this national organization, Gloria Steinem among them, believed that "women begin to make new lives for themselves by working with others who have already conquered the problems they face," and that helping women find one another and existing organizations was a key first step to "meet women's needs" and help "large numbers of women who want to change their lot in life."[69] The WAA published resources on managing and financing multifunction women's centers and undertook an ongoing project in the 1970s and 1980s of cataloging women's centers, domestic violence and rape crisis centers, counseling program training centers, women's commissions, and health centers specifically for women in an effort to "make these services visible."[70] In the course of doing this research, the WAA found that the average life span for a women's center was only two years. Of the three hundred centers it identified in 1976, only half still existed three years later. Rather than show alarm over what this might mean for women and the services to which they had access, the WAA explained that "women's centers often live and grow and change into something else—a women's bookstore or restaurant, a social action group." The WAA also noted that many broadly conceived women's centers tended to become "more specialized, offering assistance to battered women or rape victims." "For all the centers that die each year," it reported with confidence, "new ones spring up to take their place."[71] Moreover, the WAA sought to support this process, offering best practices, consulting, and other resources to those starting centers or looking to more deeply institutionalize their work. Federal funding also provided crucial support for grassroots feminist initiatives transitioning into lasting institutions; funding sources such as the 1973 Women's Educational Equity Act (funding did not start until 1976) underwrote, for example, the National Women's Centers Training Project, and grants from HUD funded the conversion of some downtown YWCAs into domestic violence shelters.

This process of institutionalization—and particularly the bureaucratization of feminist efforts such as antiviolence work—pushed social change–oriented organizations away from political organizing and into providing basic social and economic supports. As many of the early activists left these organizations, they were replaced by professional social workers and counselors. Even the repurposing of obsolete spaces for feminist initiatives took different forms than the confrontational tactics used in New York City and Boston in 1971. Brooklyn, New York, for example, turned over a shuttered maternity hospital to feminists wanting to create a domestic violence shelter called Women's Survival Space. New York City rented out an old firehouse in the Chelsea district for $1 per month to house the Women's Liberation Center.[72] In Detroit, the languishing downtown YWCA found new purpose when Jackie Washington, a local NOW activist, convinced the Y's board to turn the upper floors of the old building into the city's first shelter for domestic violence survivors and their children. As feminists successfully framed intimate partner violence, childcare, and women's health care as social issues in the 1970s and 1980s, they increasingly insisted on public resources to address the issues. In cities across the country, these resources took the form of safe "public" spaces for women who did not have safe private spaces.

Other feminist causes found a path to institutionalization through public funding sources and cooperation with public services such as law enforcement and the court system. In the 1980s and 1990s, many of these grassroots efforts, even some that were extralegal in their creation, were codified into formal and permanent institutions. Sometimes public entities took on the management of the institution, and sometimes they provided funding or other resources. Social service providers, such as rape crisis centers and shelters, became knitted into the fabric of legal and public service structures as their codification led to greater cooperation with police, departments of public health and protective services, hospitals, and the court system. Finally, others moved from the quasi-public informal realm into a more permanent state through the pressures of tax codes and similar structural forces. Charis Books & More, for example, separated out much of its activist work from its commercial enterprise by creating a nonprofit organization dedicated to social justice pursuits that operated separately from the for-profit work of the bookstore.

Institutionalization solidified some of the tangible outreach efforts of feminism, but it also deepened some of the challenges faced by the movement, especially the difficulty of inclusion. As has become more apparent in recent years, aligning services and programs with the police unintentionally (though many would argue not unpredictably) fed mass incarceration.[73] Considering the long entanglement of gender segregation with white supremacy, it perhaps should not be surprising to see that solutions built heavily around white women's experiences led to such an outcome as the system responded most readily to demands for safety by doubling down on the persecution and prosecution of men of color. Women of color certainly challenged white feminists to see their complicity in systems of racial oppression. The Combahee River Collective, a group of Black lesbian feminists, insisted that "eliminating racism in the white women's movement is by definition work for white women to do."[74] Some white feminists avoided this challenge, but others did struggle with how to do the "work." The Women's Liberation Center in New York, for example, found itself competing for affordable space with a group addressing drug addiction and other social issues among the mostly Puerto Rican residents of its Chelsea neighborhood. Lois Chaffee, a member of the center's building committee, said, "Who could be against anything that's for poor Puerto Rican mothers and children? But there isn't much feminist money around either. We can't let 'us' be pitted against 'them,' but I'm beginning to hear that word 'priorities' as an antifeminist code word for 'sexism.'"[75]

Defining the community to be served, building inclusive missions, and working beyond the boundaries created by physical geography remain ongoing challenges for many feminist-based service organizations. Nevertheless, shelters for women and centers providing key services for women created safe quasi-public spaces for women who did not have safe private spaces. In doing so, many of these institutions repurposed obsolete women's spaces to meet the needs of the late twentieth century.[76] Sometimes women demanded these institutions and services, sometimes government offered them, and sometimes it was a combination of negotiation and opportunity.

Conclusion

When it came to creating public spaces for women, the feminist movement produced two models in the 1970s: one was the nonprofit, service-oriented institution, such as a women's center, shelter, or health center, and the other was a commercial model that sought to serve and promote women and feminism through small for-profit businesses. Both models flourished into the 1980s as physical embodiments of feminist demands for women's greater access to the freedoms and services of the public sphere.

The creation of women's spaces melded the service ethic of earlier institution-building efforts from the Progressive Era with a sharper political analysis and cultural critique. Women's centers, shelters, bookstores, credit unions, health centers, restaurants, coffeehouses, and bars provided a physical location in which the feminist movement could happen. These spaces also served as psychological and social "comfort zones" in which women, as women, could feel they belonged, that their needs mattered, that they were safe, and that the stresses of functioning as a woman in other public spaces might be countered or at least held at bay. These places could serve as the social counterparts to the political work of the movement, as happened with "Gerry nights" at the Woodbridge Tavern in Detroit, or their functions in support of women might be intertwined with support services, as happened regularly in The Women's Building in San Francisco. They might also function as more straightforward service-based institutions, such as domestic violence shelters at urban YWCAs; at the same time, their very existence testified to the success of the feminists who problematized violence against women and leveraged public funds to address the issue.

Although social movements are often associated with marches and rallies, the way in which feminists sought to take up space in order to disrupt androcentric practices and institutions represented a different, yet viable, tactic for creating social change. Making this connection between controlling space and making change, folk singer Holly Near said, "If we are building a culture that is respectful of our lives then we need a respectful place in which to build it."[77] For as long as these enterprises and institutions lasted, they helped build the movement by providing spaces in which it could be built. For feminists in the 1970s and 1980s, creating and occupying space was a tactic not only for creating "comfort zones" and outposts for women outside their homes, but also for achieving the goal to establish women's physical presence in the larger public sphere.

7
Privacy in Public
The (Almost) Policy Revolution

In the waning years of the twentieth century, a remarkable thing happened: women's issues hit government with unprecedented visibility and intensity. Media dubbed 1992 the "year of the woman" as the largest number of women ever secured elected office. With women occupying congressional seats, governorships, state legislatures, mayor's offices, and city council chambers, policies specific to protecting women's rights were passed and implemented in record numbers. Controversies and high-profile incidents connected to women's presence and safety in public space often provided the spark that led to formal change. In a familiar pattern, however, protecting women in public never took center stage in the resulting policies. As much as feminists despaired over responses to sexual harassment in the workplace—revealed so starkly in the treatment of Anita Hill when she testified against Supreme Court nominee Clarence Thomas in 1991—and attacks on welfare programs, there were some developments to cheer over. New federal legislation aimed to curb violence against women and protect women's access to abortion clinics. On the state level, legislatures passed laws to protect victims of stalking, affirm the right to publicly breastfeed, and provide for more adequate public bathrooms.

Activists and reformers had been fighting for women on these issues for decades. By the 1990s, however, professionals and elected officials (at least some of whom had come from activist backgrounds) articulated a broad understanding of gender discrimination and partnered with policymakers to make substantive change. Discussions surrounding the passage and implementation of these policies brought long-standing issues associated with women's access to public space onto the public agenda. The resulting legislation responded to women's issues, but often in ways that proved more reactionary than preventative, and its implementation sometimes created controversy and backlash.

Nevertheless, the issues addressed in the 1990s disrupted traditional notions of public and private and often revealed the fictitious nature of these binary categories. At the heart of discussions of gendered access to public space at the end of the twentieth century lay competing notions of whose rights needed protection. New policies raised key aspects of the gendering of public space and its consequences for women, but public response often focused less on women's rights and more on familiar tropes of women's vulnerability and responsibility to avoid danger on their own. In sum, the design and implementation of new laws and policies in the 1990s, and the public response to them, brought uneven progress that largely left in place core assumptions about women's need for protection—and their worthiness to receive it.

"We're Like Test Pilots Sometimes": Gender Segregation and Violence against Women

In 1991, Maggie Hadleigh-West engaged in an "act of retaliation" for all the harassment she had experienced. She took a handheld video camera with her onto city sidewalks. When she encountered uninvited comments, touches, questions, or assessments of her body from men, she challenged the power dynamics of the situations by turning on her camera. She confronted men and recorded the responses provoked by her actions—the denial, the defensiveness, and the hostility. Her camera became a "tool for revenge."[1] As she explained, "I pursued as I felt pursued." Through this process, she reclaimed "the power that is taken from me every time I step out of my own house. The power over my own body, over my voice." Evoking women's continued sense of embattlement in the public spaces of American cities and American society more broadly, Hadleigh-West titled the film she made from this footage *War Zone.* As her voice-over explains, "For a woman, the streets are a war zone. Every day is a battle to stay safe, whether it is through isolation, denial, or precaution." As her title suggests, even at the end of the twentieth century women continued to experience cities as hostile and potentially violent.

Violent events leading up to the closing decade of the century reinforced a fundamental component of the twentieth-century system of gender segregation: women's fears. Moreover, the dangers of urban space for women were often painted in highly racialized terms. Between 1985 and 1988, a serial killer targeted African American sex workers in Los Angeles, murdering seven and injuring another. Police did little to seek justice for these women, despite community pressure. By contrast, when a young white woman out for an evening jog in New York City's Central Park in 1989 was severely beaten and raped, the criminal justice system leapt into action within a matter of hours. Doctors did not expect the woman to ever fully recover, and she never regained any memory of that evening. Police quickly rounded up five Hispanic and African American teenagers who were in the park that night. These young men were swiftly charged and then wrongfully convicted of the brutal attack. Years later the real assailant, a white man, confessed. The youth were exonerated, but only after spending a dozen years in prison. A fascinated public and overeager media brought all the familiar gendered and racialized tropes about public space to bear on the case of the "Central Park jogger." Immediate suspicion fell on young men of color. Plenty of people, however, even those who supposedly sympathized with the victim, raised the issue of whether the woman should have been in the park at all. The alleged perpetrators fit social stereotypes for violent criminals, and the woman victim suffered public judgment for having invited the attack by being out alone. It was a stark indicator that gender segregation and white supremacy continued to travel hand in hand.

These violent incidents were indicative of the race problem of the late twentieth century. The legal system and American society more generally did not perceive African American women as worthy victims but did view men of color as likely perpetrators. In addition to the racial implications, these incidents also say something about gender and the challenges that women continued to face in accessing public space in the late twentieth century. It is not hard to imagine the disdain with which the Black prostitutes were treated by police and the media, an issue raised jointly by white feminists and Black community members in Los Angeles during the 1980 Take Back the Night demonstration. The common perception was that, as sex workers, they had exposed themselves to danger by being on the street—a perception rooted in racist stereotypes of African American women as hypersexual that had endured since the slavery era. By contrast, the Central Park jogger was a young, white, upwardly mobile, middle-class woman. Her status evoked sympathy but did not protect her from gendered public censure. While the state was not interested in pursuing the killers of Black prostitutes and was overly determined to punish Black and brown men in the rape of a white woman, the women in both situations were blamed to some extent for being out in the first place and thereby "making" themselves victims. Despite the work of feminists over the preceding two decades—and perhaps even in response to it—the sensationalization of the Central Park jogger case and the invisibility of violence against African American women were stark indicators of how little had changed in the cultural understandings of women's presence in public spaces or the gendered and racialized terrain of public space.[2]

The case against and eventual wrongful conviction of the African American and Hispanic youth known as the "Central Park Five" clearly reveals the racial injustices and fissures of American society in the late twentieth century. The press at the time readily accepted the Black and brown teens as the culprits, calling them a "pack of wolves" and deeming the crime symbolic of a "meltdown in our cities" at the hands of people of color.[3] Any suggestion that racism might be at work in the focus on the boys during the early months of the case was met with a mocking tone as pundits cited the "desertion" of fathers of color and other failings of the "underclass" that, in their telling, had led to "anarchy in the streets."[4] A 1989 *US News & World Report* article even suggested the case against the Central Park Five might be good since it would bring the discussion of urban dysfunction front and center and finally lead to improved policing and juvenile delinquency policies.[5] After the exoneration of the youth twelve years later, a new wave of scholarship emerged exploring these aspects of the case.[6] The substantial mainstream media attention that followed—including documentaries, movies, news profiles, and talk show treatments—focused the public remembrance of the case firmly around race issues and erased the gendered aspects of the events.

Examination of the reactions to the Central Park crime between when it first broke and before the wrongful convictions came to light reveals clear links to the long-standing discussion of women's place in public and the intersections of gender with the workings of class and race. Early reports on the crime not only emphasized the jogger's youth and attractiveness, but also repeatedly signaled her class status with reference to her job as an investment banker. Columnist Gail Collins noted in 1989 that the victim's class was an essential component of public interest in the case—suggesting that the key to the case was how the crime made upper-class New Yorkers feel less safe.[7] Journalism professor Helen Benedict's content analysis of mainstream press coverage in the wake of the attack revealed the common perception at the time that, "if the jogger did not exactly deserve what happened to her, she certainly 'failed' to prevent it."[8] This sentiment, according to Greg Tate of the *Village Voice*, suggested "a silence around the issue of rights of women as human beings" in the coverage of the jogger case.[9]

News of the crime did make some women feel less safe, though not necessarily less committed to their rights to public space. *Village Voice* writer Andrea Kannapell told her readers that the jogger "could have been me." Referring to all the young white women of the city who had to prove to themselves that the "stories of unfaceable danger were lies" whenever they went out alone. She noted, "We're like test pilots sometimes, testing the limits of safety within our lives."[10] In 1989, *Glamour* named the "Central Park Jogger" one of its women of the year, bestowing recognition on her "for tragically proving that women cannot take their personal safety for granted, even if they're young, fearless, smart, upper middle class and on familiar ground."[11] This framing of her significance overtly positioned her class—and the suggestion of her whiteness—as what should have protected her. Thus, the magazine did little to disrupt the expectation that cities were dangerous for women even as they complained about it. Closing with the comment that "women are furious about having to live in fear of the dark and will fight to 'take back the night,'" the essay linked women's frustration at further evidence of their vulnerability in public space to a longer tradition of demanding access.[12]

At the close of the last decade of the twentieth century, then, narratives about the danger that women faced in public and their responsibility for avoiding such danger held strong, even alongside newer messages that women had some right to be there. What did change in the 1990s was the creation of state and federal laws seeking to address particular forms of gendered violence, including violence associated with women's presence in public space. In the late 1980s and early 1990s, for example, "stalking" entered the public lexicon to describe the act of following and intruding on another.[13] The brutal and highly publicized murder of a white Los Angeles actress by a deranged fan who followed her home from work brought attention to the issue. California subsequently passed the first anti-stalking law in the country. High-profile celebrity cases drew attention to the issue initially, but discussion of this kind of violence quickly shifted to sensationalized stories of former partners hounding ex-wives and infatuated would-be lovers pursuing the objects of their affections. The focus on distraught admirers pursuing women who had rejected them both romanticized and eroticized the crime and often suggested that some women might have been leading the men on.[14] This perpetuated the ways in which gender segregation had long been turning women from victims into perpetrators.

States did, however, respond to the sudden attention to stalking with new legal measures that expanded the reach of restraining orders, legally known as personal protection orders (PPOs). Before the 1990s, courts approved PPOs only for people in an intimate or domestic relationship with their harasser and only if the perpetrator represented a physical threat. The anti-stalking laws passed in the 1990s worked differently in different states, but they generally either revised existing laws or created new and complementary categories of restraining orders. Anti-stalking measures, whatever their format, expanded the definitions of harm warranting protection and categories of abusers against whom they might be issued. These orders allowed for court-backed injunctions against someone who was not a partner. They also recognized the "emotional distress" from being stalked. Under these laws, stalkers could be defined as anyone who engaged in "willful" and "repeated" actions that "would cause a reasonable person to feel terrorized, frightened, intimidated, threatened, harassed or molested."[15] These laws reflected an emerging willingness to confront domestic and intimate partner violence and recognize the violence women might experience outside the confines of their homes.

Once a substantial number of states had anti-stalking statutes on the books, Congress moved to improve enforcement by mandating the recognition of PPOs from other states. These laws represented a move away from the "stranger danger" understanding of rape and recognized a more complex relationship between power and violence. The laws acknowledged the ways in which public space could make an individual feel vulnerable, particularly someone from a group already thought to be "in danger" while in public, which certainly included—almost exclusively so—women. Researchers studying the phenomenon in the 1990s found that 80 percent of stalking victims were women and 8 percent of women had been stalked at some point in their lifetime.[16]

Despite the swift legal changes and the cultural recognition it bestowed, American society did not seem much surprised by the preponderance of stalking. The feminist journal *Off Our Backs* reported on stalking data in 1997 with the snarky headline "Stop the Presses: New Study Finds Men Stalk Women a Lot."[17] Over the course of the 1990s, and despite the new laws, attention to stalking normalized stalking, essentially recognizing it as a part of "normal, everyday practices of establishing, advancing, and ending relationships."[18] Activists working to eradicate domestic violence solidified this association by emphasizing that well over half of stalking victims had been pursued by a family member or intimate partner. This association framed stalking as the public manifestation of the plight of the battered woman, but in fact 23 percent of women victims had been stalked by a stranger and 19 percent by an acquaintance.[19] And the advice given to women harkened back to that offered over the preceding century whenever women's safety registered on the public radar: vary your routes home, change your routines, do not travel alone, and call the police if you feel unsafe.[20] The private and public dangers of stalking received societal attention, but not disruption.

On the federal level, a broad-ranging effort to address violence in women's lives coalesced with the Violence Against Women Act (VAWA). Initially proposed in 1990, proponents of the bill acted from—and reinforced—the idea that women naturally faced certain types of crime. Backers pointed to "several well-publicized cases of violence against women in the last two years that have crossed social and economic lines," including the Central Park jogger case.[21] Speaking on behalf of the National Organization for Women, Helen Neuborne explained: "Obviously, men fear crime in many contexts. But women have to fear virtually all of the crimes directed at men, plus all those directed at women. When a woman is attacked for being in a place where men are safe, it is just as much a bias-related crime as a racially motivated murder."[22] Then-senator Joseph Biden, who introduced the bill, expressed concern that women did not enjoy the "essential human freedom" of living without fear. "There's been an epidemic of violence against women in the last 15 years," he said. "I'm trying to make the streets a little bit safer."[23] The senator's implication was that women were generally vulnerable, especially in public, and the best they might expect was to feel just "a little bit safer."

Scholarly studies and even some probing journalism offered other interpretations by presenting more nuanced assessments of the violence women faced in the closing years of the twentieth century. Different theories of the rise in violent crimes included women's increased propensity, as a result of the feminist anti-rape movement of the 1970s, to report crimes such as rape. The ubiquity of violence toward women in the media through pornography, advertisements, and television and movies appeared in these discussions, which also often noted the economic competition between men and women and a backlash against feminism.[24] The design of VAWA, however, took little of this into account. Passed in 1994, the act claimed to address "a national tragedy played out every day in the lives of millions of American women at home, in the workplace, and on the street" by providing funds for social services to support victims and improving law enforcement practices surrounding rape, domestic violence, and harassment. It was the first piece of federal legislation to address a wide range of issues faced predominantly by women and represented a substantial victory for the women's organizations that had fought for it. The act funded studies of violence against women, improved police training, facilitated the purchase of rape kits, and supported crisis centers and shelters. It also mandated that states recognize anti-stalking and restraining orders, no matter their geographic origin.

In the end, VAWA did not make public space (or even private space) safer. Instead, it funded programs to assist women *after* they had experienced violence in public. This approach left undisturbed the fundamental assumption that public space was dangerous for women and thereby also left untouched the idea that it was up to women to avoid potential danger by restricting their presence, presentation, and use of public space. The programs funded by VAWA that sought to interrupt domestic violence in the private sphere of women's homes reinforced the message, perhaps unintentionally, that accessing public space was somehow optional for women. Attention to stalking and the funding of victim social services reinforced an association of women with vulnerability and victimization while only purporting to attend to women's safety.[25]

And as scholars in the twenty-first century have explored, antiviolence initiatives such as (and often funded by) VAWA ultimately furthered the stigmatization of women as victims of violence and led to "the unforeseen growth of a criminalized society," which manifested in the mass incarceration of men of color.[26] Esther Madriz found evidence of the impact of this growth in the "law-and-order" state of the 1990s. The African American women she interviewed expressed more fear for the safety of their Black sons than for themselves.[27] In other words, the "safetification" of American society that took place in the 1990s did little to make women feel safer and did much to make men of color and those who loved them feel even less safe, a conclusion that is reminiscent of the Central Park jogger case.[28]

Despite complicated cultural effects, passage of anti-stalking legislation and VAWA generally received high praise from feminists and pro-woman groups. It was the capstone to decades of anti-rape activism.[29] The act treated rape and domestic violence as social problems in a very public way. By targeting violence against women specifically, the act could be read as recognizing a connection between violence and women's position in American society more generally. Unsurprisingly, however, VAWA did not end violence, and the feminist antiviolence movement continues to this day.

Evidence of women's ongoing concern over violence in public spaces continued to appear throughout the 1990s and into the early 2000s. Maggie Hadleigh-West produced an expanded version of her 1991 film *War Zone* in

1998 that included the harassment stories of women of color, explored cities outside New York City, and forefronted the connections between the harassment women experienced in public and domestic violence. As African American women became far more vocal about street harassment and other types of both intra- and interracial violence they faced, they organized public demonstrations such as the Million Woman March in Philadelphia in 1997. Women of many races flooded Washington, DC, and other cities to take a stand against gun violence and its toll on their children and communities as part of the Million Mom March in 1999. Meanwhile, a robust women's peace movement opposing US-sponsored violence on the global stage emerged with groups such as CODEPINK: Women for Peace. Taken together, these actions suggest that women supported an expansive antiviolence movement at the turn of the twenty-first century, one that encompassed, but did not stop, with gender-based violence.

"Impediments to Equally Navigating the World at Large": Reopening Public Bathroom Debates

At the end of the twentieth century, the issue of public restrooms also reemerged in public debates. Rather than clubwomen and reformers leading the charge, as they had a century earlier, lawyers and architects found allies among some lawmakers. The professionals behind this effort, most of whom were academics rather than city officials or urban planning practitioners, declared public facilities inadequate and thereby "one of the last bastions of gender discrimination."[30] Public bathrooms, explained architecture professor Kathryn Anthony, "have been a taboo topic . . . they are a hidden part of our environment, a secret part of our environment that we don't talk about much. And we have to bring them out from under the rug."[31] This is precisely what some experts and lawmakers attempted to do in the 1990s.

The "rug" covering public bathrooms was first laid by the neglect that began in the middle decades of the twentieth century as the nation moved away from mass transit and toward more automobile travel. Full-scale abandonment of public facilities was common by the 1970s and 1980s, when, in the American imagination, drug users, the homeless, prostitutes, and those looking for anonymous sex took over public bathrooms. A study of public facilities in Portland, Oregon, concluded the "perception of public restrooms shifted from clean and friendly to unhygienic and dangerous."[32] That so many restrooms were located in public parks or at access points for public transportation—spaces suffering from a similar decline in reputation—certainly did not help either the perception or the actual state of these facilities.

Closing public bathrooms appeared to many public officials as a logical way to snuff out unwanted behavior and disperse undesirable populations. In the 1980s, Washington, DC, transit officials claimed that "other Metro systems have run into terrible problems with crime in their restrooms, which is why a decision was made at the beginning not to have public restrooms." All bathrooms in DC Metro stations were locked and the system's spokesperson "urge[d] folks to plan ahead and not to count on using Metro restrooms." Station attendants who were supposed to unlock the facilities for patrons in "an emergency" could essentially demand that individuals make their private needs public in order to receive accommodation. As one woman reported of her humiliating experience with this system, "I basically had to beg and plead before a (male) station attendant reluctantly let me use the bathroom."[33] After a woman was raped in a subway bathroom in Atlanta in 1982, transit officials in that city permanently closed restrooms in all stations. While this might have addressed the issue of safety in the facilities, it did so at the expense of patrons' needs and comfort. The Atlanta business community moved to quash a proposal to build new public restrooms downtown for fear that the facilities would anchor the city's substantial homeless population in the area. They argued, "It would draw winos and derelicts and other undesirables to the very area we are trying to get business to move back into."[34] Closing facilities was a far more direct, doable, and cheap approach to addressing concerns over crime (and therefore appealing to politicians and voters) than tackling the lack of social services, unemployment, and deeply embedded inequality that fed the growing homeless population and contributed to the idea that public restrooms attracted crime.

As many urbanites came to realize, however, closing public restrooms may have prevented some problems but it also created new ones, such as public urination. Residents of Washington, DC, complained mightily over their buildings' exteriors being used as urinals, and New York City police responded to complaints about those "too lazy, too rude, or too drunk to search for a restroom" by issuing more citations for public urination.[35] That virtually all individuals ticketed in New York were men is telling. Locked or nonexistent restrooms sent men to the streets, but no one seemed to ask what a lack of accessible restrooms might mean for those whose biology and gender made urinating on a city sidewalk difficult or unthinkable. Considering women's escalating fear of urban crime in this period, it is certainly likely that women accounted for the lack of facilities and the stereotype of restrooms as unsafe in devising their coping mechanisms, such as taking shorter trips and staying closer to home, going out only in the daytime (when public buildings and shops were more likely to be open), never going out alone, and avoiding parks altogether.[36] Even though men's behavior (and ideas about men's behavior) created the situation, women most certainly felt the fallout from it in ways that were often not acknowledged.[37]

By the 1990s, debates over public urination and concern over homelessness became significant enough to prompt some commentators and politicians to ask, "What about the public toilets we have?" and even to ponder the need for a new approach to public toilets.[38] Some cities and transit authorities moved to reopen their existing restrooms built earlier in the twentieth century. New controversies around whether and how to maintain useful public restrooms emerged from other quarters in the 1990s as well, leading a range of activists to call for more and better facilities. Seattle, Philadelphia, and San Francisco responded to demands by homeless advocates and distressed property owners in areas the homeless frequented by experimenting with self-cleaning public restrooms. Commuters in DC, Atlanta, Boston, and Baltimore demanded and received open facilities in light-rail stations. The success of the Americans with Disabilities Act (ADA) of 1990 also fueled a new round of restroom building. Although restrooms designed to serve the homeless, commuters, and those with disabilities have tended to be single-user, non-gender-specific facilities, the reopening of existing restrooms revived the traditional model of segregating public facilities by gender.

Tradition ensured that gender segregation for public restrooms would extend beyond the use of already segregated spaces. A century of signs—even signs on closed facilities—had conditioned Americans to expect gender-specific spaces for elimination.[39] Some good old-fashioned sexual stereotypes about which gender was messier than the other supplied another reason why Americans clung to the tradition of separate men's and women's restrooms as both men and women declared they would not share space with the other (allegedly messier) gender. Many women also believed they were physically safer in spaces reserved for women when engaged in acts that required some disrobing and the use of body parts associated with sex.[40] Finally, some women relished the homosocial world of the multi-user gendered bathroom, feeling that while these facilities might reinforce gender constructions that had disadvantaged women, they also offered welcome relief from performing gender in a patriarchal, heteronormative society. In other words, cultural support for gender-segregated bathrooms remained firmly in place as the issue of public bathrooms reemerged in public debates in the 1990s, when advocates began to call for "potty parity" between men and women.

Complaints from some women—and the men who had to wait for them—about the long restroom lines that women suffered through in large public venues fed a new movement for building public restrooms.[41] Several studies done in the 1980s revealed what most people already knew: because women took twice as long as men when using public restrooms yet generally had access to half the number of facilities, women seeking to use women's facilities often had to wait. In the 1990s and early 2000s, these studies and firsthand experiences became fodder for arguments for greater equity in access to restrooms. With increasing numbers of women holding elected office, some municipalities and twenty states passed "potty parity" legislation and building codes requiring a higher ratio of facilities for women to those provided for men.[42] These laws and building codes pertained, however, only to new construction or very significant renovations, leaving the rest of the urban environment unaltered.[43] Some critics tried to undermine the potty parity momentum by pointing out the incompleteness of the new policies, suggesting that it was not worth fixing any restrooms if we could not fix them all.

The framework of potty parity could not escape from the gender binary and the idea that women needed to be served as women specifically. By embedding in law the assumption that the only way to provide restroom facilities for large numbers of people was through gender-segregated facilities, the new legislation and building codes reinforced the idea that women needed not just different facilities than men but also "more" or "extra" when in public space.[44] Men's experiences were taken as the norm by which the needs of other groups were to be measured, and twentieth-century discussions of potty parity tended to feed into this mentality by focusing on how to serve women better rather than serve all users better.[45] New codes, for example, called for building women-specific restrooms with twice as many toilets as men's restrooms. As a result of this costly solution, builders sometimes opted to construct fewer facilities for men in order to keep space and expenditures to a minimum, leaving both men and women to stand in line or creating backlogs at men's facilities during events attended heavily by men. Some of the solutions offered by proponents—such as converting men's rooms to women's facilities—only increased gender hostility by coming directly at the expense of men, leading to a backlash against potty parity laws almost as soon as they were passed. Indicative of the hostility potty parity sometimes encountered, a state representative voted against Ohio's 1994 potty parity bill requiring more women's facilities in "big public spaces such as convention halls and theaters" because there was no policy requiring doors on men's toilets. In disingenuous reasoning that suggested women already had special treatment in public space, he argued that "men's restrooms should be brought up to the standard of women's before the alleged defects in women's are addressed."[46]

A host of other public bathroom issues based in gender discrimination were not addressed at all in potty parity policies. There were no policies, for example, requiring accommodations for women's clothing and accessories (who wants to put their purse on the dirty floor?), providing menstrual supplies, or ensuring safe and sanitary spaces for small children, who were most likely to be in the care of women. There were also no laws governing how far a woman had to travel within a public accommodation to find a bathroom.

In many ways, potty parity was doomed to fail, not only, and most obviously, because of the burden that the design of the legislation placed on some building owners and not others, but also because the approach lacked substantial support from feminist organizations or other advocacy groups. Few organized voices were arguing that the issue was an important one. Several elected officials took up the cause, but it was only one issue among many for them. Law professor John Banzhaf claimed the title "the father of potty parity" for his commitment to the issue. He declared equitable restroom access to be a "final frontier" for feminism, asking rhetorically, "Can women truly be said to be liberated when they often stand on interminable lines . . . to perform a necessary and often compelling biological function that men usually accomplish with virtually no wait?"[47] While Banzhaf assessed women's status by comparing their experiences to men's, others focused on how well public facilities served women's particular needs. As law professor Taunya Banks explained, "Women need to start measuring their degree of equality by public toilets. When the lines are gone, when each stall is clean and always has toilet tissue, when the stalls are reasonably comfortable, and when the dispensing machines are stocked with sanitary supplies, we probably will be much closer to achieving equality between the sexes than we are now."[48] These passionate legal voices, however, failed to convince feminist organizations that this was the issue on which to make a stand against gender discrimination.[49]

When the issue came before the US Congress in 2010, scholars and elected officials were the driving force behind H.R. 4869, the Restroom Gender Parity in Federal Buildings Act, a bill mandating parity in federal buildings. "Public restrooms are a fundamental part of our Nation's infrastructure, just as important as our roads and bridges," Kathryn Anthony stated during hearings. "Public restrooms are a health and safety issue," she continued. "In this respect, we lag far behind countries like Japan where clean, safe, available restrooms are integral parts of urban landscape."[50] Proponents likened the legislation's potential to the accessibility gains made in the wake of the Civil Rights Act of 1964, which outlawed racially segregated bathrooms. They also argued that just as "millions of persons with disabilities benefit every day from the [1990] Americans with Disabilities Act (ADA), millions of women and children would benefit every day from even greater potty parity laws."[51] Proponents of the federal building parity bill included a former mayor of Washington, DC, Sharon Pratt. In testifying from both her professional and personal experience, Pratt called the disparity in facilities for women "glaring . . . inconvenient . . . enormously inefficient, and . . . downright unfair." "We certainly are a society today that now genuinely supports equal rights for women," she continued. "However, it's a practical reality that a woman would be late for a meeting, miss much of a concert because there are built-in impediments to equally navigating the world at large. Stemming from an absence of parity in restrooms, women are still not equal."[52] There was not enough support, however, to encourage lawmakers to muster the will necessary to take the issue seriously as a form of gender discrimination. The bill failed to make it out of committee.[53]

As the potty parity issue of the late twentieth century suggested, gender discrimination was no longer located in women's exclusion but rather in their lack of full access to the public sphere and in the unique behaviors, institutions, and designs that inhibited their autonomy. In the early twentieth century, a lack of women's restrooms essentially excluded women from public space. By the end of the century, however, the availability of women's bathrooms was no longer the issue; instead, a demand had risen for women to have wait times for restrooms equivalent to men's. Potty parity legislation and building codes clearly recognized this issue, but like much of the policy of the 1990s, these efforts failed to achieve workable and inclusive solutions.

Despite the poor record of potty parity bills, discussions of it, revisions to existing building codes, and even an attempt at national legislation continued well into the early twenty-first century. The debate shifted dramatically after the turn of the century, however, when transgender activists successfully brought the violence against transgender individuals in gender-segregated bathrooms into public discussion.[54] Activists from LGBTQIA communities, particularly students on college campuses, joined the discussion, calling for protections for gender queer, nonbinary, or nonconforming individuals to be able to safely access the facilities of their choice. These advocates increasingly pressed for facilities not tied to gender at all, thereby eliminating the need to choose a bathroom or the possibility that one might be in the "wrong bathroom."[55] In a clear backlash against improved recognition of LGBTQIA rights in the early twenty-first century, conservative lawmakers in twenty-four states in the 2010s considered "bathroom bills" mandating that a person's biological sex as assigned at birth match the public restroom (or locker room) they used. Only North Carolina managed to pass this type of bill, but it was repealed after it triggered boycotts of the state.

The political aspects of the issue aside, solutions to the problem of equal access to public restrooms in recent years focused more broadly on increasing privacy and access for all rather than just for women (as women) through what has come to be called "universal design." Under this theory, advocates for the homeless, people with disabilities, transfolx, the gender-nonbinary, and women can unite in designs that remove physical, legal, and cultural barriers and increase privacy for all users (through fully enclosed and locking stalls, for example), while also increasing accessibility by making more facilities open to any user. Gender-segregated facilities clearly do not further any of these principles.

While gender-segregated bathrooms remain a common sight in America's public spaces, "family bathrooms" and "unisex" or "all-gender" facilities are becoming increasingly familiar on the urban landscape. The history and issues surrounding public bathrooms suggest that the path to full autonomy for women (and anyone who is not an able-bodied cis-man) might come from actually removing, in the words of law professor Mary Anne Case, the "tangible relics of gender discrimination" that activists of a century earlier fought so hard to secure.[56] The sex-segregated facilities of the turn of the twentieth century (first mandated in law in Massachusetts in 1887 but commonplace for all American municipalities in the decades that followed) represented an important physical point of access for women in urban public space, answering controversy over the meaning of women's presence in public with signs clearly indicating that women did indeed belong in parks, public buildings, and public accommodations.[57] This inclusion, along with other provisions specifically for women in public, did not quell the anxiety about women in public—and the resulting harassment—that stretched across the entire twentieth century. A 2017 study concluded that unisex bathrooms could cut down on women's wait times significantly, thereby meeting the goals of potty parity far more efficiently.[58] It is perhaps worth considering, then, that the key to securing women's autonomy might lie in disentangling the gender binary from the structures of our society.

"Here Is a Novel Idea, Don't Look at Them": Women's Bodies and Controversies around Public Breastfeeding

While dining in the restaurant of the Beverly Rodeo Hotel in 1984 in Los Angeles, Nicole Kaufman began to breastfeed her infant daughter. The hostess quickly approached and told her to either stop breastfeeding or go to the restroom, saying she would call the manager if Kaufman refused.[59] Kaufman was "shocked" to have been confronted, and she feared how the manager might react. Not wanting to endure the "discomfort" of nursing her child in the toilet or the humiliation of being evicted by the manager, Kaufman left the restaurant. She later filed a court case on her and her daughter's behalf.

Kaufman's case used arguments similar to those made in other contests over public space in which women requesting greater access couched their claims in the language of gendered respectability. She explained that, while "I'm a very quiet person and I'm certainly not a strident feminist," she wanted the courts to clarify her right to breastfeed. She framed herself as respectable, appropriately modest, demurring to the feelings of others, and thereby deserving of her presence in public. Despite her wishes, her case actually did little to clarify the issue as it wove in and out of the courts and the media over the next two decades.[60]

The case did, however, reveal the variety of views of women's bodies, their roles as mothers, and their rights in public space in the closing years of the twentieth century. The history of late twentieth- and early twenty-first-century responses to breastfeeding in public shows that women had good reason to fear harassment and censure when they chose to nurse outside their homes, but it also shows the growth in a popular movement to support women that was severely lacking in the 1980s when Kaufman filed her case.

From the perspective of the Rodeo Hotel restaurant management—and much of the public in the mid-1980s—breastfeeding was a private act to be done away from where others, particularly men and children, would see it. Virtually no attention was given to the impact of disallowing breastfeeding on women's mobility and autonomy. The manager of the Los Angeles restaurant never spoke with Kaufman on the day of the incident, but he later defended the actions of his staff and the policy of his restaurant by saying, "Breast-feeding in the restaurant in front of the public is offensive to the majority of the patrons."[61] His distaste became clearer when he likened nursing to "someone picking their nose."[62] His affidavit implied that women who breastfed in view of others were rude for ignoring their reactions to such a sight.

Considering these perceptions of breastfeeding, it is no surprise that the case put forward by Kaufman's lawyer was a relatively timid step in the effort to secure women's right to breastfeed in public. It forefronted the role of the nurturing mother, arguing that the potential harm to a "mother bonding with and tending an infant" required the courts to protect her civil rights over the potential discomfort of fellow patrons. The "remedy" requested by the plaintiffs, however, was incredibly accommodating of fellow diners who might object. The restaurant was asked merely to adopt a policy of seating women who might want to breastfeed in a more private section of the dining room and to add seating for nursing in the women's bathroom.[63] The decision was hardly supporting a forthright demand for women's rights.

From the nineteenth century until the 1970s, breastfeeding rates had been in decline in the United States. Women of the more economically comfortable classes turned to hired (or, before the Civil War, enslaved) wet nurses to feed their babies in the nineteenth century, establishing a strong connection between breastfeeding and lower socioeconomic classes. In the early twentieth century, those who could afford it increasingly turned to formula feeding, driven in no small part by both American faith that technology and science could produce the perfect baby food and an aggressive marketing campaign by formula makers.[64] Only in the mid-twentieth century did the rates of breastfeeding begin to slowly rise as the baby-centered parenting advocated by Dr. Benjamin Spock (as opposed to regimented or schedule-driven parenting) took hold and a small pro-breastfeeding movement anchored by La Leche League (founded in 1956) arose.[65] By the late twentieth century, most major health organizations, including the American Academy of Pediatrics, the American Medical Association, the US Department of Health and Human Services, and the World Health Organization, endorsed breastfeeding.

In the United States, women increasingly returned to breastfeeding; by 2015, four out of five newborns started out life at the breast. Only 57 percent were still nursing at age six months, however, and only 36 percent at one year. As Nicole Kaufman learned firsthand, women who heeded the strong "breast is best" messages often faced harsh judgment for doing so in public. In 1999, the Centers for Disease Control and Prevention (CDC) found that not quite half of the Americans it surveyed were comfortable seeing a woman nursing in a public space. As late as 2019, a national survey revealed that 30 percent of Americans still consider breastfeeding a child in a restaurant unacceptable.[66] So while women are told "breast is best" and the majority of infants have been breastfed for some of their early life, a significant number of Americans still think women should not breastfeed in public view. This sends mothers conflicting messages and sets them up for negative encounters—both fundamental characteristics of gender segregation.

Precisely because of the long-standing assumption that women do not naturally belong in public space and the myriad ways in which individuals and society have been allowed to interfere with women's presence in public, people appear to feel relatively free to criticize women breastfeeding in public. Breastfeeding in public is inherently transgressive, and lactating bodies are understood to be disorderly. As an excretory bodily function, expelling breast milk is sometimes categorized similarly to urination or defecation as something inherently private. Like menstruation, however, breastfeeding is something that some individuals can do but others cannot. By potentially exposing (or merely suggesting the possibility of exposing) a breast, areola, or nipple, breastfeeding crosses the social line between motherhood (a venerated status for women) and a forthright sexuality associated with low status and a lack of respectability. "Breasts are so over-sexualized," explained a member of the pro-breastfeeding La Leche League, that "it's hard for people to associate them with their natural function."[67] When women are turned away from spaces in which boy children are present, society's connection of breastfeeding to sexuality is further revealed. The public-private divide is transgressed when what many assume to be a private act is brought into public space and women's bodies are exposed to the public. The sense of transgression is particularly acute when body parts associated with sexual activity are exposed, but in a way that is not socially acceptable to sexualize (the act of breastfeeding). There are very real consequences in the battle over breastfeeding in public when it comes to women's rights in public space. Breastfeeding is a behavior that has a drastically different interpretation depending on the context and space in which it is happening. Seen as nurturing when done at home, breastfeeding is still often considered gross, inappropriate, sexual, and exhibitionist in a public place.

The issues raised by Nicole Kaufman's experience in the 1980s played out repeatedly and in increasingly confrontational tones in both courts of law and courts of public opinion throughout the 1990s and into the twenty-first century. These moments of conflict remained remarkably like Kaufman's experience as women from Denver to Washington, DC, were told to be more discreet, cover up, or remove themselves from shopping malls, swimming pools, bookstores, cafés, coffee shops, fast-food restaurants, recreation centers, playgrounds, and public buildings. With so many stories of harassment and humiliation for breastfeeding in the media over the last thirty years, a woman does not even need to have personally had a negative experience to sense the lack of support for breastfeeding in public.

While Kaufman struggled to make her case in the 1980s, arguments and outcomes began to shift slowly in favor of women's right to breastfeed in public in the 1990s and early 2000s. A combination of factors contributed to this change, including the increasing likelihood that mothers of young children worked for wages from economic necessity and early legislation on the state level protecting breastfeeding in public.[68] These developments may have encouraged more women to nurse when away from home, but the response they received created de facto segregation of breastfeeding women in public places. Behavioral expectations for women included being told to be discreet, to cover their nursing child, or to otherwise defer to the presence of others, particularly men and children. Physical separation was not necessarily mandated, although the calls for women to breastfeed "elsewhere" or in restrooms certainly contained elements of both performative deference and separation.

Technological and entrepreneurial innovations in the decades around the turn of the twenty-first century further revealed the public's expectation that women would hide their breastfeeding. The introduction of the electric breast pump in the 1990s, for example, allowed people to assume that there was always another option for feeding a baby.[69] Similarly, lactation rooms or "mother's rooms" offered women privacy and comfort for feeding their babies.[70] These developments allow society to believe that there have always been sufficient options to remain out of the public eye while nursing. Because these facilities are few and far between, however, they function in much the same way that ladies' windows at banks and post offices did in the nineteenth century. By promoting physical segregation of women, they implicitly encourage the exclusion of women from places not specifically marked for them. These developments may provide helpful options to nursing mothers, but they also allow society to continue skirting the fundamental issue of women's rights to bodily self-determination.

As confrontations over nursing in public made their way into the press in the 1990s and onto social media in the early 2000s, states responded. Women's groups and pro-breastfeeding organizations, from health care professionals to the La Leche League, offered enthusiastic support. Florida led the way in 1993 with legislation allowing women to breastfeed in any public or private location, followed up with an exemption of breastfeeding from indecent exposure laws in 1994. Other states followed suit, usually employing one or the other of these two approaches. In 1994, Michigan declared that public nudity laws did not apply to breastfeeding. California, where Nicole Kaufman had been shamed out of a restaurant for nursing in the 1980s, finally passed a law in 1997 that stated explicitly: "A mother may breastfeed her child in any location, public or private . . . where the mother and the child are otherwise authorized to be present."[71] Other less common protections for breastfeeding included those such as Alaska's (1998) and Kentucky's (2006) laws prohibiting local governments from enacting policies that would restrict or prohibit breastfeeding. A few laws merely stated the value of breastfeeding while offering no specific affirmation or protection of the rights invoked. Rhode Island is one of only a few states that included an enforcement clause in its legislation, allowing women to sue for compensatory damages.[72]

These state laws, even those, such as California's, that affirmed a right to breastfeed, did little to clarify the issue, and women continued to encounter harassment for nursing their babies where others might see them. In 2004, a woman in a Starbucks in Silver Springs, Maryland, was told by staff to cover her baby or nurse in the restroom, even though no customer had complained. Similar incidents happened at other businesses that purportedly served the public as the (real or imagined) comfort of others took precedence over the rights of women. When women did not perform public motherhood in ways deemed appropriately "discreet," they were called out by employees, patrons, bystanders, and commentators in the popular press. These reactions normalized the harassment of women. Researchers have clearly shown that the fear of being confronted in public while breastfeeding causes "physical and psychic discomfort" and often dissuades women from attempting it.[73] The trepidation caused some women to avoid public places or, in extreme cases, stop nursing their infants before they otherwise had wanted to wean them.[74]

Negative public responses and nursing mothers' fear of them have only increased with the advent of social media outlets in the early twenty-first century. A torrent of hostility against women has been unleashed across the internet. Comments ranging from snarky to vicious reveal in the starkest terms the judgments passed on women's bodies and behaviors in public. In response to the 2004 Starbucks incident, for example, anonymous commentators on a Starbucks gossip discussion board reveled in uncensored hostility. One declared, "I do not—repeat DO NOT—want to see your saggy udders flopping around in Starbucks . . . publicly displayed hooters should either have tassels on the end, or be jiggled around near a brass pole, or be ground into my face by a 19-year-old named Brandi in a strip club. They should NOT have a crotch-trophy stuck to the end of them. Dig?" Another stated that women needed to feed kids at home. "It may be a natural human function," he continued, "but so is urinating. I don't piss in the middle of Starbuck's—I'd appreciate it if you didn't breastfeed there, either."[75] A few individuals countered these attacks and called out the sexualization, objectification, and shaming inherent in the thread. "You are just upset that your sexual plaything is being used for more functional purposes and you're pouting," one countered. "Get over it."[76] These engagements revealed the hostility toward mothering in public and the sexualization of women's bodies, but they had little impact on actual policies relevant to women's rights.

State laws did, however, help launch a wave of activism, sometimes dubbed "lactivism," in the early 2000s that sought to assert and protect women's rights and normalize breastfeeding in public. While a few supporters bravely responded to the internet trolls, more showed up to a "nurse-in" at Starbucks, forcing the company to issue new policy for its staff in line with Maryland law. When Barbara Walters, star of ABC's *The View*, complained on air about a woman breastfeeding next to her on a plane in 2005 and making her "uncomfortable," two hundred women gathered outside the network's New York City headquarters to nurse their babies. Faced with the publicity generated by the demonstration, Walters walked back her comments and said, "No one is against breastfeeding, certainly not me."[77] Soon thereafter, in 2006, six hundred women engaged in a nurse-in in Washington, DC, to promote public breastfeeding.

Similar demonstrations took (and continue to take) place in public spaces, including YMCAs, public pools, and restaurants. One of the largest occurred at hundreds of Target stores across the country in 2011 after a woman took to the internet to share her story of being shamed by employees for nursing in a Texas store. Target responded with a public commitment to support breastfeeding in all its stores and offered more training to employees on the issue.[78] In a lesson to other retailers, Target has earned the loyalty of nursing mothers and their supporters for affirming and accommodating breastfeeding patrons in the years since.[79] Some pro-lactation organizations have built awareness campaigns around the power of women's purchasing power and now urge businesses to follow Target's lead and pledge to make their spaces comfortable and welcoming for breastfeeding.[80] As awareness and laws related to public breastfeeding spread over the last decade, demonstrations promoting public breastfeeding and responding to particular incidents of discrimination against women grew exponentially in the United States as well as in the United Kingdom, Australia, Mexico, and other countries around the world. The internet would prove to be a crucial tool for organizing public demonstrations against businesses and public accommodations that excluded breastfeeding mothers.

A variety of cultural factors have made the stigma and social sanctions around nursing particularly severe in communities of color, but another factor is the long history of harassment and violence in public faced by women of color.[81] Vanessa Simmons, a Ghanian-American activist, began the #NormalizeBreastfeeding hashtag in 2014 to capture and promote social media support for breastfeeding. This led to the creation of a formal organization dedicated to combating the stigma against breastfeeding among African American women and Latinas. This movement sought to "change the modern perception that breastfeeding is an intimate or private act" and reframe it in a way that would "positively impact public health initiatives."[82] In Los Angeles, the Breastfeeding Taskforce of Greater Los Angeles (later known as Breastfeed LA) launched a campaign to promote breastfeeding among Asian American women that included a photo exhibit of women nursing in a variety of settings.

By the 2010s, the issue of breastfeeding in public began to clearly turn in favor of nursing women's right to determine how and when to feed their children. A storm of protest in the 2010s brought an end to the censorship policies of social media platforms such as Facebook and Instagram that had banned images of breastfeeding.[83] In 2015, a diner at a Terra Haute, Indiana, TGI Fridays restaurant posted negative comments and a picture of a fellow patron nursing her child. The woman saw her picture and used Facebook to publicly call out the shaming nature of the original post, drawing sympathetic coverage from *People* magazine and ABC's *Good Morning America*. The man apologized, and the restaurant chain issued an unequivocal public statement proclaiming that "we fully support our guests in being able to breastfeed in our restaurants."[84] The contrast in the language used by this mother and that of "quiet" Nicole Kaufman demonstrates the distance traveled on the issue of public breastfeeding between 1984 and 2015. In a letter confronting her shamer, the TGI Fridays patron wrote, "You've shown your true colors to many and you've exposed others who are likewise simpleminded. . . . I get that you felt uncomfortable looking at my breasts. Here is a novel idea, don't look at them."[85] She recognized, but clearly rejected, objections to breastfeeding and called on wider audiences, through social media and the press, to support her, as they largely did.

Public breastfeeding raised issues of whose rights should prevail. At stake were the rights of women to freedom of movement and freedom to parent as they saw fit, but these rights were pitted against the unstated "right" of others to feel comfortable. Although society generally accepted the practice of breastfeeding, its association with women, nurturing, and breasts still cast

Women participating in a "nurse-in" in Philadelphia's 30th Street Station, 2016. (Photo by Vanessa Simmons, courtesy of Normalizing Breastfeeding, www.normalizebreastfeeding.org)

it as a private act and thereby profoundly disruptive when done in public. Without a well-established expectation that women belonged in the public sphere, observers of women who were breastfeeding, an action that appeared disruptive, felt entitled to shame them. The apparent irony that Americans accepted highly sexualized advertisements, including the Calvin Klein and Victoria's Secret ads that adorned bus stops and billboards in the 1990s, but were intolerant of breastfeeding can be explained this way: a woman feeding her child from her body in public was asserting a bodily autonomy at odds with historic gender roles, and therefore the act seemed confrontational to many. And it was on this level that men and women alike often sought to ease their discomfort by calling for modesty, for women to cover up, for women to be discreet—perhaps not so that a flash of breast, areola, or even nipple could be avoided, but so that the confrontational nature of the act would be hidden behind a highly gendered performance of modesty and deference to others.

Only in 2018 did the last two states (Utah and Idaho) pass laws to at least partially protect public breastfeeding.[86] Indicative of the lack of resolution around the issue, the Utah bill had a sentence struck for fear that permission to expose a breast during the act of feeding a baby would encourage immodesty. This concern is eerily similar to that raised in 1995 during California's early debate on the issue, when a legislator argued a law sanctioning breastfeeding could lead to "a situation where a woman could take her shirt off entirely."[87] The last state to protect public breastfeeding, Idaho, only exempted breastfeeding from indecency and obscenity laws. It contains no affirmation of a right to breastfeed in public. Even in states with laws specifying a right to breastfeed, the complicated relationship underlying private ownership of public accommodations continues to lead to conflicts. At a pool outside Minneapolis in the summer of 2018, a patron and a staff member told two nursing mothers to go to the locker room or cover up. The women referenced the Minnesota law that protects public breastfeeding "irrespective" of whether the breast is covered, but a police officer still asked the women to "vacate the property" at the behest of the pool management. Had they refused, the women would then have potentially been guilty of trespassing. After area families responded with a nurse-in the following Saturday, the pool staff "clarified" their position: while they "support nursing mothers," some patrons had been "uncomfortable" seeing the women breastfeeding their children.[88] The only clarity revealed here, of course, is that women's rights are often still conditional on the comfort of others and the performance of deference.

Conclusion

What the broader policy issues concerned with women's public presence reveal is the ongoing competition between notions of whose rights to public space will predominate. Despite the significant discussions of issues of access and safety and unprecedented new policy initiatives to stem harassment and violence in the 1990s and beyond, women's rights generally remained secondary to free speech, the needs of others, and law-and-order arguments. Programs ostensibly designed to aid women often maintained an image of women's status as victims and cities as dangerous spaces for women, particularly white women. As feminist scholars researching during this period learned, the fear of crime embedded in and reinforced by the antiviolence narratives and legislation of the 1990s ultimately controlled women's actions in powerful ways because women internalized those messages. Protections centered gender and often parental status, reinforcing gender stereotypes and suggesting that women's worth stemmed from their role as mothers. The policy gains at the turn of the twenty-first century came with eerily familiar caveats about women's behavior. Although they might have a right to travel safely and have their basic biological needs met, they still needed to remain vigilant and wary when in public, while also deferring to the needs (or comfort) of others.

In the 1990s, some aspects of women's rights became more palatable to the public and lawmakers when they were framed as changes good for the family or children. Laws protecting women's right to breastfeed in public often stressed the health benefits to the baby. Neither women's right to self-determination nor even the health benefits to women of breastfeeding were mentioned in these policies. Perhaps the greatest gains in access to bathrooms were made through the introduction of unisex and family bathrooms, which allowed women greater access when they were fulfilling the role of caregiver. Whatever gains women made in accessing public space during the 1990s, then, must be balanced against a failure to disrupt assumptions of women's weakness and continuing calls for protection tied more to women's vulnerability than to their rights.

Public breastfeeding, antiviolence initiatives, and potty parity offer useful windows into the issues surrounding women's rights in and to public space in the United States at the start of the twenty-first century. At first glance, the laws passed in the 1990s and early 2000s seem to signal a revolution in the protection of women's rights, particularly in light of the dearth of such policies enacted in the preceding century. Looking at the legislation for what it says and does not say, however, reveals that it was a revolution only half accomplished. Many of the laws offered only minimal protections, stopped short of affirming rights, and left unresolved long-standing assumptions about women's liminal standing as autonomous individuals in the public sphere. Few of the laws carried effective enforcement mechanisms, if any at all. Women and, increasingly, gender-nonbinary, queer, and transgender people are left on the front lines—on social media, in the press, and through activism and outreach—to work out the other half of the revolution through how they choose to live every day.

Epilogue

In the twenty-first century, some activists are rising to the challenge carried forward from the previous century. Women and other marginalized groups are forcing society to recognize the systemic causes and societal-level implica tions of the harassment, exclusion, and violence that they have faced in public spaces. This expansive understanding of the problem validates the discomfort and fear that many groups continue to experience. It also pushes the discussion away from individual reactions and toward broader solutions.

Public space in the United States has never been equally accessible to all. As a group, women have generally been told that cities were dangerous places for them, full of threats that they needed to avoid. Women who did not heed the warnings, ventured out anyway, and then encountered violence became either fodder for those pursuing "law-and-order" policies (which invariably increased police violence toward racial minorities and the urban poor) or lessons about what happened to women who did not behave properly. Looking back, however, we can be inspired by the steady stream of twentieth-century voices arguing for the rights of women to live their lives unfettered by moral judgments and threats of violence. This era's reformers and activists argued for women's essential right to determine the course of their lives, which included the ability to move about freely, safely, and without interference or even commentary as they went about their daily lives.

Although not often seen as such, this book argues that women's rights in public spaces are, at their core, civil rights. They have been overlooked for several interconnected reasons. Women's negative experiences have been dismissed as only fleeting encounters with strangers. Restrictions on women's movements have been reinforced as just "common sense" or framed as "privileges" or "protections," or they have been understood as solely stemming from race rather than more intersectional patterns of discrimination. What activists came to see as a right to access, autonomy, and expression some observers saw as breezy, humorous, or too fleeting to be consequential. Advertisers characterized "girl watching" as harmless fun, and men defended accosting women on the street as a kind of compliment. Social commentators found both mirth and scandal in the idea of women ordering a drink at a bar. Weren't women making a little too much out of the straying hand of a passerby on the subway platform? Wasn't telling a woman on the street that she'd be prettier if she smiled just a friendly observation? Once women called attention to the insidious ways in which these encounters and dismissals could eat away at their sense of self and security, they began to name the harm and imagine solutions. These remedies, not surprisingly, varied with the times. They included efforts to secure women public services, greater access, responsive policies, and social permission to use public space freely, sometimes by tackling gender norms and sometimes by addressing class- or race-based policies and practices. These efforts essentially claimed for women the right to maintain a sense of privacy when out in the world—to not have their body or their presence policed or restricted. While "privacy" was not a word twentieth-century activists often used, their implied conception of privacy pointed to the deeper goal of achieving the right to autonomy. With the overturning of *Roe v. Wade* by the *Dobbs v. Jackson* decision in 2022, this connection has returned the boundaries of privacy to the forefront of many women's consciousness and many activists' agendas.

Part of the work of twentieth-century activists and reformers in pursing privacy and autonomy was to imagine a new kind of city. Early in the century white reformers rejected protection by men and often replaced it with protection by the state in the form of better policing and women-controlled institutions. Women of color challenged the denial of access embedded in emerging Jim Crow practices. Middle-class reformers also supported better monitoring of commercial amusements, public conveyances, and public streets and sidewalks. They advocated for new laws mandating a higher age of consent and a more responsive court system, especially for protecting juveniles. For African American women, these efforts formed the bedrock of the mid-twentieth century's mass-based civil rights movement, which merged their calls for respect and access as women with a demand for racial justice. Where institutions serving women did not exist, these reformers built them, constructing libraries, lunchrooms, clubs, and boardinghouses. The framework of their goal of self-reliance rested on public recognition of and investment in women's right to function independently. Consequently, they envisioned dedicating both community and state resources to producing urban infra-structure, institutions, public accommodations, services, and policy that would support women's autonomy.

By the late twentieth century, those challenging gender segregation brought a keen eye to entrenched cultural trends that limited women's options for living and working independently. Feminists who opened bookstores, coffee shops, and restaurants successfully appealed to women as women and consumers. Shelters, health clinics, and women's centers problematized vio-lence against women from many backgrounds and many communities. They pointed to the lack of medical resources available to women and worked to leverage public funds to address these issues. Second-wave feminists also took up or took over space with marches and rallies in order to disrupt andro-centric urban practices and patriarchal institutions, creating social and cul-tural change alongside the policy. They introduced new language to speak about American society's "sexism" and "objectification" of women through practices such as "sexual harassment" (code for sexual misconduct at work) and "street harassment," and they challenged archaic practices that excluded women from bars and restaurants and other public accommodations. These twentieth-century reformers and activists called into question the ease with which men inhabited the city, something that was inaccessible to women so long as certain institutions, ideas, and practices remained unchallenged and women continued to fear for their personal safety and reputation.

Many of the questions these activists raised in challenging the formal and informal restrictions placed on women are on the public agenda yet again as we grapple with sexual harassment, restricted access to public facilities, bar-riers to access to reproductive health care, state-sanctioned violence, and a deeply entrenched rape culture, particularly in light of the #MeToo move-ment. A history of women's relationship to public space, then, offers a way to think critically about current women's movement goals by offering up the lessons gleaned from how activists confronted these issues during the last century.

One such important lesson is that social change requires many voices and approaches. The feminists, activists, and reformers in the twentieth century were not as separatist or discordant as stereotypes suggest. They created both transitory and sustained moments of collaboration and cooperation. They were often quite locally rooted in their activism, seeking to create change in and through the physical spaces in which they lived, worked, and played. Some feminists, for example, are remembered for being dismissive of mothers and childcare issues, yet the feminists who took over buildings in the 1970s always included support for working mothers, especially childcare centers, as a core element of the spaces and services they created. Progressive Era reformers, often dismissed as elitist or prudish, were far more realistic and practical than we generally recognize. They eschewed much of the social gospel–style moralizing and instead tried to work across class lines. More often than not, however, racial divisions held, and women of color often found white women to be unreliable allies. In sometimes remarkably parallel efforts, however, early twentieth-century activists argued working-class women should receive sufficient wages to pay their rent and be allowed to find lodging without having their morals questioned. While often fleeting and unstable, these alliances and moments of cooperation helped boost the issues into an arena where they could receive wider notice and sometimes even action.

In the twenty-first century, activist collaboration has blossomed into a deep attentiveness to the intersectionality of social identity and a more global perspective in discussions of rights. When a woman was raped and killed on a bus in India in 2012, gender activists around the world reeled and public condemnation came from all corners of the globe. When a Toronto police officer dredged up the old trope that women's presence in public invited rape ("women should avoid dressing like sluts in order not to be victimized," he said), women in cities around the world took to the streets in protests they dubbed "SlutWalks."[1] One scholar called these demonstrations an example of "transnational feminist solidarity," although it was a twenty-first-century type of solidarity in which some groups, particularly women of color and older women, loudly questioned the implications of using the term "slut."[2] Those who endorsed it reclaimed a pejorative term used for women whose behavior had been deemed too provocative. These protesters embraced arguments that activists had been developing for decades, ideas challenging rape culture, victim blaming, slut shaming, violence against women, and misogyny. The connections to the work of activists from the twentieth century could not have been clearer as marchers in SlutWalks in the 2010s took up the old chant from Take Back the Night marches: "Whatever we wear, wherever we go, yes means yes and no means no!"[3]

Another lesson from the twentieth century is that challenges to the dominant narratives of danger tend to coincide with historical moments when women seek other forms of social change in politics, economics, or civil rights. This should come as no surprise, really, as women's standing as full citizens lies at the root of all these issues. This explains why calls for women's access to public space crested amid the social and economic reforms of the early twentieth century, then with the protests of the 1960s and 1970s, and then again in the 2010s. Along with racial and class issues, social movements in these periods created space in which to call out gender-based harassment, violence, and exclusion, but they also rejuvenated ultraconservative cultural and political responses. The support for independent working women in the early twentieth century that led to the creation of libraries, lunchrooms, and boarding-houses for the "working girl" fell out of favor in the 1920s as the nation turned its attention to rooting out radical politics (the first Red Scare) and pursuing anti-immigrant policies following World War I. The hard-fought gains of the civil rights movement, the New Left, feminism, Black Power, and other social movements of the 1960s and 1970s were followed by serious retrenchment with the turn to the right in American politics symbolized by the election of Ronald Reagan in 1980. A sustained period of defunding, deregulation, and lack of enforcement of civil rights policies followed until the "Year of the Woman" in 1992 signaled a shift back toward the center in American politics. A fourth wave of feminism, antigovernment protests in the Arab world, anti-Donald Trump protests, the #MeToo movement, and the movement to challenge institutionalized state violence against racial minorities in the United States in the 2000s and 2010s created opportunities—and a need—to articulate issues related to safety and access to public space for all. A backlash followed with the presidency of Donald Trump, which bolstered conservative state legislatures, pulled courts away from protecting the civil rights of traditionally marginalized groups, intentionally inflamed fears of immigrants and Muslims, and emboldened extremists outside the political system.

Despite this cycle of progress and backlash, I see much to be optimistic about in the twenty-first century. The trope of cities or public space being inherently dangerous for women continues to be disrupted. Discussions about the significance of access have become markedly more expansive and inclusive in the twenty-first century. "Womyn only" spaces that exclude trans women have received scathing condemnation, most notably the Michigan Womyn's Music Festival (Michfest). Ideas have been cross-pollinating across national, racial, and ethnic boundaries, fostered in no small part by the opportunities for remote organizing via social media. Language has become much more nuanced and, by extension, inclusive. Although the experiences of women are still central in some of today's issues, there is a new sensitivity to how that category can exclude and clear efforts are being made to do better. Proponents of public breastfeeding, for example, are shifting their language to be more inclusive of those who present as gender-nonbinary or as men and who "chestfeed" their babies.[4]

Finally, and perhaps most exciting to me personally, is the revival of

Twenty-first-century demonstrations continue to challenge the message that women are responsible for the harassment and violence they encounter. (Photo by Diane Smithers)

grassroots organizing. Some of these protests, such as the SlutWalks, take on familiar forms, but others have incorporated new technology options to build a base, foster a sense of identity, and bring awareness to issues. One example is the success of the anti–street harassment organization Hollaback! Founded in New York City in 2005, the group has since spread to over sixty cities in twenty-two countries and in 2022 changed its name to Right To Be. Reminiscent of Hadleigh-West and her film *War Zone*, this organization urges women to use their cell phones to take pictures of anyone who makes them "scared or uncomfortable" with anything from making "comments . . . to groping, flashing and assault" and then post the pictures to social media.[5] Other groups have followed, creating blogs where women can post their stories of harassment and interactive maps to identify "harassment zones." One marked difference in this revival of the anti–street harassment campaign is the enthusiastic participation of women and girls of color, groups that were reluctant to engage during criticisms of mashers in the early 1900s or the "ogle-ins" of the 1970s.[6] LGBTQ+ activists have also joined this wave of organizing, including those raising awareness of the disproportionate harassment and horrific violence faced by transgender individuals, especially transgender women of color, in public spaces.[7]

What is remarkable is how many of the social, cultural, political, and economic issues identified by reformers and feminists in the previous century have found new life in the twenty-first century. In their latest iteration, however, advocates still work on behalf of women, but they also call the gender binary into question and recognize the global reach of many issues. They take seriously how the intersection of identities shapes experiences and makes finding one-size-fits-all solutions difficult. Twenty-first-century efforts blend the opportunities of social media as a base for communication and raising awareness with older forms of activism, including street art, guerrilla theater, and political lobbying. For example, Collective Action for Safe Spaces, a Washington, DC organization formed in 2009, conducted a "safety audit" around the city in 2011 in order to encourage women to tell their stories and raise awareness of harassment on mass transit. The group then launched a successful campaign to lobby the Washington Metropolitan Area Transit Authority to address harassment on the city's public transportation.[8] Metro Transit police chief Michael Taborn minimized the problem when he told a local TV reporter, "One person's harassment is another person's flirtation."[9] Local anti-harassment activists responded to this dismissive remark on social media. The public relations fiasco that followed prompted Metro officials to launch a formal official anti-harassment campaign. Under similar pressure from grassroots groups, Chicago, Boston, and New York City transit launched analogous campaigns in the 2010s.

In raising challenges to the status quo, twenty-first-century grassroots movements, from Occupy Wall Street to Black Lives Matter, have also been remarkably attentive to validating the experiences of those who face harassment in public. Many of the last decade's hashtag movements—which ignite communication across social media by using a shared hashtag—convene the power of individuals and their stories without needing formal organizations to guide the work. In the United States, Feminista Jones began #YouOKSis to encourage women of color to speak out about the street harassment they experience, watch out for one another, and learn tools for intervening and de-escalating situations when they see them happening.[10] In 2017, when an Indian public official opined that a stalking victim had brought it on herself by being out at midnight, women's responses went viral as thousands posted pictures of themselves in public late at night and defiantly tagged them with #AintNoCinderella Hashtags provide accessible avenues for challenging restrictive norms of behavior and enable women to support one another in claiming their autonomy. In other words, they cut through a core issue of gender segregation, namely, the way gendered codes hold women individually responsible for anything bad that happens to them in public. The blame and shame society heaps on women who have been harassed, attacked, or raped has kept many women from sharing their stories. Hashtags send a message to the world, but perhaps more importantly, they create a sense of connection and solidarity between victims every time someone tweets #ItsNotYourFault or #MeToo.[11]

While some of the issues documented in *Breaking the Gender Code* might seem quaint, the work of challenging gender assumptions laid the groundwork for the questions being asked now. At the turn of the twentieth century, women demanded inclusion in public space through the construction of public restrooms for women where none had existed before. In the potty parity debates of the 1990s, women and their allies took note of how gender-segregated facilities underserved women, but they never questioned that bathrooms were segregated by gender. In the twenty-first century, discussion about a lack of public facilities has reemerged. Pointing the way toward solutions that advocates for women rarely considered before, activists working on behalf of the rights of the homeless and for trans* rights in the last fifteen years have endorsed more single-user facilities, secure high-privacy stalls, and gender-neutral bathrooms as a means of making facilities easier to clean and ensuring that no one is ever in the "wrong" bathroom because of gender.[12] Shifting the discussion to access and safety and away from equity presents compelling reasons to loosen the gender distinction for toilet facilities, either by allowing individuals to choose which bathroom to use or by removing the gendered labels on facilities altogether. If all facilities are open to all potential users, the wait times are equalized, no one needs to match the labels on the doors to feel safe, and all users get more privacy through more inclusive designs—goals that potty parity advocates supported but never achieved as they clung to the old tradition of multi-user, gender-segregated bathrooms.

There have been times in our history when making space for women in public meant making space for women as women first and foremost: women's bathrooms, women's trains, and women's centers. But now, between the problematizing of classless, race-blind conceptions of "woman," particularly by women of color, and challenges to the existence of a gender binary at all, primarily by queer, nonconforming, and intersex activists, this approach is proving archaic, too narrow, and too reductive. The question for the twentieth century might have been how to include women, as women, in public space, but it seems that the question emerging in the twenty-first century is how to understand women as one part of a spectrum of identities that have been denied full and equal access to the public sphere.

The coalitions emerging around issues of access in the twenty-first century reveal many of the threads connecting this work to earlier waves of activism. Conservatives often used reactionary tactics around bathrooms in the twentieth century, including Phyllis Schlafly when she argued against the Equal Rights Amendment in the 1970s and opponents of state and municipal human rights ordinances who argued in the 1990s that cross-dressing men would use the laws to enter women's bathrooms and rape women.[13] Efforts to delegitimize the gender expression of transgender people, especially transgender women, by invoking the "need" to protect cisgendered women appeared again in 2016 when the Republican-controlled legislature of North Carolina made it illegal to use a public facility that did not match one's birth sex. This time a broad coalition of civil rights groups, including venerable organizations rooted deeply in the twentieth century, such as the National Organization for Women, sprang into action and successfully used both political and economic pressure to force a repeal of the so-called bathroom bill.[14] Earlier waves of activism around traditional gender identities helped move American society from exclusion to segregation, and then toward various forms of inclusion. As the widespread condemnation of the transphobic bathroom policies in the 2010s suggests, that earlier process of increasing inclusion, far from being repudiated, continues today.

At the intersection of the hashtags, grassroots organizations, media attention, and ongoing legal battles in the twenty-first century lie deep cultural issues touching on who belongs, what behaviors will be tolerated, and whose rights will prevail. It is not surprising that change happens slowly and that laws, where they do exist, generally fall short (as we saw in the 1990s). This is amply demonstrated in the responses to the twenty-first-century phenomenon known as "upskirting." With small but powerful cell phones in hand, men in grocery stores, on subways, and even at protest rallies were taking pictures and videos under women's clothing without their permission.[15] A few of the perpetrators were arrested and charged with various invasions of privacy, but state courts overturned the convictions in Massachusetts, Georgia, Tennessee, and Wisconsin in the 2010s. Although there seemed to be widespread public agreement that the practice was "appalling," courts noted that the practice was not specifically restricted; a Georgia court even ruled that "a woman's body was not a 'private place.'"[16] If someone was in public, they had no right to stop someone else from taking a picture of them and posting it to social media or even pornography websites. "Peeping Tom" laws prohibited spying on people in public bathrooms or changing rooms, where some nudity might occur and the occupants would expect privacy, but when fully clothed and out in public, courts told women, they could not expect their underwear, inner thighs, buttocks, or breasts to be off limits, even if they were covered. Over the last decade, legislatures in twenty-eight states did attempt to update or create new laws to guard against the practice.[17] But that such legislation was even necessary speaks volumes about the ongoing linkages of privacy to space, the continued sexualization of women's bodies, particularly when in public, and the connections between the old tropes of the twentieth century and the meaning of urban public space today.

An analysis of the arguments and actions of groups that have confronted gender segregation in modern urban America reveals compelling arguments for why these issues mattered in the past and are still relevant today. The long history of the fights for the dignity of access and full standing in the public sphere also offers examples of a diverse set of tactics, from developing new analyses and language to challenge culture to holding public protests, pushing for policy, occupying space, and building alternative institutions. As broad as these tactics were, all worked toward a remarkably consistent goal: ensuring women's bodily integrity and right to privacy while in public. If we understand these calls for privacy as more than just a right to exist or even be safe but also as a right to self-define, to practice autonomy, and to belong fully in the public sphere, then the connections become clear between activists of the twentieth century and those fighting today for transgender rights and those telling their stories of harassment on social media; those continuing to call for desexualizing women's bodies (#FreeTheNipple is one example); and activists demanding recognition of and accountability for violence against women of color with calls to #SayHerName (reminiscent of the work of LA community members who tried to bring attention to the 1980s serial killer who preyed on African American sex workers).[18] In the realm of policy, anti-harassment groups pressured lawmakers to strengthen "invasion of privacy" statutes and mass transit companies to launch anti-harassment campaigns. All of these efforts incorporate and legitimate the arguments about the negative psychological impact of harassment that feminists have been making for decades.

After more than a century of activism, the goal of so many of the organized attempts to make urban public space more accessible to women, ensuring their right to privacy, has yet to be fully achieved. Considering the very nature of public space, however, that goal is unlikely to ever be fully achieved, not just for women but for anyone. Privacy in public is, at its core, a myth built more out of customs and rituals than out of any possibility of physical privacy. It is a psychological privilege more than a physical reality. Beyond its unattainability, the goal of privacy raises hard questions. First, privacy is a rather individualistic approach to life. And it is this focus on the individual that groups may need to trade away in order to reach a state of actual "empowerment" in the public sphere. To be empowered, to actually participate in democratic decision-making, we need to get messy. We need to expose the parts of ourselves and our identities that we hide behind the veil of "privacy," and we need to see what others keep private as well. That means we need to be in messy spaces, places where boundaries are challenged, because it is only when boundaries are crossed that we can clearly see where they are. This is an important reason why I see the wealth of grassroots activism in the twenty-first century as so encouraging: it is questioning the traditional boundaries of social identity. It is only when we recognize these boundaries and the inequities built into them that we can set about changing how hierarchies of power have been naturalized in our social spaces. We make cities better, we make them feel safe for all, when we make them feel safe for the most vulnerable and disempowered populations among us.

Acknowledgments

The work that went into this book has been the most rewarding and challenging of my career. I am humbled by the generosity of activists who shared their stories with me and validated many of the questions I ask in this book. I am deeply indebted to the archivists at all the institutions cited in the notes, especially the staff of the Mardigian and Harlan Hatcher Libraries at the University of Michigan. I am grateful to my students, who, whether they knew it or not, worked through some of the project's thorniest material with me (and extra love to those who sent me pictures of public bathrooms they've encountered in their travels). Several students also worked as research assistants, including Hannah Aronson, Tiffany Martek, and Very Raft. Finally, it has been only with the unfailing support (and a bit of nagging) from family, friends, colleagues, and the most kick-ass writing group a scholar could ever hope for that this project reached completion. Thank you all.

And now, the list. Each of these people deserves special recognition for doing some heavy lifting to help bring this book into existence: Danielle Anderson (a research assistant but so much more), Pam Aronson, Gerry Barons (who welcomed me into the world of Detroit feminists), Deirdre Climer, Lora Lempert, Maureen Linker, Clay McShane (an early believer), Warren Nelson, Liz Rohan, Patricia Smith, Jaqueline Vansant, Nathan Voght, and Victoria Wolcott (who, at a few crucial moments, said, "Finish the book so I can use it in class").

This book is dedicated to my children, Emma and Owen Nelson, and the world their generation is building, a world that is calling into question so many of the old rules about who must fit where and why. Keep making it complicated.

Notes

Introduction

1. Robert Macoy, *History of and How to See New York and Its Environs* (New York: R. Macoy, 1876), reprinted in *The American Urban Reader: History and Theory*, ed. Steven H. Corey and Lisa Krissoff Boehm (New York: Routledge, 2011), 62–63.

2. Glenna Matthews, *The Rise of Public Woman: Woman's Power and Woman's Place in the United States, 1630–1970* (New York: Oxford University Press, 1992), 7.

3. Mary Ryan, *Women in Public: Between Banners and Ballots, 1825–1880* (Baltimore: Johns Hopkins University Press, 1990), 75.

4. Barbara Welke, "When All the Women Were White and All the Blacks Were Men: Gender, Class, Race, and the Road to Plessy, 1855–1914," *Law and History Review* 13 (1995): 275–276.

5. The scholarly literature on racial segregation inspired many of my questions about gender segregation. While gender segregation ultimately works differently from racial segregation (and often reinforces it), these studies of systems of power and social organizations helped me find a way in. See Leon Litwack, *Been in the Storm So Long: The Aftermath of Slavery* (New York: Vintage, 1980); Howard Rabinowitz, *Race Relations in the Urban South, 1865–1890* (Athens: University of Georgia Press, 1996); Jennifer Ritterhouse, *Growing Up Jim Crow: How Black and White Southern Children Learned Race* (Chapel Hill: University of North Carolina Press, 2006); and Paula Austin, *Coming of Age in Jim Crow DC: Navigating the Politics of Everyday Life* (New York: New York University Press, 2019).

6. Susan Brownmiller, interview with the author, August 10, 2004, New York, NY.

7. Sarah Deutsch, *Women and the City: Gender, Space, and Power in Boston, 1870–1940* (Oxford: Oxford University Press, 2000), 78; Jessica Sewell, *Women and the Everyday City: Public Space in San Francisco, 1890–1915* (Minneapolis: University of Minnesota Press, 2001), xiv–xxii; LaKisha Michelle Simmons, *Crescent City Girls: The Lives of Young Black Women in Segregated New Orleans* (Chapel Hill: University of North Carolina Press, 2015), 25–29.

8. Nan Enstad, *Ladies of Labor, Girls of Adventure: Working Women, Popular Culture, and Labor Politics at the Turn of the Twentieth Century* (New York: Columbia University Press, 1999).

9. Christine Stansell, *City of Women: Sex and Class in New York, 1789–1860* (Urbana: University of Illinois Press, 1986); Kathy Peiss, *Cheap Amusements: Working Women and Leisure in Turn-of-the-Century New York* (Philadelphia: Temple University Press, 1986); Joanne Meyerowitz, *Women Adrift: Independent Wage Earners in Chicago, 1880–1930* (Chicago: University

of Chicago Press, 1988); see also Ryan, *Women in Public*; Maureen Flanagan, *Seeing with Their Hearts: Chicago Women and the Vision of the Good City, 1871–1933* (Princeton, NJ: Princeton University Press, 2002); Daphne Spain, *How Women Saved the City* (Minneapolis: University of Minnesota Press, 2001); Jessica Sewell, *Women and the Everyday City: Public Space in San Francisco, 1890–1915* (Minneapolis: University of Minnesota Press, 2011); and A. Finn Enke, *Finding the Movement: Sexuality, Contested Space, and Feminist Activism* (Durham, NC: Duke University Press, 2007).

10. Deutsch, *Women and the City*, 24.

11. These approaches, while more theoretical, are not entirely new. Jane Addams, *Twenty Years at Hull House* (New York: Macmillan, 1911), Mary Ritter Beard, *Woman's Work in Municipalities* (New York: D. Appleton and Co., 1915); Mary S. Sims, *The Natural History of a Social Institution—The YWCA* (New York: Woman's Press, 1936), and many early histories of the YWCA recognized the power of space in enacting reform and shaping political dialogues.

12. Leila Rupp, *A Desired Past: A Short History of Same-Sex Love in America* (Chicago: University of Chicago Press, 1999), 153.

Chapter 1: Right and Reason

1. "Her Sister in the Country Who Wants to Come to the City to Make Her Way," *Ladies' Home Journal*, August 1911, 16, 45.

2. Emmett J. Scott, "Additional Letters of Negro Migrants of 1916–1918," *Journal of Negro History* 4 (October 1919): 457.

3. Claudia Goldin, "Female Labor Force Participation: The Origin of Black and White Differences, 1870 and 1880," *Journal of Economic History* 37, no. 1 (1977): 87.

4. Meyerowitz, *Women Adrift*, 5.

5. US Bureau of the Census, *Statistics of Women at Work*, cited in Meyerowitz, *Women Adrift*, 4.

6. Theodore Dreiser, *Sister Carrie* (1900; Philadelphia: University of Pennsylvania Press, 1988), 3.

7. "D.M., Athens, PA" (writing about New York), *Harper's Bazaar*, April 1908, 397.

8. US Department of Labor, Bureau of Labor Statistics, "The Share of Wage-Earning Women in Family Support," Bulletin 23 (Washington, DC: US Government Printing Office, 1922), 1.

9. Leslie Woodcock Tentler, *Wage-Earning Women: Industrial Work and Family Life in the United States, 1900–1930* (New York: Oxford University Press, 1982), 13–25.

10. "W.T., Spokane, Wash." *Harper's Bazaar*, July 1908, 695.

11. Lillie McKnight, interview with Charles Hardy III, August 2, 1983, "Goin' North: Tales of the Great Migration Oral History Project," Louie B. Nunn Center for Oral History, University of Kentucky Libraries).

12. Ella Lee, interview with Diane Turner, June 15, 1984, "Goin' North"; "M.E.C. Saginaw, Mich." *Harper's Bazaar*, June 1908, 594; "E.S., Fort Scott, Kans." *Harper's Bazaar*, April 1908, 394.

13. Eric Silverman, *A Cultural History of Jewish Dress* (New York: A&C Black, 2013), 76.

14. "Elizabeth R., New York, N.Y." *Harper's Bazaar*, February 1908, 171.

15. Dorothy Richardson, *The Long Day: The Story of a New York Working Girl* (Charlottesville: University of Virginia Press, 1990), 17.

16. Edith B. Ordway, *The Etiquette of To-Day* (New York: Sully and Kleinteich, 1913), 122.

17. Ibid., 134.

18. Emily Holt, *Everyman's Encyclopedia of Etiquette* (New York: Doubleday, Page, 1920), 403.

19. Emily Post, *Etiquette in Society, in Business, in Politics, and at Home* (New York: Funk and Wagnalls, 1922), 8.

20. Deutsch, *Women and the City*, 81.

21. Holt, *Everyman's Encyclopedia of Etiquette*, 1920.

22. Glenda Gilmore, *Gender and Jim Crow: Women and the Politics of White Supremacy, 1896–1920* (Chapel Hill: University of North Carolina Press, 1996); Ritterhouse, *Growing Up Jim Crow*, chap. 1; Victoria Wolcott, *Remaking Respectability: African American Women in Interwar Detroit* (Chapel Hill: University of North Carolina Press, 2001), chap. 2; Michele Mitchell, *Righteous Propagation: African Americans and the Politics of Racial Destiny after Reconstruction* (Chapel Hill: University of North Carolina Press, 2004).

23. Charlotte Hawkins Brown, *The Correct Thing to Do—to Say—to Wear* (Sedalia, NC: The author, 1940).

24. Robert Orsi, *The Madonna of 115th Street: Faith and Community in Italian Harlem* (New Haven, CT: Yale University Press, 1988).

25. Rosalind S. Chou, *Asian American Sexual Politics* (Lanham, MD: Rowman & Littlefield, 2012), 32–34.

26. Erika Lee, *At America's Gates: Chinese Immigration during the Exclusion Era, 1882–1943* (Chapel Hill: University of North Carolina Press, 2003), 93–94.

27. Rebecca Chiyoko King-O'Riain, *Pure Beauty: Judging Race in Japanese American Beauty Pageants* (Minneapolis: University of Minnesota Press, 2006), 51.

28. "New Orleans, La., May 7, 1917," reprinted in Emmett J. Scott, "Letters of Negro Migrants of 1916–1918," *Journal of Negro History* 4 (July 1919): 317.

29. "S.H.R., Los Angeles, Cal." (reflecting on her time in Boston), *Harper's Bazaar*, July 1908, 693.

30. Richardson, *The Long Day*, 34.

31. Estelle B. Freedman, *Redefining Rape: Sexual Violence in the Era of Suffrage and Segregation* (Cambridge, MA: Harvard University Press, 2013), 196.

32. "Girl Beats 'Masher,'" *Chicago Daily Tribune*, October 17, 1903.

33. Fannie Dickerson Chase, *Good Form and Social Ethics* (Washington, DC: Review and Herald Publishing Assn., 1913), 80.

34. Arney H. Ritchie, "How a Masher Was Punished," *Chicago Daily Tribune*, March 17, 1907.

35. "Masher Badly Beaten by Girl He Insulted," *Atlanta Constitution*, February 19, 1913.

36. "Girl Mashes Masher on Car," *Chicago Daily Tribune*, December 3, 1912.

37. "E.E.E., N.Y.," *Harper's Bazaar*, July 1908, 693; "N.R.A., Allston, Mass.," *Harper's Bazaar*, November 1908, 1140; "A.R.F., Baltimore, MD" *Harper's Bazaar*, November 1908, 1142; "H.S., Atlantic City, N.J." *Harper's Bazaar*, August 1908, 777.

38. "The Masher," *Chicago Defender*, July 31, 1926.

39. "Bold Flirt Taken to Jail," *Chicago Defender*, April 12, 1924.

40. Eugene Harris, *An Appeal for Social Purity in Negro Homes* (n.p., 1898), 7.

41. "Bishop Hughes Flays Mashers," *Afro-American*, November 5, 1920; "Plucky Elevator Girl Fights off White Masher," *Afro-American*, November 1, 1918; also quoted in Freedman, *Redefining Rape*, 206, 207.

42. Elizabeth Kytle, *Willie Mae* (Athens: University of Georgia Press), 140–141.

43. Blanche Ashby, as quoted in Elizabeth Clark-Lewis, *Living In, Living Out: African American Domestics in Washington, DC, 1910–1940* (Washington, DC: Smithsonian Books, 2010), 165.

44. "It is Time to Act," *Atlanta Evening News*, September 21, 1906.

45. See Susan Porter Benson, *Counter Cultures: Saleswomen, Managers, and Customers in American Department Stores* (Urbana: University of Illinois Press, 1986); William Leach, *Land of Desire: Merchants, Power, and the Rise of a New American Culture* (New York: Vintage Books, 1994); and Sharon Zukin, *Point of Purpose: How Shopping Changed America* (New York: Routledge, 2004).

46. Ryan, *Women in Public*, 76–77, 82; Rachel Shteir, *The Untold History of the Girlie Show* (New York: Oxford University Press, 2004), 72.

47. As quoted in Anthony J. Stanonis, *Creating the Big Easy: New Orleans and the Emergence of Modern Tourism, 1918–1945* (Athens: University of Georgia Press, 2006), 127.

48. My interest is in the impact of sensationalized stories of white slavery on women's access to public space. Historian Ruth Rosen explores the panics in relation to evidence of sex trafficking. See *The Lost Sisterhood: Prostitution in America, 1900–1918* (Baltimore: Johns Hopkins University Press, 1982), chap. 7.

49. Kevin Mumford, *Interzones: Black/White Sex Districts in Chicago and New York in the Early Twentieth Century* (New York: Columbia University Press, 1997); Brian Donovan, *White Slave Crusades: Race, Gender, and Anti-Vice Activism, 1887–1917* (Urbana: University of Illinois Press, 2006). See also Rosen, *The Lost Sisterhood*, chap. 7; Barbara Meil Hobson, *Uneasy Virtue: The Politics of Prostitution and the American Reform Tradition* (New York: Basic Books, 1987), 143–147.

50. M. Joan McDermott and Sarah J. Blackstone, "White Slavery Plays of the 1910s: Fear of Victimization and the Social Control of Sexuality," *Theatre History Studies* 16 (1996): 141–156.

51. Clifford G. Roe, *Panders and Their White Slaves; or, Fighting for the Protection of Our Girls* (New York: Fleming H. Revell Co., 1910), 94.

52. O. Edward Janney, *The White Slave Traffic in America* (New York: National Vigilance Committee, 1911), 83.

53. Roe, *Panders and Their White Slaves*, 79, 80, 93. Roe helped draft the legislation that would become the White Slave Traffic Act, more commonly known as the Mann Act of 1910. Jessica Pliley, *Policing Sexuality: The Mann Act and the Making of the FBI* (Cambridge, MA: Harvard University Press, 2014), 61–67.

54. Peggy Pascoe, *Relations of Rescue: The Search for Moral Authority in the American West, 1874–1939* (New York: Oxford University Press, 1990).

55. Nayah Shah, *Contagious Divides: Epidemics and Race in San Francisco Chinatown* (Berkeley: University of California Press, 2001).

56. W.E.B. Du Bois, quoted in Cheryl D. Hicks, *Talk with You Like a Woman: African American Women, Justice, and Reform in New York, 1890–1935* (Chapel Hill: University of North Carolina Press, 2010), 91–103.

57. "Adventuresome Girls Big Headache to DC Police," *Afro-American*, September 4, 1943.

58. Some histories of the gendered aspects of racial uplift focus on the ways in which respectability politics judged, managed, and controlled working-class women's bodies in the name of racial advancement. See, for example, Hazel Carby, "Policing the Black Woman's Body in an Urban Context," *Critical Inquiry* 18 (Summer 1992): 738–755.

59. Ibid., 739.

60. Harris, *An Appeal for Social Purity in Negro Homes*, 7–8, 14, 15.

61. Nazera Sadiq Wright, *Black Girlhood in the Nineteenth Century* (Urbana: University of Illinois Press, 2016), 150–165.

62. "Calls Modern Society Women Gold Diggers," *Chicago Defender*, September 30, 1933.

63. Mary E. Odem, *Delinquent Daughters: Protecting and Policing Adolescent Female Sexuality in the United States, 1885–1920* (Chapel Hill: University of North Carolina Press, 1995);

Georgina Hickey, "Waging War on 'Loose Living Hotels' and 'Cheap Soda Water Joints': The Criminalization of Working-Class Women in Atlanta's Public Space," *Georgia Historical Quarterly* 82 (Winter 1998): 775–800; Ernest A. Bell, *Fighting the Traffic in Young Girls; or, War on the White Slave Trade* (G. S. Ball, 1910); Robert A. Woods and Albert J. Kennedy, *Young Working Girls: A Summary of Evidence from Two Thousand Social Workers* (Boston: Houghton Mifflin, 1913), chap. 8. Forty-three cities established a vice commission between 1910 and 1917. Pliley, *Policing Sexuality*, 5.

64. 1903 headline from *The Leader*, quoted in Sharon E. Wood, *Freedom of the Streets: Work, Citizenship, and Sexuality in a Gilded Age City* (Chapel Hill: University of North Carolina Press, 2005), 240.

65. National Women's History Museum, "Pedaling the Path to Freedom," June 27, 2017, https://www.womenshistory.org/articles/pedaling-path-freedom.

66. Thomas A. Edison, Inc., *What Happened on Twenty-Third Street, New York City* (film), 1901, National Audio-Visual Conservation Center, Niver Collection and Paper Print Collection, Library of Congress, https://www.loc.gov/item/00694379.

67. Anzia Yezierska, *Bread Givers: A Novel* (New York: Persea, 1925; reprinted 1994), 18–19.

68. "G.E.D.," *Harper's Bazaar*, March 1908, 277.

69. Laura Hapke, *Tales of the Working Girl: Wage-Earning Women in American Literature, 1890–1925* (New York: Twayne Publishers, 1992), 31.

70. Richardson, *The Long Day*, 23.

71. Jane Addams, *The Spirit of Youth and the City Streets* (New York: Macmillan, 1909; reprint, Urbana: University of Illinois Press, 2001), 14.

72. For a critique of Addams's "sloppy, contradictory, sentimental, hyperbolic" views on prostitution, see Victoria Bissell Brown, "Sex and the City: Jane Addams Confronts Prostitution," in *Feminist Interpretations of Jane Addams*, ed. Maurice Hamington (University Park: Pennsylvania State University Press, 2010), 126.

73. Addams, *The Spirit of Youth and the City Streets*, xx.

74. For more on cross-class arguments over fashion in this period, see Nan Enstad, *Ladies of Labor, Girls of Adventure: Working Women, Popular Culture, and Labor Politics at the Turn of the Twentieth Century* (New York: Columbia University Press, 1999); Lauren Rabinowitz, *For the Love of Pleasure: Women, Movies, and Culture in Turn-of-the Century Chicago* (New Brunswick, NJ: Rutgers University Press, 1998); and Peiss, *Cheap Amusements*.

75. Addams, *The Spirit of Youth and the City Streets*, 8.

76. Jane Addams, quoted in Elizabeth Wilson, *Sphinx in the City: Urban Life, the Control of Disorder, and Women* (Berkeley: University of California Press, 1991), 74.

77. "The Strange Girl in the Large City: A Word to Those Who Might Help Her," *Ladies' Home Journal*, January 1907.

78. "Fannie Barrier Williams Lauds Chicago Women," *Chicago Defender*, October 10, 1914.

79. Jane Edna Hunter, *A Nickel and a Prayer* (Cleveland, OH: Elli Kani Publishing, 1940), 77.

80. Fannie Barrier Williams, "The New Black Woman," reprinted in Gerda Lerner, *Black Women in White America: A Documentary History* (New York: Vintage Books, 1992), 575.

81. Mary Church Terrell, quoted in Alison M. Parker, *Unceasing Militant: The Life of Mary Church Terrell* (Chapel Hill: University of North Carolina Press, 2020), 132.

82. Freedman, *Redefining Rape*, 202.

83. "Civic Centers Should Displace Cheap Shows," *Atlanta Journal*, September 21, 1912.

84. "Mrs. W. B. Lowe Will Take Up the Case of Dolly Pritchard," n.d. (probably 1900), Atlanta Woman's Club Scrapbook 2, Atlanta Woman's Club Collection, Atlanta History Center.

85. Quoted in Gilmore, *Gender and Jim Crow*, 75.

86. Wolcott, *Remaking Respectability*, 57.

87. Mabel Dodge, quoted in Sheila Rothman, *Woman's Proper Place: History of Changing Ideals and Practices, 1870 to the Present* (New York: Basic Books, 1980), 79.

88. "The Strange Girl in the Large City: A Word to Those Who Might Help Her," *Ladies' Home Journal*, January 1907.

89. "Separate Cars for Women," *New York Times*, March 21, 1909. Clifton Hood argues that the segregated cars offered a means for encouraging women to behave more demurely when in public. Clifton Hood, "Changing Perceptions of Urban Space on the New York Rapid Transit System," *Journal of Urban History* (March 1996): 320.

90. "Fair Sex Opposes Car Segregation," *Chicago Daily Tribune*, March 19, 1909.

91. Hood, "Changing Perceptions of Urban Space," 330n39.

92. "Cars for Women Prove a Success," *New York Times*, April 1, 1909.

93. "Women Divide on Car Segregation," *Chicago Daily Tribune*, April 24, 1909.

94. "Misogynist in the Subway," *New York Times*, March 31, 1909.

95. "Women Divide on Car Segregation," *Chicago Daily Tribune*, April 24, 1909; "Testing Subway Manners," *New York Times*, May 16, 1909.

96. "Giving Up One's Seat," *New York Times*, November 26, 1909.

97. Other cities watched these events closely, but most commentators dismissed the idea as unworkable. See, for example, "Women Want Car on Each Express," *Chicago Daily Tribune*, March 27, 1909.

Chapter 2: Building Women into the City

1. "Subway May Run Cars for Women," *Chicago Daily Tribune*, April 7, 1909.

2. Damon Scott, "When the Motorman Mayor Met the Cable Car Ladies: Engendering Transit in the City That Knows How," *Journal of Urban History* 40 (2014): 65–96.

3. Maureen Flanagan, "Private Needs, Public Space: Public Toilets Provision in the Anglo-Atlantic Patriarchal City: London, Dublin, Toronto, and Chicago," *Urban History* 41, no. 2 (2014): 266.

4. Mildred Andrews, *Seattle Women: A Legacy of Community Development* (Seattle, WA: YWCA of Seattle-King County, 1984), 26.

5. Cleveland YWCA yearbook, 1898, quoted in "Women Involved in the Real World: A History of the Young Women's Christian Association of Cleveland, Ohio, 1868–1968," compiled by Mildred H. Esger, YWCA papers, Sophia Smith Collection, Smith College, Northampton, MA; Seattle YWCA, quoted in Andrews, *Seattle Women*, 26.

6. "Women Involved in the Real World," 80–81, YWCA papers.

7. "The Stranger at Our Door," June 1903, Minneapolis YWCA.

8. "Two Hours from a Travelers' Aid Worker's Life," *Los Angeles Times*, October 19, 1924.

9. Andrews, *Seattle Women*, 28.

10. "Women Involved in the Real World," 52–53, YWCA papers.

11. "Women Dissolve Body Organized in City in 1908," undated/unattributed clipping [c. 1926], Business Women's Building and Rest Room Association (BWBRRA) papers, Center for Archival Studies, University Libraries, Bowling Green State University, Sandusky, OH.

12. "Women's Body Given $120,000," undated/unattributed clipping [c. 1926], BWBRRA.

13. Georgina Hickey, *Hope and Danger in the New South City: Working-Class Women and Urban Development in Atlanta, 1890–1940* (Athens: University of Georgia Press, 2003), chap. 4.

14. Karen McNeill, "Julia Morgan: Gender, Architecture, and Professional Style," *Pacific Historical Review* 76, no. 2 (May 2007): 229–268; Sara Holmes Boutelle, *Julia Morgan: Architect* (New York: Abbeville Press, 1988).

15. "History of Origin of Grace Dodge Hotel," 1922, YWCA papers.

16. Clare Crane, "Early Days of the San Diego YWCA," unpublished paper, YWCA papers.

17. Spain, *How Women Saved the City*, 3.

18. "San Diego's Greatest Need," fundraising pamphlet, 1925, San Diego YWCA papers, San Diego State University Archives, San Diego, CA.

19. Clare Crane, *The San Diego YWCA: A Short History, 1907–1982* (San Diego, CA: YWCA of San Diego County, 1982), 12–13.

20. Hunter, *A Nickel and a Prayer*, 107.

21. Minneapolis YWCA, "History," https://www.ywcampls.org/about_us/history (accessed December 12, 2022).

22. "Women Involved in the Real World," 55, YWCA papers; Blanche Geary, "Handbook of the Association Cafeteria" (New York: National Board of the Young Women's Christian Associations, 1917), 85, YWCA papers.

23. "Women Involved in the Real World," 55, 56, YWCA papers.

24. Geary, "Handbook of the Association Cafeteria," 85, YWCA papers.

25. Hunter, *A Nickel and a Prayer*, 108.

26. "Survey of Rooming and Boarding Houses in the Vicinity of Northwestern Knitting Company Plant Central District, Minneapolis, 1919," 159, Minneapolis YWCA.

27. Ruth B. Griffin, "The Northeast District," Minneapolis YWCA survey, 1919, 26, Minneapolis YWCA.

28. In the Northeastern District, where a new branch was recommended, 520 of the 952 women surveyed worked for wages in "factory and mechanical work." Ibid., 25.

29. "Mrs. Matzger's Annual Report 'To the President, Board of Directors, and Members of the Federation of Jewish Charities'" (1938), Emanuel Residence Records, 1902–1969, Collection 70/11, Judah L. Magnes Museum, Berkeley, CA; see also Linda Borish, "Jewish American Women, Jewish Organizations, and Sports, 1880–1940," in *Sports and the American Jew*, ed. Steve A. Riess (Syracuse, NY: Syracuse University Press, 1998): 105–131.

30. Some clubs functioned independently, and others were part of the YWCA. Nina Mjagkij, *Organizing Black America* (New York: Garland Publishing, 2001); Nina Mjagkij, *Portraits of African-American Life since 1895* (Wilmington, DE: Scholarly Resources, 2003); Deborah Gray White, *Too Heavy a Load: Black Women in Defense of Themselves 1894–1994* (New York: W. W. Norton & Company, 1999).

31. "History of Origin of Grace Dodge Hotel," YWCA papers.

32. The Grace Dodge Hotel in Washington, DC, had the additional goal of providing professional women with a place to learn and demonstrate their skill at hotel management.

33. Edith Hatley, quoted in Mary Ritter Beard, *Woman's Work in Municipalities* (New York: D. Appleton & Company, 1915), 201.

34. "Handbook for the YWCA Movement," 1919, 51, YWCA papers.

35. Ibid., 46.

36. Elizabeth Wilson, *The Sphinx in the City: Urban Life, the Control of Disorder, and Women* (Berkeley: University of California Press, 1991), 46.

37. George W. Simons, "More Public Convenience Stations Needed," *The American City* 23, no. 5 (1920): 472; Civic League of St. Louis Street Improvement Committee, *Public Comfort Stations for Saint Louis* (St. Louis: Civic League of St. Louis, 1908), 203.

38. Simons, "More Public Convenience Stations Needed," 472.

39. Civic League of St. Louis, *Public Comfort Stations for Saint Louis*, 13; J. J. Cosgrove, "The Comfort Station as a Public Utility," *The American City* 16 (February 1917)" 180.

40. Frederick L. Ford, "Public Comfort Stations," Department of City Making Leaflet 14, 2nd ed., January 1908, American Civic Association, 3, Library of Congress.

41. Nineteenth-century "Sanitarians," the reformers behind the early public bath movement, generally endorsed building public comfort stations, but the issue was clearly never a priority for them. Marilyn Thornton Williams, *Washing "The Great Unwashed": Public Baths in Urban America, 1840–1920* (Columbus: Ohio State University Press, 1991), 36–37, 155n25. On women's sanitation efforts, see Suellen Hoy, *Chasing Dirt: The American Pursuit of Cleanliness* (New York: Oxford University Press, 1997).

42. F. L. Hays Jr., "Wants Public Comfort Stations," *Chicago Daily Tribune*, November 25, 1908.

43. "Vote for Public Comfort Stations," clipping from the Central Press Bureau, October 11, 1912, Civic Club of Allegheny County Collection, Archives Service Center, University of Pittsburgh, Pittsburgh, PA.

44. City of Chicago, "Public Comfort Stations," *Bulletin of the Department of Public Welfare City of Chicago* 1, no. 3 (October 1916): 1–25.

45. "Bathing Beaches and Public Comfort Stations Committee," *Woman's City Club Bulletin* (January 1917): 8.

46. Ibid., 3.

47. Louise Osborne Rowe, "Public Comfort Stations," *Bulletin of the Department of Public Welfare City of Chicago* 1, no. 3 (October 1916): 26.

48. "$90,000 Asked for Public Comfort," *Pittsburgh Gazette Times*, November 3, 1912.

49. Chicago Woman's Club, minutes of meeting, March 25, 1908, Chicago Woman's Club records, 1876–1998, Chicago History Museum, Chicago, IL.

50. "Public Comfort Station," uncited clipping, October 1912, Civic Club of Allegheny County Records, 1896–1974, AIS.1970.02, Archives & Special Collections, University of Pittsburgh Library System, Pittsburgh, PA.

51. Flanagan, "Private Needs, Public Space," 273. Maureen Flanagan argues that, in refusing to build toilets for women, the male power structure protected the androcentric city and its privileging of profit over the more "feminine" goals of comfort and safety. While Chicago was very slow to build stations, the objections to spending money on comfort stations waylaid projects for both men's and women's facilities.

52. A Man, "Complaint of a Man" (letter to the editor), *Pittsburgh Post*, December 7, 1913, Civic Club of Allegheny County Records.

53. "An Indignant Taxpayer," *Pittsburgh Post*, December 4, 1913.

54. "They are a public necessity and to close them because between council and the administration no provision was made in the annual budget to keep them open would be too raw a performance even for the patient Pittsburg public." *Pittsburg Press*, January 7, 1916.

55. Wisconsin State Board of Health, Plumbing and Domestic Sanitary Engineering Division, "Wisconsin Public Comfort Station Code and Rest Room Suggestions," Madison, WI, 1920, 5, Library of Congress.

56. In the 1890s and 1900s, underground comfort stations were tried in many cities. By the 1910s, most advocates and design professionals supported only aboveground facilities, citing better visibility (easier to find) and ventilation.

57. Harry F. Bascom, "Features of the New Comfort Station in Allentown, PA," *The American City* 22 (January 1922): 47.

58. "Elmira's Rest Room Proves Popular," *The American City* 24 (June 1921): 627. For Progressive Era–standards in outfitting men's and women's facilities and recommendations for location, size, funding sources, staffing, and so on, see Frank R. King, "Public Comfort Stations," *The American City* 33(July–December 1925), 618; Wisconsin State Board of Health, "Wisconsin Public Comfort Station Code and Rest Room Suggestions"; Ford, "Public Comfort Stations"; Civic League of St. Louis, *Public Comfort Stations for Saint Louis*; and City of Chicago, "Public Comfort Stations."

59. There is something of a catch-22 with women's facilities. There were fewer accommodations for women, so women might plan not to use them, but with fewer women using them, justification grew to build fewer facilities. Studies from the early twentieth century do cite significant numbers of women using the facilities, but their use was much lower than men's. Women accounted for about 12 percent of the attendance at Brooklyn's six public comfort stations in 1915. Rowe, "Public Comfort Stations," 12.

60. Simons, "More Public Convenience Stations Needed," 472.

61. Wisconsin State Board of Health, "Wisconsin Public Comfort Station Code and Rest Room Suggestions," 5.

62. Ford, "Public Comfort Stations."

63. "Bulletin of the Department of Public Welfare, City of Chicago, Public Comfort Stations," October 1, 1916, 20, Chicago Historical Museum, Chicago, IL.

64. Royal S. Copeland, "The City Rest House," *The American City* 53 (February 1938): 16.

65. "Bathing Beaches and Public Comfort Stations Committee," *Woman's City Club Bulletin* 7 (June 1918).

66. Ruth Colker, "Public Restrooms: Flipping the Default Rules," Ohio State Public Law Working Paper 388, March 20, 2017, 2. http://moritzlaw.osu.edu/sites/colker2/files/2017/04/Public-Restrooms.pdf.

67. Anna Julia Cooper, *A Voice from the South* (Xenia, OH: Aldine Printing House, 1892), 69.

68. Mary McLeod Bethune, "Closed Doors" (1936 speech), reprinted in *Sisters in the Struggle: African American Women in the Civil Rights–Black Power Movement*, ed. Bettye Collier-Thomas and V. P. Franklin (New York: New York University Press, 2001), 15, 14.

69. Mary Burks, "Trailblazers: Women in the Montgomery Bus Boycott," in *Women in the Civil Rights Movement: Trailblazers and Torchbearers, 1941–1965*, ed. Vicki L. Crawford, Jacqueline Anne Rouse, Barbara Woods, and Broadus N. Butler (Bloomington: Indiana University Press, 1993), 76.

70. Burroughs's 1908 speech is quoted in Evelyn Brooks Higginbotham, *Righteous Discontent: The Women's Movement in the Black Baptist Church 1880–1920* (Cambridge, MA: Harvard University Press, 1993), 223.

71. Leon Litwack, *Been in the Storm So Long: The Aftermath of Slavery* (New York: Vintage, 1980), 233.

72. For reflections on African American responses to the signs of racial segregation, see ibid.; Ritterhouse, *Growing Up Jim Crow*; Austin, *Coming of Age in Jim Crow DC*. Section II of the Civil Rights Act of 1964 outlawed discrimination in public accommodations, including public restrooms, on the basis of race, but unlike Title VII of the same act, sex discrimination was not included.

73. On reasons for building public facilities underground, see Andrew Brown May and Peg Fraser, "Gender, Respectability, and Public Convenience in Melbourne, Australia, 1859–1902," in *Ladies and Gents: Public Toilets and Gender*, ed. Olga Gershenson and Barbara Penner (Philadelphia: Temple University Press, 2009), 75–89.

74. The Civil Rights Act of 1875 outlawed racial discrimination in public accommodations,

including trains, but the Supreme Court nullified the law in 1883, thereby opening the door to the era of Jim Crow segregation.

75. Welke, "When All the Women Were White," 267.

76. Patricia Schechter, *Ida B. Wells-Barnett and American Reform, 1880–1930* (Chapel Hill: University of North Carolina Press, 2001), 43–44.

77. *Chesapeake, Ohio, & Southwestern Railroad Company v. Ida B. Wells*, 85 Tenn. 613 (1887), 615.

78. Crystal Feimster, *Southern Horrors: Women and the Politics of Rape and Lynching* (Cambridge, MA: Harvard University Press, 2011), 88; Paula Giddings, *When and Where I Enter: The Impact of Black Women on Race and Sex in America* (New York: HarperCollins/William Morrow, 1984), 262.

79. Alfreda M. Duster, ed., *Crusader for Justice: The Autobiography of Ida B. Wells* (Chicago: University of Chicago Press, 1991), 21.

80. Cooper, *A Voice from the South*, 30.

81. Ibid., 37.

82. Feimster, *Southern Horrors*, 103.

83. Martha Jones, *All Bound Up Together: The Woman Question in African American Public Culture, 1830–1900* (Chapel Hill: University of North Carolina Press, 2007), 9; Treva B. Lindsay, *Colored No More: Reinventing Black Womanhood in Washington, DC* (Urbana: University of Illinois Press, 2017), 11–18; and Elsa Barkley Brown, "Negotiating and Transforming the Public Sphere: African American Political Life in the Transformation from Slavery to Freedom," *Public Culture* 7 (1994): 107–146.

84. Mia Bay, "Gender, Jim Crow, and Public Protest," in *Becoming Visible: Women's Presence in Late Nineteenth-Century America*, ed. Janet Floyd, Alison Easton, R. J. Ellis, and Lindsay Traub (New York: Rodopi, 1994), 113.

85. Darlene Clark Hine labeled this tradition the "culture of dissemblance." Hine, "Rape and the Inner Lives of Black Women in the Middle West: Preliminary Thoughts on the Culture of Dissemblance," *Signs* 14, no. 4 (Summer 1989): 912–920.

86. Ida B. Wells, *The Red Record: Tabulated Statistics and Alleged Causes of Lynching in the United States* (Chicago: Donohue & Henneberry, 1894), available as a Gutenberg Project ebook, https://www.gutenberg.org/files/14977/14977-h/14977-h.htm.

87. Lindsay, *Colored No More*, 13.

88. Ibid., 100.

89. Bay, "Gender, Jim Crow, and Public Protest," 106. Mary Church Terrell often passed as white when traveling. She argued that she owed it to her family, her community (race), and the audiences that hired her to speak to stay safe and to make it to her destination, and that this larger need justified passing as white. Anna Julia Cooper, *Beyond Respectability: The Intellectual Thought of Race Women* (Urbana: University of Illinois Press, 2017), 77.

90. Cooper, *A Voice from the South*, 63.

91. Mary Church Terrell, *A Colored Woman in a White World* (1940; reprint, Lanham, MD: Rowman & Littlefield, 2005), 308.

92. Cooper, *A Voice from the South*, 66–67.

93. Williams, quoted in Lerner, *Black Women in White America*, 575.

94. Lottie Wilson Jackson, "An Appeal," *National Association Notes* 3, no. 1 (June 1899): 5.

95. Susan B. Anthony and Ida Husted Harper, *History of Woman Suffrage*, vol. 4, *1883–1900* (Rochester, NY: n.p., 1902), 342–343. The description of the incident includes a note that Lottie Jackson had a very light complexion, apparently appearing to the note taker as white. There is no direct indication of why this mattered, but suggests the note taker thought Jackson's skin tone bolstered her standing as a respectable woman.

96. Blair L. M. Kelley, *Right to Ride: Streetcar Boycotts and African American Citizenship in the Era of "Plessy v. Ferguson"* (Chapel Hill: University of North Carolina Press, 2010), 10.

97. August Meier and Elliott Rudwick, "The Boycott Movement against Jim Crow Streetcars in the South, 1900–1906," *Journal of American History* 55 (March 1969):756–775. Meier and Rudwick focus on streetcar boycotts as conservative, elite efforts in which Blacks lost, but Blair Kelley makes an effective argument for their inclusive nature and foundational role in the civil rights movement. Kelley, *Right to Ride*, 5–6.

98. Quoted in Kelley, *Right to Ride*, 11.

99. Ibid., 106–107.

100. S. A. Gates, quoted in ibid., 107.

101. Ibid., 154.

102. Anne Valk and Leslie Brown, *Living with Jim Crow: African American Women and Memories of the Segregated South* (New York: Palgrave Macmillan, 2010), 8–9.

103. Ritterhouse, *Growing Up Jim Crow*, 93.

104. Terrell, *A Colored Woman in a White World*, 26.

105. Ritterhouse, *Growing Up Jim Crow*, 93.

106. Nannie Helen Burroughs, "Not Color but Character," *Voice of the Negro* 1 (July 1904): 279.

107. Freedman, *Redefining Rape*, 203.

108. Elsie Johnson McDougald, "The Double Task" (1925), reprinted in Lerner, *Black Women in White America*, 171.

109. Quoted in Parker, *Unceasing Militant*, 90–91.

Chapter 3: The City and the Girl

1. Roberta Lee, "Getting On and Off the Streetcar," *Afro-American*, March 25, 1950.

2. Carolyn Herbst Lewis, *Prescriptions for Heterosexuality: Sexual Citizenship in the Cold War Era* (Chapel Hill: University of North Carolina Press, 2010), 4.

3. Leila Rupp and Verta Taylor, *Survival in the Doldrums: The American Women's Rights Movement, 1945 to the 1960s* (New York: Oxford University Press, 1987).

4. Robyn Muncy, "The Long Progressive Era," paper presented at Organization of American Historians conference, San Francisco, April 2013.

5. Dorothy Sue Cobble, *The Other Women's Movement: Workplace Justice and Social Rights in Modern America* (Princeton, NJ: Princeton University Press, 2004); Landon Storrs, "Left-Feminism, the Consumer Movement, and Red Scare Politics in the United States, 1935–1960," *Journal of Women's History*, 18 (Fall 2006): 40–67; Annelise Orleck, *Common Sense and a Little Fire: Women and Working-Class Politics in the United States, 1900–1965* (Chapel Hill: University of North Carolina Press, 1995).

6. "Genora (Johnson) Dollinger Remembers the 1936–37 General Motors Sit-Down Strike," as told to Susan Rosenthal, February 1995, History Is a Weapon, http://www.historyisaweapon.com/defcon1/dollflint.html#thewomen.

7. Amy Swerdlow, *Women Strike for Peace: Traditional Motherhood and Radical Politics in the 1960s* (Chicago: University of Chicago Press, 1993).

8. Freedman, *Redefining Rape*, 29.

9. Bethune, "Closed Doors," 15.

10. Pauli Murray, "Jim Crow and Jane Crow" (1964), reprinted in Lerner, *Black Women in White America*, 595.

11. Dara Abubakari, quoted in Jane J. Mansbridge, "'You're Too Independent'!: How Gender, Race, and Class Make Many Plural Feminisms," in *The Cultural Territories of Race: Black and White Boundaries*, ed. Michèle Lamont (Chicago: University of Chicago Press, 1999), 295.

12. Fannie Lou Hamer, quoted in Danielle McGuire, *At the Dark End of the Street: Black Women, Rape, and Resistance—A New History of the Civil Rights Movement from Rosa Parks to the Rise of Black Power* (New York: Knopf, 2010), 192.

13. Robin D. G. Kelley, *Race Rebels: Culture, Politics, and the Black Working Class* (New York: Free Press, 1994), 56.

14. McGuire, *At the Dark End of the Street*, 53–56.

15. Jo Ann Gibson Robinson, *The Montgomery Bus Boycott and the Women Who Started It: The Memoir of Jo Ann Gibson Robinson* (Knoxville: University of Tennessee Press, 1987), 8; Willi Coleman, "Black Women and Segregated Public Transportation: Ninety Years of Resistance," reprinted in *Black Women in United States History*, ed. Darlene Clark Hine (Brooklyn, NY: Carlson Publishers, 1990), 295.

16. Northern cities did not enforce legal segregation and seem to have had less sustained racial friction—except during the World War II years, when severe overcrowding on public conveyances opened the door to expressions of white anxiety over African American demands for social equality. Sarah Fohardt-Lane, "Close Encounters: Interracial Contact and Conflict on Detroit's Public Transit in World War II," *Journal of Transport History* 33 (December 2012): 212–275.

17. "Man Bound over for Striking Woman on Car," *Atlanta Daily World*, March 17, 1943.

18. "Bill Seeks Choice Seats," *Atlanta Daily World*, July 25, 1956.

19. Crystal Feimster, *Southern Horrors: Women and the Politics of Rape and Lynching* (Cambridge, MA: Harvard University Press, 2011).

20. Mary-Elizabeth Murphy, *Jim Crow Capital: Women and Black Freedom Struggles in Washington, DC, 1920–1945* (Chapel Hill: University of North Carolina Press, 2018), 173–177.

21. "Part II: Branch File, 1940–1955," NAACP records, 1842–1999, Library of Congress.

22. Kelley, *Race Rebels*, 72.

23. Willi Coleman draws a straight line from Black women's refusal to leave first-class cars and ride in segregated (Jim Crow) cars in the nineteenth century to the 1955 bus boycott: "The pattern of confrontational behavior begun in the nineteenth century surfaced surprisingly intact in the middle of the twentieth century." Coleman, "Black Women and Segregated Public Transportation," 300.

24. Marisa Chappell, Jenny Hutchinson, and Brian Ward, "'Dress Modestly, Neatly . . as if You Were Going to Church': Respectability, Class, and Gender in the Montgomery Bus Boycott and the Early Civil Rights Movement," in *Gender and the Civil Rights Movement*, ed. Peter J. Ling and Sharon Monteith (New Brunswick, NJ: Rutgers University Press, 1999), 88.

25. *Browder, et al. v. Gayle et al.*, 142 F. Supp. 707 (1956).

26. Simmons, *Crescent City Girls*, 63.

27. Aline St. Julien, as quoted in Simmons, ibid., 62.

28. Robinson, *The Montgomery Bus Boycott and the Women Who Started It*, 43.

29. Mary Burks, "Trailblazers: Women in the Montgomery Bus Boycott," in *Women in the Civil Rights Movement: Trailblazers and Torchbearers, 1941–1965* (Brooklyn, NY: Carlson Publishers, 1990), 75.

30. Kelley, *Race Rebels*, 68–69, 73.

31. McGuire, *At the Dark End of the Street*, 34.

32. Miriam Thaggert, *Riding Jane Crow: African American Women on the American Railroad* (Urbana: University of Illinois Press, 2022), 12–13.

33. Murray, "Jim Crow and Jane Crow," 593.

34. Chappell, Hutchinson, and Ward, "'Dress Modestly, Neatly . . as if You Were Going to Church,'" 69.

35. Amanda H. Littauer, *Bad Girls: Young Women, Sex, and Rebellion before the Sixties* (Chapel Hill: University of North Carolina Press, 2015), 19–23, 26–30.

36. Marilyn E. Hegarty, *Victory Girls, Khaki-Wackies, and Patriotutes: The Regulation of Female Sexuality during World War II* (New York: New York University Press, 2008), 87.

37. Margaret Fishback, *Safe Conduct: When to Behave and Why* (New York: Harcourt, Brace, 1938), 32–35.

38. Alice-Leon Moats, *No Nice Girl Swears* (New York: Alfred A. Knopf, 1935), 184–185.

39. Millicent Fenwick, *Vogue Book of Etiquette* (New York: Simon & Schuster, 1948), 35.

40. Elinor Ames, *Book of Modern Etiquette Illustrated* (Toronto: C. Van Nostrand, 1948), 91.

41. Eleanor Harris, "Women without Men," *Look*, July 5, 1960, 43, 44, 45, 46.

42. "Cities and the Single Girl," *Newsweek*, November 15, 1965, 120.

43. "Bachelor Girl," *Ebony*, August 1966, 103.

44. "Cities and the Single Girl," *Newsweek*, November 15, 1965, 120.

45. John Kronenberger, "Memo from a Bachelor: The Singles Scene," *Look*, February 6, 1968, 80.

46. "Lonely Girl in the Big City," *Ladies' Home Journal*, May 1962, 28; Harry F. Waters, "Disenchanted: Girls in the City," *New York Times Magazine*, February 6, 1966, 28.

47. Rickie Solinger, *Wake Up Little Susie: Single Pregnancy and Race before "Roe v. Wade"* (New York: Routledge, 2000).

48. "Bachelor Girl," *Ebony*, 108.

49. Littauer, *Bad Girls*, 16.

50. Ibid., 152–155.

51. Marc Stein, *City of Sisterly and Brotherly Love: Lesbian and Gay Philadelphia, 1945–1972* (Philadelphia: Temple University Press, 2004), 86.

52. Littauer, *Bad Girls*, 4, 43; John Costello, *Love, Sex, and War: Changing Values, 1939–1945* (London: William Collins Sons and Co. Ltd., 1985); Leisa Meer, *Creating GI Jane: Sexuality and Power in the Women's Army Corps during World War II* (New York: Columbia University Press, 1996), chap. 7.

53. Lillian Faderman, *Odd Girls and Twilight Lovers: A History of Lesbian Life in Twentieth-Century America* (New York: Columbia University Press, 1991), 161, 163; see also Janet Kahn and Patricia A. Gozemba, "In and around the Lighthouse: Working-Class Lesbian Bar Culture in the 1950s and 1960s," in *Gendered Domains: Rethinking Public and Private in Women's History: Essays from the Seventh Berkshire Conference on the History of Women*, ed. Dorothy Helly and Susan Reverby (Ithaca, NY: Cornell University Press, 1992): 90–106; Marie Cartier, *Baby, You Are My Religion: Women, Gay Bars, and Theology before Stonewall* (Abingdon, UK: Acumen Press, 2013); Gwendolyn Stegall, "A Spatial History of Lesbian Bars in New York City," master's thesis, Columbia University, 2019.

54. Rochella Thorpe, "A House Where Queers Go: African-American Lesbian Nightlife in Detroit, 1940–1975," in *Inventing Lesbian Cultures in America*, ed. Ellen Lewin (Boston: Beacon Press, 1996), 41.

55. Marc Stein, *City of Sisterly and Brotherly Love*, 86. The term "reterritorialize" is taken from Lauren Berlant and Elizabeth Freeman, "Queer Nationality," *Boundary* 19, no. 1 (1992): 149–180, quoted in Phil Hubbard, *Cities and Sexuality* (New York: Routledge, 2011), 106.

56. Nan Alamilla Boyd, *Wide Open Town: A History of Queer San Francisco to 1965* (Berkeley: University of California Press, 2003), 71.

57. Faderman, *Odd Girls and Twilight Lovers*, 165.

58. Leslie Feinberg, *Stone Butch Blues* (New York: Firebrand Books, 1993), 8, 10.

59. Arlene Stein, *Sex and Sensibility: Stories of a Lesbian Generation* (Berkeley: University of California Press, 1997), 29; Alix Genter, "Appearances Can Be Deceiving: Butch-Femme Fashion and Queer Legibility in New York City, 1945–1969," *Feminist Studies* 42 (2016): 604–631.

60. Lillian Faderman and Stuart Timmons, *Gay LA: A History of Sexual Outlaws, Power Politics, and Lipstick Lesbians* (New York: Basic Books, 2006), 94.

61. Joan Nestle, *A Restricted Country* (New York: Firebrand Books, 1987; reprint, San Francisco: Cleis Press, 2003), 100.

62. Judith Butler, *Gender Trouble: Feminism and the Subversion of Identity* (New York: Routledge, 1999), 140.

63. Nestle, *A Restricted Country*, 102.

64. Toni, quoted in Elizabeth Lapovsky Kennedy and Madeline D. Davis, *Boots of Leather, Slippers of Gold: The History of a Lesbian Community* (New York: Routledge, 1993), 181.

65. Matty, quoted in ibid., 181.

66. Stormy, quoted in ibid., 178.

67. Genter, "Appearances Can Be Deceiving," 79–80.

68. Thorpe, "A House Where Queers Go," 42.

69. "Purpose of the Daughters of Bilitis," *The Ladder*, January 1959, 2; Martin Meeker, *Contacts Desired: Gay and Lesbian Communications and Community, 1940s–1970s* (Chicago: University of Chicago Press, 2006).

70. Dee, quoted in Kennedy and Davis, *Boots of Leather, Slippers of Gold*, 172.

71. Koreen Phelps, interview with Scott Paulsen, November 5, 1993, Twin Cities Gay and Lesbian Community Oral History Project, University of Minnesota, Minneapolis, MN. On partial passing, see Sherrie Inness, *The Lesbian Menace: Ideology, Identity, and the Representation of Lesbian Life* (Amherst: University of Massachusetts Press, 1997), 158.

72. Adrienne Rich, "Compulsory Heterosexuality and Lesbian Existence," in *The Lesbian and Gay Studies Reader*, ed. Henry Abelove, Michele Aina Barale, and David M. Halperin (New York: Routledge, 1993), 238.

73. Arlene Stein, *Sex and Sensibility*, 68, 83.

74. Ibid., 78.

75. Don Sauers, *The Girl Watcher's Guide* (New York: Harper, 1954).

76. Ibid., 10, 7.

77. Ken Lubas, "Girl Watchers International: Furtive Leer Comes Out in Open," *Los Angeles Times*, August 7, 1969; Hal Boyle (for the Associated Press), "Girl-Watching: Has Turned into Fine Art," *Biloxi-Gulfport Daily Herald*, April 9, 1968; Hal Boyle, "Plain Bloomer Uniform Urged for Office Girls," *Washington Post*, June 7, 1955.

78. "What Kind of Girl Watcher Are You?," *Girl Watcher*, March 1959, 8.

79. See, for example, Ordway, *The Etiquette of To-Day*, 134; Moats, *No Nice Girl Swears*, 116; and Chase, *Good Form and Social Ethics*, 243.

80. John Kasson, *Rudeness and Civility: Manners in Nineteenth-Century Urban America* (New York: Hill and Wang, 1990), 127. New Orleans, San Francisco, and New York passed laws in the nineteenth century prohibiting "public insults" against women in the streets. Mary Ryan notes that there were twice as many arrests for such offenses than for rape. Ryan, *Women in Public*, 69.

81. Sauers, *The Girl Watcher's Guide*, 8.

82. "Standing on the Corner," lyrics and music by Frank Loesser, 1956.

83. Sauers, *The Girl Watcher's Guide*, 35 (emphasis in original).

84. "Introduction to Girl Watching," *The Girl Watcher*, March 1959, 6.

85. Sauers, *The Girl Watcher's Guide*, 13, 19.

86. Overviews of this theme can be found in Joanne Meyerowitz, "Introduction: Women and Gender in the Postwar United States," in *Not June Cleaver: Women and Gender in Postwar America*, ed. Joanne Meyerowitz (Philadelphia: Temple University Press, 1994): 1–16; Winifred Breines, "Introduction," in Breines, *Young, White, and Miserable: Growing Up Female in the Fifties* (Chicago: University of Chicago Press, 1992); and Nathan Abrams and Julie Hughes, ed., *Containing America: Cultural Production and Consumption in 50s America* (Birmingham, UK: University of Birmingham Press, 2000), 1–3.

87. Breines, *Young, White, and Miserable*, 11.

88. Michael Kimmel, *Manhood in America: A Cultural History* (New York: Free Press, 1997), 262.

89. Philip Wylie, *Generation of Vipers* (New York: Farrar & Rinehart, 1942; rev. ed., New York: Rinehart, 1955).

90. Bill Osgerby, *Playboys in Paradise: Masculinity, Youth, and Leisure-Style in Modern America* (New York: Oxford, 2001), 4; Carrie Pitzulo, *Bachelors and Bunnies: The Sexual Politics of Playboy* (Chicago: University of Chicago Press, 2011).

91. Barbara Ehrenreich, *The Hearts of Men: American Dreams and the Flight from Commitment* (New York: Anchor Press, 1983), 3.

92. Beth Bailey, *From Front Porch to Back Seat: Courtship in Twentieth-Century America* (Baltimore: Johns Hopkins University Press, 1988), 96.

93. Enid A. Haupt, "Young Living: Fundamentals of Flirting," *Washington Post*, July 5, 1964.

94. Joanne Meyerowitz, "Beyond the Feminine Mystique: A Reassessment of Postwar Mass Culture, 1946–1958," in Meyerowitz, *Not June Cleaver*, 244.

95. Boyle, "Plain Bloomer," 15.

96. Sauers, *The Girl Watcher's Guide*, 39.

97. "An Introduction to Girl Watching," *Girl Watcher*, March 1959, 4.

98. "More about Collecting Pretty Girls," *Girl Watcher*, June 1959, 18.

99. Michael Davidson, *Guys Like Us: Citing Masculinity in Cold War Poetics* (Chicago: University of Chicago Press, 2004), vii.

100. Breines, *Young, White, and Miserable*, 11; Susan Douglas, *Where the Girls Are: Growing Up Female with the Mass Media* (New York: Random House, 1994), esp. chap. 3; Elaine Tyler May, *Homeward Bound: American Families in the Cold War Era* (New York: Basic Books, 1988), esp. chap. 4; and Bill Osgerby, "Muscular Manhood and Salacious Sleaze: The Singular World of the 1950s Macho Pulps," in Abrams and Hughes, *Containing America*, 125–150. For an examination of women's disparate reactions to the sexual representation of women in mass media, see Joanne Meyerowitz, "Women, Cheesecake, and Borderline Material: Responses to Girlie Pictures in the Mid–Twentieth Century," *Journal of Women's History* 8 (Fall 1996): 9–35.

101. Michael Johns, *Moment of Grace: The American City in the 1950s* (Berkeley: University of California Press, 2003), 1.

102. Dick Kidson, "Farmers Market Today," *Los Angeles Times*, October 11, 1958.

103. Sauers, *The Girl Watcher's Guide*, 30.

104. Jack Smith, "Watcher or the Watched?," *Los Angeles Times*, September 28, 1970.

105. Sauers, *The Girl Watcher's Guide*, 15; Frank Loesser, "Standing on the Corner," 1956.

106. May, *Homeward Bound*, 10.

107. On gender hierarchies in business, see Angel Kwolek-Folland, *Engendering Business: Men and Women in the Corporate Office, 1870–1930* (Baltimore: Johns Hopkins University Press, 1994), chap. 4.

108. Yvonne Rainer, "Skirting," in *The Feminist Memoir Project: Voices from Women's Liberation*, ed. Ann Snitow and Rachel Duplessis (New York: Three Rivers Press, 1998), 444.

109. "The Hunter and the Hunted," *Girl Watcher*, March 1959, 6.

110. On Cold War sexuality for women, see May, *Homeward Bound* 93–99; and Donna Penn, "The Sexualized Woman: The Lesbian, the Prostitute, and the Containment of Female Sexuality in Postwar America," in Meyerowitz, *Not June Cleaver*, 358–381.

111. McGuire, *At the Dark End of the Street*, 51.

112. John D'Emilio and Estelle Freedman, *Intimate Matters: A History of Sexuality in America* (New York: Harper & Row, 1988), 242.

113. Don Sauers, "The Birth of Girl Watching," March 2004, https://www.renevanmaars-seveen.nl/wp-content/uploads/overig7/The%20Birth%20of%20Girl%20Watching.pdf.

114. Patricia McCormack, "Boots March to Fashion Frontline," *Atlanta Daily World*, July 11, 1963; Steve Snider, [untitled], *Atlanta Daily World*, March 29, 1970.

115. "Champ," *Los Angeles Sentinel*, March 25, 1971.

116. Theresa Fambro Hooks, "Black-Rimmed Spectacles for 'Girl Watching,'" *Chicago Daily Defender*, November 4, 1968.

117. Ken Lubas, "Girl Watchers International: Furtive Leer Comes Out in Open," *Los Angeles Times*, August 7, 1969.

118. "60s Classic Diet Pepsi Commercial," YouTube, https://youtu.be/jNyosJw6YuU.

119. See, for example, "No Rental Agency Runaround," *Los Angeles Sentinel*, May 15 1969.

120. "Too Much Girl Watching?" (advertisement), *Chicago Daily Defender*, November 10, 1964.

121. "Folding Binoculars" (advertisement), *New York Amsterdam News*, October 1, 1960.

122. *Glamour*, January 1969, 138–139, quoted in Carol Brooks Gardner, *Passing By: Gender and Public Harassment* (Berkeley: University of California Press, 1995), 22–23.

123. "Gimbels Wonderful World of New York" (advertisement), *New York Times*, February 16, 1969.

Chapter 4: When Girls Became Women

1. Beth Bailey, *Front Porch to Back Seat: Courtship in Twentieth-Century America* (Baltimore: Johns Hopkins University Press, 1988), 116.

2. Susan Brownmiller, interview with the author.

3. Erving Goffman, *Behavior in Public Places: Notes on the Social Organization of Gatherings* (New York: Free Press, 1963), 8, 87.

4. Etiquette limited women's ability to respond to the furtive touching. Frotteurs count on women ignoring their behavior since etiquette has generally taught women that it is rude to be confrontational or make a scene, especially in a situation where it is difficult to judge with certainty whether the touch is intentionally violating her personal space or she has merely been jostled in a crowd. Gardner, *Passing By*, 138–141.

5. Marge Piercy, "An Open Letter," in *Take Back the Night: Women on Pornography*, ed. Laura Lederer (New York: William Morrow, 1980), 7; quoted in Leslie Weisman, *Discrimination by Design: A Feminist Critique of the Man-Made Environment* (Urbana: University of Illinois Press, 1992), 67.

6. Betsy Israel, *Bachelor Girl: 100 Years of Breaking the Rules, A Social History of Living Single* (New York: Perennial, 2003), 230.

7. Brownmiller, interview with the author.

8. Israel, *Bachelor Girl*, 227.

9. Mary Conroy, *The Rational Woman's Guide to Self-Defense* (New York: Grosset & Dunlap, 1975), 8.

10. Israel, *Bachelor Girl*, 241.

11. Peter Braunstein, "'Adults Only': The Construction of an Erotic City in New York during the 1970s," in *America in the 70s*, ed. Beth Bailey and David Farber (Lawrence: University Press of Kansas, 2004), 130.

12. Bill Osgerby, *Playboys in Paradise: Masculinity, Youth, and Leisure Style in Modern America* (New York: Berg Publishers, 2001), 39; Elizabeth Fraterrigo, *Playboy and the Making of the Good Life in Modern America* (New York: Oxford University Press, 2009), 172.

13. Susan Brownmiller, *In Our Time: Memoir of a Revolution* (New York: Random House, 1999), 201.

14. Elizabeth Stanko, *Everyday Violence: How Women and Men Experience Sexual and Physical Danger* (San Francisco: Pandora, 1990); and Esther Madriz, *Nothing Bad Happens to Good Girls: Fear of Crime in Women's Lives* (Berkeley: University of California Press, 1997), esp. chap. 6.

15. Activism on this issue reveals key fissures and characteristics of the feminist movement of the late 1960s and early 1970s, including debates over the role of lesbians, prostitution, and race. See Sara Evans, *Tidal Wave: How Women Changed America at Century's End* (New York: Free Press, 2003), 50–53; Alice Echols, *Daring to Be Bad: Radical Feminism in America, 1969–1975* (Minneapolis: University of Minnesota Press, 1989), 194; Val Jenness, *Making It Work: The Prostitutes' Rights Movement in Perspective* (Piscataway, NJ: Aldine Transaction, 1993); Stephanie Gilmore, "Bridging the Waves: Sex and Sexuality in a Second Wave Organization," in *Different Wavelengths: Studies of the Contemporary Women's Movement*, ed. Jo Reger (New York: Routledge, 2005), 107; Ruth Rosen, *The World Split Open: How the Modern Women's Movement Changed America* (New York: Viking, 2000), 87; Barbara Ryan, *Feminism and the Women's Movement: Dynamics of Change in Social Movement Ideology and Activism* (New York: Routledge, 1992), 40–41; Stephanie Gilmore, "The Dynamics of Second-Wave Feminist Activism in Memphis, 1971–1982," *NWSA Journal* 15 (Spring 2003): 94–117; and Judith Ezekiel, *Feminism in the Heartland* (Columbus: Ohio State University Press, 2002), 37–40.

16. Many hotels still refused to let rooms to lone women, assuming they were prostitutes. Perry R. Duis, *The Saloon: Public Drinking in Chicago and Boston, 1880–1920* (Urbana: University of Illinois Press, 1983), 186–187.

17. Howard Chudacoff, *The Age of the Bachelor: Creating an American Subculture* (Princeton, NJ: Princeton University Press), 108, 113.

18. Madelon Powers, *Faces along the Bar: Lore and Order in the Workingman's Saloon, 1870–1920* (Chicago: University of Chicago Press, 1998); Duis, *The Saloon*, 276–277; and Paul Groth, *Living Downtown: The History of Residential Hotels in the United States* (Berkeley: University of California Press, 1994).

19. Odem, *Delinquent Daughters*, chap. 4; Hickey, *Hope and Danger in the New South City*, 122; and Littauer, *Bad Girls*, chap. 2.

20. Mary Murphy, *Mining Cultures: Men, Women, and Leisure in Butte, 1914–1941* (Urbana: University of Illinois Press, 1997), chap. 2.

21. As late as 1970, for example, one-quarter of the licenses in Boston went to male-only establishments. "Men-Only Boston Bars Carry on Tradition," *Wall Street Journal*, September 4, 1970; Women's Ephemera Folders (WEF), McCormick Library, Northwestern University.

22. Susan Brownmiller describes being humiliated when her mother took her out for a fancy birthday lunch and the pair was turned away from the Café de la Paix in the Saint Moritz Hotel because they were "unescorted." Brownmiller, *In Our Time*, 208–209.

23. Dolores Alexander, "Her Pause for Refreshment Leads to Fight for Equality," *Newsday*, June 13, 1968.

24. Karen DeCrow, interview with the author, July 20–21, 2004, Jamestown, NY.

25. Ibid., and "Public Accommodations" (unpublished manuscript), Frances Arick Kolb Papers, Schlesinger Library, Radcliffe Institute, Harvard University, Cambridge, MA.

26. Georgina Hickey, "The Respectability Trap: Gender Conventions in 20th Century Movements for Social Change," *Journal of Interdisciplinary Feminist Thought* 7 (Summer 2013), article 2, http://digitalcommons.salve.edu/jift/vol7/iss1/2.

27. "People," *Time*, February 21, 1969, 33; *Parade*, April 6, 1969; Betty Friedan, "Up from the Kitchen Floor," *New York Times*, March 4, 1973; "Memo to Aileen Hernandez," March 6, 1971, National Organization for Women Collection, Schlesinger Library, Radcliffe Institute, Harvard University, Cambridge, MA.

28. NOW, "The National Organization for Women's 1966 Statement of Purpose," *http://now.org/about/history/statement-of-purpose.*

29. *NOW ACTS* 3 (July 1970), 7.

30. Sara Evans, *Personal Politics: The Roots of Women's Liberation in the Civil Rights Movement and New Left* (New York: Vintage Books, 1979), 193–211; Alice Echols, *Daring to Be Bad: Radical Feminism in America, 1967–1975* (Minneapolis: University of Minnesota Press, 1989), 23–50.

31. Brownmiller, interview with the author; "Libs Lose Stein Room Battle," *Los Angeles Herald Examiner*, November 21, 1970.

32. Andrew Tully, "Libbers Silly about Bars" (uncited clipping), October 13, 19[71], WEF.

33. Karen DeCrow to Frances Kolb, March 6, 1981, and DeCrow, "Memo to Aileen Hernandez," NOW Collection.

34. "NOW Gals Liberate a Lounge," *Reporter Dispatch* (White Plains, NY), May 22, 1971.

35. On the chronology of women-of-color feminisms, see Ann Valk, *Radical Sisters: Second-Wave Feminism and Black Liberation in Washington, DC* (Urbana: University of Illinois Press, 2010); Kimberly Springer, *Living for the Revolution: Black Feminist Organizations, 1968–1980* (Durham, NC: Duke University Press, 2005); Benita Roth, *Separate Roads to Feminism: Black, Chicana, and White Feminist Movements in America's Second Wave* (New York: Cambridge University Press, 2004).

36. The role of the public sphere in shaping and transmitting societal norms is addressed by Jürgen Habermas, "The Public Sphere: An Encyclopedia Article," *New German Critique* 5, no. 2 (1974): 49–55. Feminist theorists have thoroughly called Habermas to task for ignoring or dismissing women's lack of standing, and that of other disadvantaged groups, in the public sphere. See Nancy Fraser, *Unruly Practices: Power, Discourse, and Gender in Contemporary Social Theory* (Minneapolis: University of Minnesota Press, 1989); and Joan B. Landes, "The Public and the Private Sphere: A Feminist Reconsideration," in *Feminists Read Habermas: Gendering the Subject of Discourse*, ed. Johanna Meehan (New York: Routledge, 1995): 91–116.

37. Lizabeth Cohen, *A Consumer's Republic: The Politics of Mass Consumption in Postwar America* (New York: Knopf, 2003), 167.

38. *Seidenberg and DeCrow v. McSorely's Old Ale House, Inc.*, No. 69 Civ. 2728 (1970).

39. DeCrow to Kolb, NOW Collection.

40. Brownmiller, interview with the author; Betty Friedan and Nita Ladewig to Richard Swig (president of Fairmont Hotel), July 1, 1969, Carabillo/Meuli Files, Dismore Archives (formerly the Feminist History E-mail Archives), https://www.veteranfeministsofamerica.org/legacy/Dismore.htm; NOW press release, n.d., NOW Collection; "They'd Make Public Bars Coed," *New London Day*, n.d., Karen DeCrow's private papers.

41. Nancy Baltad, "Women Stage Protest Demonstration in Bar," *Hollywood (CA) Citizen-News*, February 21, 1969.

42. Karen DeCrow to "Nan," July 24, 1968, DeCrow's private papers.

43. The activists I interviewed, including DeCrow and Brownmiller, resisted questions about the racial and class implications of these protests.

44. Joanne Undercoffler, "NOW Gals Liberate a Lounge," *Reporter-Dispatch* (White Plains, NY), May 22, 1971.

45. Pauli Murray, *Song in a Weary Throat: An American Pilgrimage* (New York: Harper & Row, 1987), 183.

46. NOW, "New York City Goals," [1969], NOW Collection.

47. "Two Women Storm Sanctum Reserved for Men—and Lose," *Cleveland Press*, April 22, 1971, WEF.

48. Brownmiller, interview with the author; Brownmiller, *In Our Time*, 209.

49. Nancy Ballard, "Women Stage Protest Demonstration in Bar," *Hollywood Citizen-News*, February 21, 1969.

50. DeCrow, interview with the author.

51. "Lib Wins Another Round," *Sacramento (CA) Union*, February 17, 1971.

52. "Two Beers, Please," *Manhattan Tribune*, May 2, 1970, WEF.

53. John R. Coyne Jr., "Ale, Cheese, Onions, and Women," *National Review*, September 22, 1970, 997.

54. Uncited clipping, July 20, 1971, WEF.

55. DeCrow, interview with the author.

56. Sookie Stambler, "Liberating McSorley's: Return to the Scene of the Crime," *Manhattan Tribune*, August 22, 1970.

57. "Gals Rapping Restaurants over Men-Only Policies," *Nation's Restaurant News*, March 3, 1969, 3.

58. Stambler, "Liberating McSorley's."

59. William S. White, "Gone Is Man's Last Hope," *Syracuse Herald Journal*, June 30, 1970.

60. "Council Approves Bill Barring Discrimination against Women," *New York Times*, July 22, 1970, WEF.

61. DeCrow, interview with the author.

62. *Debra Millenson v. The New Hotel Monteleone, Inc.*, No. 72-3131 (E.D La. 1973, affirmed by 5th Cir. Ct. App., 1973).

63. *Village Voice*, August 26, 1971, 3.

64. "News Release, Commission on Human Rights: '21' Club and the Biltmore Hotel Are Charged with Sex Discrimination," May 20, 1971, WEF.

65. Karen DeCrow, "Task Force on Public Accommodations," March 16, 1970, and Jean Witter, "Pittsburgh Chapter–NOW, 11-70 to 9-71 Report," NOW Collection.

66. Karen DeCrow, "Task Force on Public Accommodations," NOW Collection.

67. Tully, "Libbers Silly about Bars."

68. "Is the Absurd Now Treated Seriously?" *Miami Herald*, August 16, 1970.

69. "Gals Rapping Restaurants over Men-Only Policies."

70. "NOW girls" appears in "People," *Time*, February 21, 1969, 33; "Spokesgal" appears in "Gals Rapping Restaurants over Men-Only Policies."

71. "Let's Do It," *Newsweek*, July 13, 1970, 34.

72. Karen DeCrow, "Memo to NOW Board of Directors Re: Public Accommodations Week, February 9–15, 1969," March 21, 1969, and minutes of the Southern California Chapter, April 8, 1969, NOW Collection.

73. *Gallagher v. The City of Bayonne, NJ*, No. C1956-65 (1968), discussed in E. J. Farians, "Memorandum to All Stout-Hearted Women and Their Friends," WEF.

74. Faith Seidenberg, "The Federal Bar v. the Ale House Bar: Women and Public Accommodations," *Valparaiso University Law Review* 5 (1971): 318–325; see also *DeCrow v. Hotel Syracuse Corp.*, 59 Misc. 2d 383, 386, 298 N.Y.S.2d 859, 862–863 (Sup. Ct. 1969).

75. Joseph Mitchell, *Up in the Old Hotel and Other Stories* (New York: Vintage, 1993), 4.

76. Ibid., 11.

77. McSorley's is still open (it claims to be the oldest continuously operating bar in the city) and still wringing all it can from its reputation. It incorporated the story of its gender integration into its larger mythology, and newspaper clippings pertaining to the issue are displayed in the front window.

78. "Notice of Motion for Summary Judgement," *Seidenberg v. McSorley's*, 9.

79. Judge Charles H. Tenney, quoted in Faith Seidenberg, "The Federal Bar v. the Ale House Bar: Women and Public Accommodations," *Valparaiso University Law Review* 5 (1971): 321; see also Leo Kanowitz, *Sex Roles in Law and Society: Cases and Materials* (Albuquerque: University of New Mexico Press, 1973), chap. 7.

80. This strategy for addressing racial discrimination had been made obsolete by the passage of the 1964 Civil Rights Act, which specifically outlawed discrimination in public accommodations based on race. See Thomas P. Lewis, "The Sit-In Cases: Great Expectations," in *1963: The Supreme Court Review*, ed. Philip B. Kurland (Chicago: University of Chicago Press, 1963), 101–151.

81. *Millenson v. The New Hotel Monteleone, Inc.*, No. 72-3131 Summary Calendar, 475 F. 2d 736 (US App., 1973). A lower federal court did, however, rule that if the police got involved in the exclusion or segregation of women (by taking down names or asking women to leave an establishment), the equal protection clause of the Fourteenth Amendment would apply.

82. Joseph P. Fried, "Following Up," *New York Times*, June 23, 2002; "Male Bastion Falls," *Post-Standard* (Syracuse, NY), June 16, 1970.

83. WBAI Consciousness Raising, "Men and Violence," in *Radical Feminism*, ed. Anne Koedt, Ellen Levine, and Anita Rapone (New York: Quadrangle Books, 1973), 64.

84. "D," "Street Hassling," *Women's Center Newsletter*, Women's Liberation Collection (WLC), Sophia Smith Collection, Smith College, Northampton, MA.

85. "Rape Is the Ugliest Four-Letter Word in the English Language," *Womankind* (Chicago), July 1972, Labadie Collection, Harlan Hatcher Graduate Library, University of Michigan, Ann Arbor, MI; Lisa Leghorn, "I Am a Woman," *No More Fun and Games* 3 (November 1969).

86. Roxanne Dunbar, "Female Liberation as the Basis for Social Revolution," in *Sisterhood Is Powerful: An Anthology of Writings from the Women's Liberation Movement*, ed. Robin Morgan (New York: Vintage Books, 1970), 537.

87. WBAI Consciousness Raising, "Men and Violence," 64; "D," "Street Hassling."

88. Madriz, *Nothing Bad Happens to Good Girls*, 153–154.

89. Laura Mulvey, "Visual Pleasure and Narrative Cinema" (1976), reprinted in Laura Mulvey, *Visual and Other Pleasures* (Bloomington: Indiana University Press, 1989), 20, 25, 16.

90. WBAI Consciousness Raising, "Men and Violence," 64. Privacy, as Gwendolyn Pough notes in her study of hip-hop culture, is a marker of privilege and one long denied minorities and women. Pough, *Check It While I Wreck It: Black Womanhood, Hip-Hop Culture, and the Public Sphere* (Boston: Northeastern University Press, 2004), 33.

91. *She Is Beautiful When She Is Angry* (DVD), directed by Mary Dore, distributed by Cinema Guild, 2015.

92. Roxanne Dunbar, "Outlaw Woman: Chapters from a Feminist Memoir-in-Progress," in *The Feminist Memoir Project: Voices from Women's Liberation*, ed. Rachel Blau DuPlessis and Ann Snitow (New York: Three Rivers Press, 1998), 112.

93. Madriz, *Nothing Bad Happens to Good Girls*, 51–57.

94. In this very Foucault-like description of public space, etiquette acts as a "disciplinary power" that promotes docility. See Linda McDowell, "Spatializing Feminism: Geographic Perspectives," in *BodySpace: Destabilizing Gender Geographies of Gender and Sexuality*, ed. Nancy Duncan (New York: Routledge, 1996), 33. On how power relations are built into spatial arrangements in ways that make them appear "natural" and "real" and therefore hard to challenge, see Barbara Hooper, "The Poem of Male Desire," in *Making the Invisible Visible: A Multicultural Planning History*, ed. Leonie Sandercock (Berkeley: University of California Press, 1998), 232–233.

95. Shirley Ardner, ed., *Women and Space: Ground Rules and Social Maps* (New York: St. Martin's Press, 1981), 11–12; Hooper, "The Poem of Male Desire," 231; Jos Boys, "Women and Public Space," in Matrix, *Making Space: Women and the Man-Made Environment* (London: Pluto Press, 1984), 49.

96. Jürgen Habermas narrowly ties the "standing" or "competency" to participate in the public sphere to the concept of the "rational individual." This is one of the key areas where feminists have critiqued his theory for failing to see the ways in which this restricts the public sphere to white, middle-class men. See Habermas, *The Structural Transformation of the Public Sphere: An Inquiry into a Category of Bourgeois Society* (Cambridge, MA· MIT Press, 1991); and Meehan, *Feminists Read Habermas*.

97. Nancy Duncan, "Renegotiating Gender and Sexuality in Public and Private Space," in Duncan, *BodySpace*, 127.

98. "'Ogling,'" *Guardian*, reprinted in *Everywoman* 1 (July 10, 1970).

99. Ann Forfreedom, "First L.A. Ogle-in," *Everywoman* 7 (September 11, 1970).

100. *ABC News*, "Women's Liberation" (video recording), c. 1971, distributed by Xerox Films, 2002.

101. "Bod Squad vs. Verbal Rapists," *Everywoman* 32 (May 1972): 32.

102. Detroit Women Against Rape (WAR), 1971, quoted in Maria Bevacqua, *Rape on the Public Agenda: Feminism and the Politics of Sexual Assault* (Boston: Northeastern University Press, 2000), 71.

103. Elizabeth Kissling, "Street Harassment: The Language of Sexual Terrorism," *Discourse and Society* 2, no 4. (1991): 452–460; Cynthia Bowman, "Street Harassment and the Informal Ghettoization of Women," *Harvard Law Review* (January 1993): 517–577.

104. Carol Weston, "Viewpoint," *Glamour*, July 1981; Karin Winegar, "What I Want Is an Hour on the Jogging Path without Men's Catcalls. Is That Too Much to Ask?" *Glamour*, June 1980; "Verbal Abuse on the Street: How to Talk Back," *Glamour*, February 1984.

105. Mary K. Blakely, "True or False: "All Men Like to Girl-Watch and Girls Don't Mind It," *Vogue*, January 1982, 56, 58; Gwenda Blair, "Street Hassling: Putting Up with Put Downs," *Mademoiselle*, July 1984, 118–119.

106. Elizabeth Kuster, "Don't 'Hey, Baby' Me: How to Fight Street Harassment," *Glamour*, September 1992, 308–311, 332–334.

107. See, for example, Carol Dana, "Talking Back to Street Harassers," *Washington Post*, August 19, 1986.

108. Christina Del Sesto, "Our Mean Streets: DC's Women Walk through Verbal Combat Zones," *Washington Post*, March 18, 1990.

109. Kuster, "Don't 'Hey, Baby' Me," 309.

110. Courtland Milloy, "The Ugly Sounds of Summer," *Washington Post*, May 31, 1990.

111. Don Sauers, "The Death of Girl Watching," 2001, https://www.renevanmaarsseveen.nl /wp-content/uploads/overig7/The%20Death%20of%20Girl%20Watching.pdf.

Chapter 5: The Public Is Political

1. Carol Hanisch, "The Personal Is Political," in *Notes from the Second Year: Women's Liberation*, ed. Shulamith Firestone and Anne Koedt (New York: Radical Feminism, 1970), 76–77.

2. Betty Friedan, quoted in Simon Hall, *American Patriotism, American Protest: Social Movements since the Sixties* (Philadelphia: University of Pennsylvania Press, 2010), 52.

3. Brownmiller, *In Our Time*, 296.

4. Carolyn Bronstein, *Battling Pornography: The American Feminist Anti-Pornography Movement, 1976–1986* (New York: Cambridge University Press, 2011), 64.

5. Kathleen Keefe Burg, *The Womanly Art of Self-Defense: A Commonsense Approach* (New York: A&W Visual Library, 1979), 146–147.

6. Mary Conroy, *The Rational Woman's Guide to Self-Defense: A Commonsense Approach* (New York: Grosset & Dunlap, 1975), 6.

7. Chester W. Krone, *The Womanly Art of Self-Defense* (New York: Award Books, 1967), cover.

8. Ibid., 25.

9. Conroy, *The Rational Woman's Guide to Self-Defense*, cover.

10. Israel, *Bachelor Girl*, 208, 234.

11. Teresa Amott and Julie Matthaei, *Race, Gender, and Work: A Multicultural Economic History of Women in the United States* (Boston: South End Press, 1991), 305.

12. Marcia M. Gallo, *No One Helped: Kitty Genovese, New York City, and the Myth of Urban Apathy* (Ithaca, NY: Cornell University Press, 2015).

13. Conroy, *The Rational Woman's Guide to Self-Defense*, 9.

14. Burg, *The Womanly Art of Self-Defense*, 145.

15. S. Margaret Heyden and Allan V. Tarpenning, *Personal Defense for Women* (Belmont, CA: Wadsworth Publishing, 1970), 69.

16. Conroy, *The Rational Woman's Guide to Self-Defense*, 8.

17. Ibid.

18. Ibid., 37.

19. Heyden and Tarpenning, *Personal Defense for Women*, 74.

20. Conroy, *The Rational Woman's Guide to Self-Defense*, 30.

21. Heyden and Tarpenning, *Personal Defense for Women*, 74.

22. Lisa Sliwa, *Attitude: Commonsense Defense for Women* (New York: Crown Publishers, 1986), 84; Jim Bullard, *Looking Forward to Being Attacked: Self-Protection for Every Woman* (New York: M. Evans and Co., 1977), 119.

23. Bullard, *Looking Forward to Being Attacked*, 120.

24. Beth Bailey, "She 'Can Bring Home the Bacon': Negotiating Gender in Seventies America," in Bailey and Farber, *America in the 70s*, 117–119.

25. Susan Faludi, *Backlash: The Undeclared War against Women* (New York: Crown Publishing Group, 1991), xxii.

26. Madriz, *Nothing Bad Happens to Good Girls*, 19.

27. Rachel Moon Pascale and Leslie B. Tanner, "Self-Defense for Women," in Morgan, *Sisterhood Is Powerful*, 527.

28. Susan Smith, *Fear or Freedom: A Woman's Options in Social Survival and Physical Defense* (Racine, WI: Mother Courage Press, 1986), 13.

29. Ibid., 5–6.

30. Martha McCaughey, *Real Knockouts: The Physical Feminism of Women's Self-Defense* (New York: New York University Press, 1997), 55–56.

31. Py Bateman, *Fear into Anger: A Manual of Self-Defense for Women* (Chicago: Nelson-Hall, 1978), 4.

32. Ibid., 2; Smith, *Fear or Freedom*, 6.

33. Carrie Bronstein, "No More Black and Blue," in *Violence Against Women* 14 (April 2008): 418–436.

34. Anne Pride, "Women Take Back the Night," *Feminist Alliance Against Rape Newsletter*, November/December 1977, 18–19.

35. Brownmiller, *In Our Time*, 301–302.

36. Lynn Campbell, quoted in Bronstein, *Battling Pornography*, 166.

37. Estelle B. Freedman, *No Turning Back: The History of Feminism and the Future of Women* (New York: Ballantine Books, 2002), 286.

38. Take Back the Night pamphlet, publicizing a march on Saturday, November 18 (likely 1978), Women Against Violence in Pornography and the Media (WAVPM) Records, GLBT Historical Society, San Francisco, CA.

39. On the evolution of TBN from political action to memorialization, see Anne Valk, "Remembering Together: Take Back the Night and the Public Memory of Feminism," *US Women's History: Untangling the Threads of Sisterhood*, ed. Leslie Brown, Jacqueline Castledaine, and Anne Valk (New Brunswick, NJ: Rutgers University Press, 2017).

40. Linda Tessier, email message to WMST list serve, September 25, 1997, archived at Internet Archive, Wayback Machine, http://web.archive.org/web/20070630022550/http:// research.umbc.edu/~korenman/wmst/takenite2.html.

41. Holly Near, "Fight Back," from *Imagine My Surprise* (Redwood Records, 1978). Lyrics to the song appear on a flyer in the Organizing Against Pornography (OAP) collection, "Chants and Songs for Take Back the Night," n.d.

42. Marge Piercy, email message to WMST list serve, September 25, 1997, archived at Internet Archive, Wayback Machine, http://web.archive.org/web/20070630022550/http:// research.umbc.edu/~korenman/wmst/takenite2.html.

43. David Johnston, "5,000 March through Hollywood to Protest Nighttime Attacks on Women," *Los Angeles Times*, April 20, 1980.

44. Lynn Smith, "Action: Anti-Rape March a Move to Substitute Strength for Fear," *Los Angeles Times*, December 1, 1983.

45. "Take Back the Night," history folder, Coalition to Take Back the Night records (Boston), Northeastern University Archives and Special Collections, Northeastern University, Boston, MA.

46. See, for example, Stephanie Gilmore, ed., *Feminist Coalitions: Historical Perspectives on Second Wave Feminism in the United States* (Urbana: University of Illinois Press, 2008); and Tamar Carroll, *Mobilizing New York: AIDS, Anti-Poverty, and Feminism Activism* (Chapel Hill: University of North Carolina Press, 2015).

47. Untitled "History" of marches in the 1980s, Coalition to Take Back the Night records, Northeastern University.

48. Bevacqua, *Rape on the Public Agenda*, 72.

49. Smith, "Action."

50. Nkenge Toure, staff member from DC Rape Crisis Center, quoted in Martin Weil and Peter Eng, "Women March Against Pornography," *Washington Post*, September 27, 1981.

51. I. Rajeswary, "Anti-Rape Week Will Target Verbal Abuse," *Washington Post*, September 20, 1985.

52. "Afraid to Go Out at Night," *Chicago Tribune*, September 27, 1980.

53. Weil and Eng, "Women March against Pornography."

54. "Women Unite—Reclaim the Night," March 29, 1978, Coalition to Take Back the Night records.

55. "Take Back the Night," history folder, Coalition to Take Back the Night records.

56. WAVPM Action Committee, minutes, February 11, 1980.

57. Dolores Alexander, interview with Kelly Anderson (transcript), March 20, 2004, Voices of Feminism Oral History Project, Sophia Smith Collection, Smith College, Northampton, MA.

58. Quoted in Bronstein, *Battling Pornography*, 4.

59. Women Against Violence in Pornography and the Media, "Statement of Purpose," August 5, 1978.

60. Laurence Senelick, "Private Parts in Public Places," in *Inventing Times Square: Commerce and Culture at the Crossroads of the World*, ed. William R. Taylor (New York: Russell Sage Foundation, 1991), 346.

61. Whitney Strub, *Perversion for Profit: The Politics of Pornography and the Rise of the New Right* (New York: Columbia University Press, 2013), 243.

62. Josh Sides, *Erotic City: Sexual Revolutions and the Making of Modern San Francisco* (Oxford: Oxford University Press, 2009), 144, 151.

63. On the ways in which these factors contributed to inner-city decline in the 1960s and 1970s, see Thomas J. Sugrue, *The Origins of the Urban Crisis: Race and Inequality in Postwar Detroit* (Princeton, NJ: Princeton University Press, 1998), 48; and Raymond Mohl, "Planned Destruction: The Interstates and Central City Housing," in *From Tenements to the Taylor Homes: In Search of an Urban Housing Policy in Twentieth-Century America*, ed. John F. Bauman, Roger Biles, and Kristin M. Szylvian (University Park: Pennsylvania State University Press, 2000), 226–245.

64. Mark Simons (owner of Robert's Shoes), interview with the author, June 11, 2008, Minneapolis, MN. Simons's store has anchored the Lake Street–Chicago Avenue intersection since the 1930s. One of the most controversial adult businesses, Ferris Alexander's Chicago-Lake Bookstore, was across the street from Simons's store. Simons also rented space above his store to one of the feminist antipornography groups in 1984 and 1985. Wizard Marks (activist and Central neighborhood resident since 1979), interview with the author, June 11, 2008, Minneapolis, MN.

65. Statistics from a 1984 study of the Lake Street commercial strip referenced in "Once-Maligned Developer Is Backed by Neighborhood," *Minneapolis Star and Tribune*, July 8, 1985.

66. Judith A. Martin and Antony Goddard, *Past Choices/Present Landscapes: The Impact of Urban Renewal on the Twin Cities* (Minneapolis: Center for Urban and Regional Affairs, 1989), 89–90; and Mickey Lauria, "Community Controlled Redevelopment: South Minneapolis," PhD dissertation, University of Minnesota, 1980, 110–112.

67. Linda Wejcman, interview with the author, June 15, 2008, Minneapolis, MN.

68. Ruth Hammond, "Porn Arouses Neighborhood Passion," *Minneapolis Tribune*, January 31, 1981.

69. Wejcman, interview with the author.

70. Helen Robinson and Ann Stumme, "Seventh Annual Urban Journalism Workshop Report on 'Adult Bookstores in Minneapolis,'" *Minneapolis Star*, August 4, 1977.

71. Joan Gilbertson (officer of the Powderhorn Park Neighborhood Association), interview with the author, June 15, 2008, Minneapolis, MN. Gilbertson wrote about the pornography issue for the neighborhood paper and organized pickets against the Chicago-Lake Bookstore.

72. Ruth Hammond, "Porn Arouses Neighborhood Passion," *Minneapolis Tribune*, January 31, 1981.

73. Teri Mach, "Powderhorn Fights Live Sex Shows," *Twin Cities Reader*, October 16, 1985.

74. Sharon Sayles Belton (neighborhood activist, city council member, and mayor), interview with the author, June 6, 2007, Minneapolis, MN; Wizard Marks, interview with the author, June 11, 2008, Minneapolis, MN.

75. Vernon Watternach (staffer on Sharon Sayles Belton's campaigns and a member of the Men's Auxiliary for the South Side Sewing Circle), interview with the author, June 6, 2007, Minneapolis, MN.

76. Gilbertson, interview with the author; Wejcman, interview with the author.

77. Gilbertson, interview with the author.

78. "City Officials Visit Adult Bookstore," *Minneapolis Star and Tribune*, September 23, 1983.

79. These laws succeeded in locating most new adult businesses on the edge of downtown, in the warehouse district, although a few "saunas" and massage parlors still dot the smaller commercial districts of the city.

80. Marks, interview with the author.

81. Paul Brest and Ann Vandenberg, "Politics, Feminism, and the Constitution: The Anti-Pornography Movement in Minneapolis," *Stanford Law Review* 39 (February 1987): 616; Charlee Hoyt to unnamed, n.d. (template for a letter that could be sent to anyone inquiring about the 1983 civil rights ordinance), OAP, Minnesota Historical Society, St. Paul, MN.

82. Ordinance of the City of Minneapolis, amending title 7, chap. 139 of "Minneapolis Code of Ordinances Relating to Civil Rights: In General" (first reading: 11-23-83, 1983). The full text of the proposed revisions to the ordinance can be found in Catharine A. MacKinnon and Andrea Dworkin, *In Harm's Way: The Pornography Civil Rights Hearings* (Cambridge, MA: Harvard University Press, 1997), 426–432.

83. Pamela Butler argues that a major rift developed between gay men and lesbians in the Twin Cities over lesbian feminist anti-porn work. At the time when the move to close the adult bookstores and theaters was at its peak, so was the harassment of the gay men who frequented these establishments. Pamela Butler, "Sex and the Cities : Reevaluating 1980s Feminist Politics in Minneapolis and St. Paul," in *Queer Twin Cities: Twin Cities GLBT Oral History Project*, ed. Kevin P. Murphy, Jennifer L. Pierce, and Larry Knopp (Minneapolis: University of Minnesota Press, 2010), 220–221. The activists I interviewed claimed to not be aware of how important the businesses might have been in gay social life. As one explained years later, "What we didn't think about at the time was that probably a lot of those people [patronizing the stores] were gay, and that was not our issue—most of us were very pro-gay, but that was a different time." Wejcman, interview with the author.

84. Political Scientist Donald Downs points to the haste of the hearings to consider the ordinance as the single largest factor in its ultimate failure. The city council did not take the time to properly investigate and deliberate. Donald Alexander Downs, *The New Politics of Pornography* (Chicago: University of Chicago Press, 1989), 51–52; Mayor Donald Fraser to Honorable Alice Rainville, January 5, 1984, Office of the City Clerk, Minneapolis, MN.

85. Janet R. Shaddix & Associates, transcription of public hearings, June 1984, 66–67, Pornography Resource Center Collection, Minnesota Historical Society, St. Paul, MN.

86. The beginnings of these trends in Minneapolis are outlined in Martin and Goddard, *Past Choices/Present Landscapes*, 137–146. A detailed analysis of another Minneapolis neighborhood appears in Randy Stoecker, *Defending Community: The Struggle for Alternative*

Redevelopment in Cedar-Riverside (Philadelphia: Temple University Press, 1994). On the national trends, see Alice O'Connor, "Swimming against the Tide: A Brief History of Federal Policy in Poor Communities," in *Urban Problems and Community Development*, ed. Ronald Ferguson and William Dickens (Washington, DC: Brookings Institution Press, 1999): 77–137.

87. Harry Boyte's work on "citizen advocacy" reveals that groups' shift from work on single issues to broader campaigns to tackle the sources of decline was a common pattern in neighborhood organizing in these decades. Harry C. Boyte, *The Backyard Revolution: Understanding the New Citizen Movement* (Philadelphia: Temple University Press, 1981), 45–46.

88. Laura Mansnerus, "For Lawyers, Crime May Not Pay," *New York Times*, December 17, 1989; Arthur Hayes and Bob Hagerty, "LAW: Obscenity Case May Affect Media Firms," *Wall Street Journal*, July 8, 1992.

89. The literature on feminism and pornography is voluminous and often quite strident. In her careful account of the early years of the movement, Carolyn Bronstein shows how feminist critiques of a culture of male violence led to a focus on representations of women and gender in the media and then eventually became the antipornography movement. Bronstein, *Battling Pornography*; see also Ronald J. Berger, Patricia Searles, and Charles E. Cottle, *Feminism and Pornography* (New York: Praeger, 1991); and Rosen, *The World Split Open*, 191–194. Feminist defenses of pornography (especially through the lens of free speech) appear in Nadine Strossen, *Defending Pornography: Free Speech, Sex, and the Fight for Women's Rights* (New York: Anchor Books, 1996); Alan Soble, *Pornography, Sex, and Feminism* (Amherst, NY: Prometheus Books, 2002); Lisa Duggan and Nan D. Hunter, *Sex Wars: Sexual Dissent and Political Culture*, rev. ed (New York: Routledge, 2006); and Drucilla Cornell, *Feminism and Pornography* (New York: Oxford University Press, 2000). MacKinnon and Dworkin's work remains the most visible representation of the antipornography camp. See Catharine A. MacKinnon, "The Roar on the Other Side of Silence," and Andrea Dworkin, "Suffering and Speech," in MacKinnon and Dworkin, *In Harm's Way*, 3–24, 25–36.

90. For an early and widely read explanation of the connection that some feminists saw between pornography and violence against women, see Susan Brownmiller, *Against Our Will: Men, Women, and Rape* (New York: Ballantine Books, 1975), 389–396.

91. Bay Area Feminist Anti-Censorship Taskforce (BA-FACT), "Feminism and Censorship: Strange Bedfellows?" (marked draft), c. 1985, Phyllis Lyon and Del Martin Papers, GLBT Historical Society, San Francisco, CA.

92. BA-FACT minutes, November 25, 1985.

93. Nancy Weisman, *Discrimination by Design: A Feminist Critique of the Man-Made Environment* (Urbana: University of Illinois Press, 1994), 70.

94. Sides, *Erotic City*, 131.

95. "Take Back the Night," Coalition to Take Back the Night records.

Chapter 6: Taking Up Space and Making Place

1. Holly Near, quoted in "What Are Leading Women in the Community Saying about the Women's Building?" Women's Building of the Bay Area [1978?], San Francisco Women's Building/Women's Centers Records (WBWCR), Gay, Lesbian, Bisexual, Transgender Historical Society, San Francisco, CA.

2. "Actions," *Everywoman* 1, no. 13 (January 22, 1971).

3. Roberta Gold, *When Tenants Claimed the City: The Struggle for Citizenship in New York City Housing* (Urbana: University of Illinois Press, 2014), 198.

4. "Westside Women's Liberation Center," *Rat*, June 14–July 10, 1971.

5. Quoted in Roberta Gold, "'I Had Not Seen Women Like That Before': Intergenerational Feminism in New York City's Tenant Movement," *Feminist Studies* 35, no. 2 (2009): 387.

6. "Westside Women's Liberation Center, *Rat*, June 14-July 10, 1971.

7. Minda Bickman, "New Years on 5th: Enter through the Window," *Village Voice*, January 7, 1971.

8. There is no indication that the organizers saw their removal of the homeless people who had been using the building for shelter in the middle of a New York City winter as problematic.

9. Anonymous person in The Fifth Street Women's Building Film (1972), quoted in Liz Cowan, "Side Trip: The Fifth Street Women's Building Takeover: A Feminist Urban Action, January 1971," paper written in 1992 for the course "Urban Social Movements" taught by Professor Diane Davis, Graduate Faculty, New School for Social Research, New York, NY.

10. Bickman, "New Years on 5th."

11. "The City," *Rat*, February 3–20, 1971.

12. *Rat*, February 3–20, 1971.

13. "24 Arrested as Police End Feminist Demonstration," *New York Times*, January 14, 1971, 41.

14. Cowan, "Side Trip: The Fifth Street Women's Building Takeover."

15. "Fifth Street Action," 1971, Florence Rush Feminism and Women's Liberation Collection, Cache Digital Archive, Kalamazoo College, Kalamazoo, MI, http://hdl.handle.net /10920/28112.

16. "Gimme Womans Shelter," *Rat*, January 12–29, 1971.

17. "Fifth Street Action," 1971

18. *Left on Pearl* (documentary), directed by Susan Rivo, 888 Women's History Project, 2017.

19. West Side Women's Center publicity materials, quoted in "We Raise Our Voices: Celebrating Activism for Equality & Pride in Boston's African American, Feminist, Gay & Lesbian, & Latino Communities" (online exhibit), Northeastern University Libraries, Archives and Special Collections, Boston, MA.

20. Some accounts suggest that Harvard agreed to supply the down payment but other sources indicate that the feminists' actions motivated a private donor to offer the money to the center through Harvard.

21. Flyer quoted in Cowan, "Side Trip: The Fifth Street Women's Building Takeover."

22. "Actions," *Everywoman* 1, no. 13 (January 22, 1971).

23. Cowan, "Side Trip: The Fifth Street Women's Building Takeover."

24. *Rat*, March 30–April 30, 1971.

25. See, for example, Valk, *Radical Sisters*, chap. 6.

26. Judy Smith, "We Marched Right into a Little-Used Building That Harvard Owned, and the Rest Is History," Left on Pearl: Women Take over 888 Memorial Drive, Cambridge (blog), April 4, 2013, http://leftonpearl.blogspot.com/2013/04/welcome-to-left-on-blog-hope-this -will.html.

27. Adrienne Rich, quoted in Nedra Reynolds, *Geographies of Writing: Inhabiting Places and Encountering Difference* (Carbondale: Southern Illinois University Press, 2007), 11.

28. Saralyn Chesnut, Amanda C. Gable, and Elizabeth Anderson, "Atlanta's Charis Books and More: Histories of a Feminist Space," *Southern Spaces*, November 3, 2009, https:// southernspaces.org/2009/atlantas-charis-books-and-more-histories-feminist-space.

29. Dolores Alexander, interview with Kelly Anderson, transcript of video recording, March 20, 2004, Voices of Feminism Oral History Project, Sophia Smith Collection, Smith College, Northampton, MA.

30. Ibid.

31. Ibid.

32. Jim Jerome, "Feminists Hail a Restaurant Where the Piece de Resistance Is an Attitude, Not a Dish," *People*, June 2, 1975, 10–11.

33. Bloodroot, "About Bloodroot," https://www.bloodroot.com/about.

34. Chesnut, Gable, and Anderson, "Atlanta's Charis Books and More."

35. Jerome, "Feminists Hail a Restaurant Where the Piece de Resistance. . ."

36. A customer of the first feminist restaurant in Los Angeles, the Los Angeles Women's Saloon & Parlor, quoted in Sharon Johnson, "In Los Angeles Saloon Women Get the Red Carpet," *Lakeland Ledger*, June 1976.

37. Enke, *Finding the Movement*, 63.

38. The store grew under this status until 1981, when it reorganized as a for-profit business.

39. Candice Reed, "Society and Credit Unions Have Come a Long Way, Baby," *Credit Union Times Magazine*, December 12, 2012, 6.

40. Enke, *Finding the Movement*, 86. The feminist publication *Off Our Backs* erroneously reported that some Chicago feminists refused to go to the Susan B. because of the men there, falsely implying that the restaurant was struggling for want of customers for this reason. The authors later recanted. In reality, the restaurant was well patronized, and the owner called it quits in part because it was too busy and chaotic for its tiny space. Ibid., 87.

41. Jerome, "Feminists Hail a Restaurant Where the Piece de Resistance. . ."

42. Alexander, interview with Kelly Anderson.

43. Sharon Davenport, "LGBT Pride: Remembering the Brick Hut Café—Part 1," *Bay Area Bites*, June 23, 2011, http://ww2.kqed.org/bayareabites/2011/06/23/lgbt-pride-remembering-the-brick-hut-cafe-part-1.

44. Marcia Cron and Gerry Barrons, interview with the author, May 11, 2015, Detroit, MI.

45. Ibid.

46. Ibid.

47. Barrons, quoted in Veteran Feminists of Michigan, *Passing the Torch: Feminism in Michigan since the 1960s* (documentary), 2006.

48. Cron and Barrons, interview with the author.

49. Jane and Anne [pseud.], interview with Saralyn Chesnut, tape recording, Atlanta, GA, March 22, 1990, quoted in Chesnut, Gable, and Anderson, "Atlanta's Charis Books and More."

50. In 1979, the Women's Action Almanac listed seventy feminist bookstores across the country. Women's Action Alliance, *Women's Action Almanac: A Complete Resource Guide*, ed. Jane Williamson, Diane Winston, and Wanda Wooten (New York: William Morrow and Company, 1979), 317–319.

51. Davenport, "LGBT Pride."

52. Enke, *Finding the Movement*, 86.

53. For a detailed study of the Dayton Women's Center—a good example of this kind of institution—see Judith Ezekiel, *Feminism in the Heartland* (Columbus: Ohio State University Press, 2002), chap. 3.

54. Women's Action Alliance, *Women's Action Almanac*, 319.

55. Ibid.

56. Enke, *Finding the Movement*, 177.

57. "New Women's Center in the Oranges," *New York Times*, December 10, 1972.

58. Ibid.

59. Sylvia Hartman, "Women's Center Planned," Register of the Los Angeles Women's Liberation Movement Collection, 1970–1976, MSS 023, California Library for Social Studies and Research, Los Angeles, CA.

60. Marilyn Bender, "Women's Liberation Headquarters," *New York Times*, July 1, 1970.

61. Daphne Spain, "Women's Rights and Gendered Spaces in 1970s Boston," *Frontiers* 32 (Winter 2011): 155.

62. "Review of Strategic Planning Process and Outcomes: The Women's Building, 1982–1988," September 22, 1988, WBWCR.

63. "Continuation of the Definition of the Greater Environment," meeting no. 2, August 23, 1982, WBWCR.

64. "Review of Strategic Planning Process and Outcomes: The Women's Building, 1982–1988," September 22, 1988, WBWCR.

65. "Plan for Expansion for the Collective 4/28/87," unpublished report, p. 4, WBWCR.

66. "Continuation of the Definition of the Greater Environment," meeting no. 2, August 1982, p. 8, WBWCR.

67. On October 28, 1980, the Planning and Women's Division of the American Planning Association presented an award to SFWC for TWB as part of a national competition called "Planning to Meet the Changing Needs of Women." Carmen Vazquez, "Dear Friend" (fund-raising letter), n.d., p. 2, WBWCR.

68. Enke, *Finding the Movement*, 178.

69. Women's Action Alliance, *Women Helping Women: A State-by-State Directory of Services* (New York: Neal-Schuman Publishers, 1981), x, xi; "large numbers," from Marla Miller, "Tracking the Women's Movement through the Women's Action Alliance," *Journal of Women's History* 14 (Summer 2002): 154–156.

70. Women's Action Alliance, *Women Helping Women*, ix, x.

71. Ibid., 320.

72. Laurie Johnston, "Groups Seeking a Firehouse Here," *New York Times*, October 28, 1973.

73. Aya Gruber, *The Feminist War on Crime: The Unexpected Role of Women's Liberation in Mass Incarceration* (Berkeley: University of California Press, 2021).

74. "The Combahee River Collective Statement," April 1977, Library of Congress, Web Archive, https://www.loc.gov/item/lcwaN0028151.

75. Johnston, "Groups Seeking a Firehouse Here."

76. See, for example, Brownmiller's discussion of Women's Survival Space in Brooklyn in *In Our Time*, 272.

77. Holly Near quoted in "What are leading women in the community saying about the Women's Building?" Women's Building of the Bay Area [1978?], WBWCR.

Chapter 7: Privacy in Public

1. *War Zone* (documentary short), directed by Maggie Hadleigh-West, 1991.

2. Freedman, *Redefining Rape*, 289.

3. Mortimer B. Zuckerman, "Meltdown in Our Cities," *US News & World Report* 106 (May 29, 1989): 74.

4. Charles Krauthammer, "Crime and Responsibility," *Time*, May 8, 1989.

5. Zuckerman, "Meltdown in Our Cities," 74.

6. Natalie P. Byfiled, *Savage Portrayals: Race, Media, and the Central Park Jogger Story* (Philadelphia: Temple University Press, 2014), and Kristin Bumiller, *In an Abusive State: How Neoliberalism Appropriated the Feminist Movement against Sexual Violence* (Durham, NC: Duke University Press, 2008), provide critical insights into the structural racism of the wrongful convictions while largely overlooking gender.

7. Gail Collins, "Gifted, Black, and Angry," *New York Daily News*, April 26, 1989, 5.

8. Helen Benedict, *Virgin or Vamp: How the Press Covers Sex Crimes* (New York: Oxford

University Press, 1993), 195. The premise of Benedict's book is that society's true feelings about women's place emerges when we look at sex and sex-related crimes. The book focuses on the "pervasiveness of rape myths and [how] the habits of the newsroom have led the press to consistently cover these crimes with bias and, sometimes, even cruelty" (ibid., 3). Her approach was to look at how attitudes toward women shaped coverage (in the media and in popular culture) of the case. Chapter 6 is on the Central Park jogger case, but Benedict wrote the book *after* the convictions of the five youth and *before* the real assailant came to light; thus, she accepts the guilt of the five teenagers. So, while her book gets that part of the story very wrong, it does set the episode within the historical moment, a time when New York was hyper-focused on race relations, tensions, and violence. Benedict argues that, "as soon as the racial difference between the jogger and her assailants came to light, therefore, the story was slotted into a racial profile" (ibid., 191).

9. Greg Tate, "Sexism: The Forbidden Issue," *Village Voice*, May 9, 1989.

10. Andrea Kannapell, "She Could Have Been Me, 28 and White," *Village Voice*, May 9, 1989, 37, as quoted in Benedict, *Virgin or Vamp*, 196.

11. The press convention of not printing the names of victims of sexual assault was partly a response to the lingering shame suffered by rape victims, but it also purportedly protected the victim from unwanted attention. Keeping a victim nameless, however, gave the press free rein to invoke her image for their own purposes.

12. Charla Krupp, "Women of the Year, 1989," *Glamour* 87 (December 1989): 155.

13. Paul E. Mullen and Michele Pathé, "Stalking," *Crime and Justice* 29 (2002): 275.

14. For a similar argument on the eroticization of rape, see Madriz, *Nothing Bad Happens to Good Girls*, 18.

15. Michigan Penal Code, Act 328 of 1931, Section 750.411h, effective March 31, 1998, http://www.legislature.mi.gov/(S(c5wh4qo412mwkcmnftqnrrpk))/mileg.aspx?page=getObject&objectName=mcl-750-411h.

16. Patricia Tjaden and Nancy Thoennes, "Stalking in America: Findings from the National Violence against Women Survey," National Institute of Justice, Centers for Disease Control and Prevention, April 1998, 17, https://www.ncjrs.gov/pdffiles/169592.pdf. Interestingly, the rates of women being stalked did not change across racial or ethnic lines.

17. Whitney George, "Stop the Presses," *Off Our Backs* 27 (December 1997): 3.

18. Robert M. Emerson, Kerry O. Ferris, and Carol Brooks Gardner, "On Being Stalked," *Social Problems* 45 (August 1998): 289–314, 290.

19. Tjaden and Thoennes, "Stalking in America," 2.

20. "General Advice for Victims," Stalking Risk Profile, 2011, https://www.stalkingriskprofile.com/victim-support/general-advice-for-victims.

21. "Biden Proposes New Law on Assault," *Sun Sentinel*, December 13, 1990; Ruth Lopez, "Landmark Bill Would Attack Escalating Violent Crime," *Chicago Tribune*, July 1, 1990.

22. Ruth Lopez, "Landmark Bill Would Attack Escalating Violent Crime," *Chicago Tribune*, July 1, 1990.

23. Leslie Phillips, "Crime against Women Target of New Bill," *USA Today*, June 20, 1990.

24. Susan Baer, "Freedom from Fear: Psychologists, Lawmakers, and Women Themselves Face the Issue of Violence," *The Sun*, October 2, 1990.

25. Rose Corrigan, *Up against a Wall: Rape Reform and the Failure of Success* (New York: New York University Press, 2013), 4.

26. Kristen Bumiller, *In an Abusive State: How Neoliberalism Appropriated the Feminist Movement against Sexual Violence* (Durham, NC: Duke University Press, 2008), xii. For an assessment of this literature and the neoliberal "state's use of feminist ideas and energies for its own

ends," see Ruthann Robson, "Feminist Struggle to Be Revolutionary," *Women's Studies Quarterly* 39 (Spring/Summer 2011): 262–269.

27. Madriz, *Nothing Bad Happens to Good Girls*, 51.

28. Robson, "Feminist Struggle to Be Revolutionary."

29. Bevacqua, *Rape on the Public Agenda*, 170.

30. US House of Representatives Committee on Oversight and Government Reform, "Hearing on H.R. 4869 to Provide for Restroom Gender Parity in Federal Buildings," May 12, 2010, serial no. 111-108, prepared statement of Kathryn Anthony, 111th Cong., 2nd sess., https://www.govinfo.gov/content/pkg/CHRG-111hhrg63145/html/CHRG-111hhrg63145.htm. The connection of public facilities to belonging has also been developed in disability studies; see, for example, Phillippa Wiseman, "Lifting the Lid: Disabled Toilets as Sites of Belonging and Embodied Citizenship," *Sociological Review* 67, no. 4 (July 2019): 788–806.

31. House Committee on Oversight and Government Reform, "Hearing on H.R. 4869," Anthony statement.

32. Josh Ahmann, Kevin Bond, Warren Greaser, Sarah Selden, Amber Springberg, Katrik Srinivas, and Jon Swae, "Going Public! Strategies for Meeting Public Restroom Need in Portland's Central City" January 1, 2006, Master of Urban and Regional Planning Workshop Projects 5, http://archives.pdx.edu/ds/psu/8664.

33. Ron Shaffer (aka Dr. Gridlock), "When You've Got to Go, Metro Stations Aren't the Best Place to Be," *Washington Post*, October 20, 1989.

34. William E. Schmidt, "Atlanta's Lack of Public Toilets Spurs Debate," *New York Times*, December 19, 1983. Seattle is another good example of these trends. It opened state-of-the-art public toilets in 1909, closed them off and on in the 1920s and 1930s, permanently shuttered them in 1945, installed portable toilets in the 1980s after public outcry around public urination and defecation, installed automated public toilets (APTs) in 2004, abandoned the expensive and hard-to-maintain APT project, and sold off the units in 2009. Alberta Bleck and Sally Bagshaw, "Public Restrooms Are an Urban Necessity," *The Urbanist*, December 2, 2006, https://www.theurbanist.org/2016/12/02/public-restrooms-are-an-urban-necessity; Noelene Clark, "Seattle's $5 million Automated Public Toilets Sold for $12,000," *Seattle Times*, August 16, 2008.

35. Pat Durkin, "Foul Smells Angering Residents," *Washington Post*, September 20, 1990; Nick Ravo, "Perplexing Problem: When Streets Become Public Urinals," *New York Times*, December 29, 1986. Conviction for public urination carried fines of between $50 and $250 in the mid-1980s.

36. Madriz, *Nothing Bad Happens to Good Girls*, 117–124; Gardner, *Passing By*, 202–205.

37. Judith Plaskow, "Embodiment Elimination and the Role of Toilets in Struggles for Social Justice," *Cross Currents* 58 (July 8, 2008): 60.

38. James Munves, "What about the Public Toilets We Have?," *New York Times*, March 8, 1994.

39. Prior to the twentieth century, most businesses—offices, saloons, even city buildings—would have had little cause to specify gender. The nature of the entity would have dictated who used it, and the rooms would have been labeled by function. For example, in the House of Representatives wing of the US Capitol Building, no restrooms for women were located anywhere near the House chambers until after Nancy Pelosi became Speaker of the House. The roughly seventy female House members had to bypass a full-service restroom for men located right outside the chambers and go down long corridors filled with tourists to find a bathroom.

40. Alexander Kira, *The Bathroom* (New York: Viking Press, 1976). As sociologist Erving Goffman theorized in the 1960s, restrooms are a space to which we retreat, without entirely

leaving public space, when we need to adjust our public self. Society generally concurs with this use of restroom spaces, and that is why we respect the illusion of privacy by ignoring the sights, sounds, and smells that would otherwise diminish our public "game face." Erving Goffman, *Behavior in Public Places: Notes on the Social Organization of Gatherings* (London: Free Press of Glencoe, 1961).

41. On the popular reaction to the passage of "potty parity" laws, see Garth Johnston, "Potty Parity Prevails," *The Gothamist*, January 8, 2006; and John Hoff, "Double the Women's Rest Rooms," *Minnesota Daily*, June 14, 2006.

42. As of this writing, plumbing codes and legislation are being revised to adjust that ratio for the type and size of the venue. For codes and other current information, see American Restroom Association, "Potty Parity: Overview." http://www.americanrestroom.org/parity/index.htm.

43. Kathryn H. Anthony and Meghan Dufresne, "Potty Privileging in Perspective: Gender and Family Issues in Toilet Designs," in *Ladies and Gents: Public Toilets and Gender*, ed. Olga Gershenson and Barbara Penner (Philadelphia: Temple University Press, 2009), 58.

44. Ibid., 59.

45. John F. Banzhaf III, "Final Frontier for the Law?" *National Law Journal*, April 18, 1990.

46. Junda Woo, "'Potty Parity' Lets Women Wash Hands of Long Loo Lines," *Wall Street Journal*, February 24, 1994.

47. Banzhaf famously sued the University of Michigan for "unlawful gender discrimination" and violation of the equal protection clause of the Fourteenth Amendment by not including more women's restrooms in the renovation of the university's Hill Auditorium. John F. Banzhaf III, "Final Frontier for the Law?," *National Law Journal*, April 18, 1990, reprinted at Potty Parity, Restroom Equity, Squatters Rights, http://banzhaf.net/docs/potty_parity.html (accessed April 18, 2020).

48. Taunya Lovell Banks, "Toilets as a Feminist Issue: A True Story," *Berkeley Women's Law Journal* 236 (1990–1991): 267.

49. Banzhaf, "Final Frontier for the Law?"

50. House Committee on Oversight and Government Reform, "Hearing on H.R. 4869," Anthony statement. Indicating that the United States had fallen behind on an issue had been a successful strategy during the restroom building era of the early twentieth century. See "H.R. 4869, The Restroom Gender Parity in Federal Buildings Act," part 2, posted by GOP Oversight, https://www.youtube.com/watch?v=_uZAgzUqicU&list=LLB6a6gYkpUihL8hg1RRs TLg&index=114.

51. House Committee on Oversight and Government Reform, "Hearing on H.R. 4869," Anthony statement.

52. House Committee on Oversight and Government Reform, "Hearing on H.R. 4869," prepared statement of Sharon Pratt (former DC mayor). Pratt continued: "With regards to the disparity in restrooms, you can characterize it as follows: It is glaring, it is inconvenient, it is enormously inefficient, and it is downright unfair."

53. House Committee on Oversight and Government Reform, "Hearing on H.R. 4869," prepared statement of Chairman Edolphus Towns.

54. See, for example, the National Center for Transgender Equality, "Know Your Rights: Public Accommodations," https://transequality.org/know-your-rights/public-accommodations.

55. Mary Anne Case, "Why Not Abolish the Laws of Urinary Segregation?," in *Toilet: Public Restrooms and the Politics of Sharing*, ed. Harvey Molotch and Laura Noren (New York: New York University Press, 2010): 211–225. Shani Heckman also used the phrase "wrong

bathroom" as the title of her 2005 documentary short on challenges faced by transgender individuals (https://youtu.be/yFDaYIsOWQk).

56. Case ponders the costs and benefits of segregation and comes to much the same conclusion in her essay "Why Not Abolish Laws of Urinary Segregation?," in Molotch and Noren, *Toilet*, 211–225. For a reactionary feminist argument against gender-neutral bathrooms that essentializes biological sex, see Sheila Jeffreys, "The Politics of the Toilet: A Feminist Response to the Campaign to 'Degender' a Women's Space," *Women's Studies International Forum* 45 (July/August 2014): 42–51.

57. Terry S. Kogan, "Sex Separation: The Cure-all for Victorian Social Anxiety," in Molotch and Noren, *Toilet*, 145.

58. Rebecca Flood, "Scientists Claim Unisex Toilets Would Cut Queuing Time for Women to One Minute," *Express*, July 18, 2017, https://www.express.co.uk/news/uk/829816/toilet-queue-women-unisex-bathroom-gender-transgender-slash.

59. This version of the story comes from documents filed with the courts in 1984. In her appellant brief filed in 1989, Kaufman claims that she asked to see the manager and the hostess refused to get him. Although there might be many explanations for the differing stories, it is worth considering that Kaufman felt more emboldened in the subsequent case and more willing to craft a version of her experiences in which she claimed her rights.

60. The case was filed in 1984, with a ruling in favor of the restaurant. Kaufman appealed in 1990.

61. *Kaufman v. Beverly Rodeo Hotel*, 2d Civil B 045379 (1990), 12.

62. Ibid., 15.

63. Even supportive public responses proved to be limited in their recognition of women's rights. The LA restaurateur Wolfgang Puck, himself a new father in 1984, supported breastfeeding in public. He recognized that it made some people uncomfortable, but said, "It is the man's problem, not the mothers'. She shouldn't have to change the way she acts." Laurie Ochoa, "Restaurants Rethink Their Nursing Policies in Wake of Lawsuit," *Los Angeles Times*, June 28, 1989. Letters to the editor of the *Los Angeles Times* on the Kaufman case offered far more tepid support. One writer proclaimed that "right or wrong" did not matter in these situations. Rather, it was the mother's duty to be "gracious" in thinking of the comfort of those around her by practicing discretion. "Letters: Nursing Mothers in Restaurants," *Los Angeles Times*, April 21, 1984.

64. Rima D. Apple, *Mothers and Medicine: A Social History of Infant Feeding, 1890–1950* (Madison: University of Wisconsin Press, 1987).

65. For a broader history, see Jessica Martucci, *Back to the Breast: Natural Motherhood and Breastfeeding in America* (Chicago: University of Chicago Press, 2015).

66. YouGov, "Breastfeeding," August 8–9, 2019, https://d25d2506sfb94s.cloudfront.net/cumulus_uploads/document/5cr8rm2f72/Results%20for%20YouGov%20RealTime%20(Breastfeeding)%20194%209.8.2019.xlsx%20%20[Group].pdf. A CDC survey conducted in 2018 found that only 68 percent of respondents believed women should have the right to breastfeed in public, while just over 25 percent said that they neither agreed nor disagreed; over 10 percent of respondents said that, in their opinion, women should not have this right. Centers for Disease Control and Prevention, "Public Opinions about Breastfeeding," November 15, 2021, https://www.cdc.gov/breastfeeding/data/healthstyles_survey/index.htm.

67. Mary Lofton, quoted in Juhie Bhatia, "Moms Fight to Breastfeed in Public," *Women's News*, November 22, 2004, https://womensenews.org/2004/11/moms-fight-breastfeed-public.

68. The number of women in the paid labor force peaked in the late 1990s. Both single and married women with children increased their representation in the workforce in the 1970s and 1980s at a faster rate than women without children, with their employment rates peaking in 1999. "Employment Rates of Women by Marital Status and Children," The Hamilton Project, March 2, 2017, https://www.hamiltonproject.org/charts/employment_rates_of_women _by_marital_status_and_children.

69. Jill Lepore, "Baby Food," *The New Yorker*, January 12, 2009, https://www.newyorker .com/magazine/2009/01/19/baby-food.

70. Congress amended the Fair Labor Standards Act in 2010 to require workplaces with more than fifty employees to make lactation rooms available. These rooms are an almost uniquely American development, largely because of the minimal maternity leave available in the United States, substantial numbers of women working for wages, and barebones regulations for employers to accommodate nursing mothers. Recently, entrepreneurs have sought to capitalize on this situation by selling portable, podlike lactation spaces, such as "the Mamava" (https://www.mamava.com).

71. California Assembly Bill 157, July 14, 1997, http://www.leginfo.ca.gov/pub/97-98/bill /asm/ab_0151-0200/ab_157_bill_19970714_chaptered.pdf.

72. Most of these laws have been cataloged at National Conference of State Legislatures, "Breastfeeding State Laws," August 26, 2021, https://www.ncsl.org/research/health /breastfeeding-state-laws.aspx.

73. Kate Boyer, "'I Don't Want to See You Flashing Your Bits Around': The Emotional Resonances of Breastfeeding in Public," *Emotion, Space, and Society* 26 (February 2018): 33, https://doi.org/10.1016/j.emospa.2016.09.002; Lucille R. Marchand and Marina Helen Morrow, "Infant Feeding Practices: Understanding the Decision Making Process," *Family Medicine* 26, no. 5 (1994): 319–324, 33–40.

74. Michele Acker, "Breast Is Best … but Not Everywhere: Ambivalent Sexism and Attitudes toward Private and Public Breastfeeding," *Sex Roles*, 61 (2009): 476–490; Judy Sheeshka, Beth Potter, Emilie Norrie, Ruta Valaitis, Gerald Adams, and Leon Kuczynski, "Women's Experiences Breastfeeding in Public Places," *Journal of Human Lactation* 17, no. 1 (2001): 31–38, https://www.ncbi.nlm.nih.gov/pubmed/11847849.

75. "Writer Doesn't Want to See Moms Nursing at Starbucks," Starbucks Gossip, August 11, 2004, https://starbucksgossip.typepad.com/_/2004/08/writer_doesnt_w.html.

76. Ibid.

77. Amy Harmon, "'Lactivists' Taking Their Cause, and Their Babies, to the Streets," *New York Times*, June 7, 2005.

78. "Got Milk? Target Does! Readers Share Stories from the Target Nurse-in," *Today*, December 29, 2011, https://www.today.com/news/got-milk-target-does-readers-share -stories-target-nurse-1C7397908.

79. Target's employee handbook offers clear instructions on how to protect nursing parents from customer complaints and accommodate those who want a more private or quiet area to feed. Employees are instructed to never recommend that someone use the restroom to nurse. Laura T. Coffey, "Moms Get Pumped about Target's Breastfeeding Policy," *Today*, July 15, 2015, https://www.today.com/parents/moms-love-targets-breastfeeding-policy-shoppers-t32561.

80. "Breastfeeding Welcomed Here," Southern Nevada Breastfeeding Coalition, https:// nevadabreastfeeds.org/business-resources/breastfeeding-welcomed-here.

81. Nicole Owens, Shannon Carter, and Chelsea Nordham, "Neutralizing the Maternal Breast: Accounts of Public Breastfeeding by African American Mothers," *Journal of Family Issues* 39, no. 2 (2018): 430–450.

82. See the Normalizing Breastfeeding website at https://www.normalizebreastfeeding.org (accessed April 8, 2020).

83. The issue has come up several times since 2009 as social media policies evolve. See, for example, Svetlana Mintcheva, "Nipplephobia—Facebook and Beyond," National Coalition Against Censorship, January 14, 2009, https://ncac.org/news/blog/nipplephobia-facebook-and-beyond; and Soraya Chemaly, "How Women Got Facebook to Tackle Their Nipple Problem," MIC, June 11, 2014, https://www.mic.com/articles/90795/how-women-got-facebook-to-tackle-their-nipple-problem.

84. Marcia Mercedes Lara, "Young Mother Responds to Male Stranger Who Shamed Her for Breastfeeding in Public on Facebook," *People*, May 30, 2015.

85. Ibid.

86. As of 2022, all laws protecting breastfeeding conceive of those needing protection to be women and their biological children. As with other issues of gender in public space, transgender and gender-nonconforming or nonbinary individuals and rights organizations have offered us a significant challenge to this essentialization of gender. A more inclusive term of "chestfeeding" is emerging to reflect a broader understanding of who might nurture children and thereby need to be included in this discussion of public behavior in the future. La Leche League International, "Support for Transgender & Non-Binary Parents," https://www.llli.org/breastfeeding-info/transgender-non-binary-parents (accessed December 2, 2022).

87. Jerry Gillam Times, "Panel Rejects Bill Establishing Right to Breast-Feed in Public," *Los Angeles Times*, March 31, 1995.

88. Christina Zhao, "Breastfeeding Mothers Stage 'Nurse-In' Protest at Minnesota Pool after Woman Told to Cover Up," *Newsweek*, July 24, 2018.

Epilogue

1. Sarah Miller, "Police Officer's Remarks at York Inspire 'SlutWalk,'" *Toronto Star*, March 17, 2011.

2. Joetta L. Carr, "The SlutWalk Movement: A Study in Transnational Feminist Activism," *Journal of Feminist Scholarship* 4 (Spring 2013): 24–38.

3. Janelle Crubaugh, "Take Back the Night," *The Carolinian*, August 30, 2017.

4. La Leche League International, "Support for Transgender & Non-Binary Parents."

5. Right To Be, formerly Hollaback! (https://righttobe.org), has steadily increased its reach and now also offers policy recommendations, resources for bystander training, case studies, and guides for handling harassment at work.

6. See, for example, Girls for Gender Equity, https://www.ggenyc.org.

7. Barbara Perry and D. Ryan Dyck, "I Don't Know Where It Is Safe": Trans Women's Experiences of Violence," *Critical Criminology* 22 (2014): 49–63.

8. Georgina Hickey, "Privacy in Public: Anti-Harassment Campaigns for Mass Transit in the 21st Century US," *Women's Issues in Transportation: Summary of the 5th International Conference*, vol. 2, *Technical Papers* (February 2015): 365–379.

9. "Is Sexual Harassment a Problem on Metro?" WUSA*9, February 21, 2012.

10. Britni Daniell, "You OK, Sis? Why Those Three Words Can Save a Woman's Life," *Reader Supported News*, July 20, 2014, https://readersupportednews.org/news-section2/318-66/24882-you-ok-sis-why-those-three-words-can-save-a-womans-life.

11. Jamillah Bowan Williams, Lisa Sing, and Naomi Mezey, "#MeToo as Catalyst: A Glimpse into 21st Century Activism," *University of Chicago Legal Forum* 22 (2019): 371–393; "Beauty with a Purpose, #Itsnotyourfault," SABC News, November 17, 2019, https://youtu.be/cYEP_PhwK90. Reflective of twenty-first-century approaches, Sasha-Lee Laurel Olivier,

who won the Miss South Africa title in 2019, acknowledged that men and boys have also survived harassment and sexual abuse, which often goes unrecognized, when she said, "This is an issue that transcends gender."

12. See the work of the Sylvia Rivera Law Project (srlp.org). I use "trans*" here as an umbrella term to capture identities beyond cisgender.

13. Tim Retzloff, "Remembering the History of Michigan's LGBT Ballot Fights," *Between the Lines*, January 14, 2016.

14. Richard Fausset, "Bathroom Law Repeal Leaves Few Pleased in North Carolina," *New York Times*, March 30, 2017; National Organization for Women, "Ensuring Transgender Students' Safety and Dignity" (press statement), May 13, 2016, https://now.org/media-center/press-release/ensuring-transgender-students-safety-and-dignity.

15. Joseph Cox, "People Are Filming Creepshots of Women at BLM Protests," *Vice*, June 18, 2020.

16. Kimberly Lawson, "In Many States, It's Still Legal for Creeps to Photograph Up Your Skirt," *Vice*, July 20, 2016.

17. Wesley McCann, Amelie Pedneault, Mary K. Stohr, and Craig Hemmens, "Upskirting: A Statutory Analysis of Legislative Responses to Video Voyeurism 10 Years Down the Road," *Criminal Justice Review* 43, no. 4 (2018): 399–418.

18. Kimberlé Crenshaw and Andreain J. Ritchie. *Say Her Name: Resisting Police Brutality against Black Women* (New York: African American Policy Forum, 2015).

Index